The
Short Stack
Cookbook

The
Short Stack
Cookbook

Ingredients that Speak Volumes

Nick Fauchald & Kaitlyn Goalen

—

Photography by Noah Fecks

ABRAMS, NEW YORK

TABLE OF CONTENTS

IT STARTS WITH INGREDIENTS

• • •

We're romantics when it comes to cooking at home.
Unapologetically sentimental and downright enthusiastic.

We love the process of choosing our food, whether it's carefully sourcing ingredients for a recipe or doing a routine refill on the things we always want around (nothing is nicer than a fully stocked fridge, right?). And we fall—hard, every time—for the act of cooking itself, the muscle memory that clicks on when we begin to dice an onion, the music we like to play while bouncing around the kitchen, the secret self-congratulatory thoughts when we manage to keep the kitchen clean while we cook. But most of all, we love that cooking offers a clear and immediate way to create, to take raw materials and transform them into an end result that satisfies on multiple levels.

Recipes are the trail maps that lead us to this success and inspire a sense of mastery—bragging rights and all. And there's plenty of romance in that. Recipes can be time capsules, scribbled over with notes in the margin from a grandmother, friend or a complete stranger. And a good recipe offers both consistency, producing the same result time after time, and flexibility, as we riff and refine with each use. When we pine for familiarity, that guarantee of comfort is a powerful force. Isn't that the same stuff that love stories are made of?

Even more evocative than recipes, though, are ingredients themselves. For most of us, ingredients are the entry point to a passion for cooking. As kids, we fixate on what we like and dislike, and that instinctive pull continues throughout adulthood, guiding our choices and helping us find the recipes that become our staples.

Anyone who cooks with any regularity hits a tipping point where they relinquish the safety of recipes and charge into the kitchen without them. In these moments, ingredients become even more critical, whether you're making something from memory or completely improvising. We rely on them to remind us how to get from point A to point B. It requires a level of trust, some intuition and a lot of paying attention to what you're cooking—all things that imbue the process with a sense of magic, particularly when you end up with something delicious—or at least pleasantly edible.

These days, our decision of what to cook very often starts with an ingredient, whether it's a beautiful piece of fruit or vegetable from the market, a wedge of exciting cheese we've stumbled across or a craving for a specific cut of meat. Only once we've chosen the lead actor is the script written and the cast assembled. We'll either seek out a recipe that spotlights our muse, or wing it based on our previous knowledge of the ingredient's potential in the kitchen.

This is not a new way of thinking about ingredients (although the extreme fetishization and documentation of them might be); it's really more a return to a former relationship with food. A few generations ago, most home cooks had a limited selection of ingredients to choose from—almost exclusively grown, raised or caught nearby—and this supply shifted with the seasons. Every year, mothers and grandmothers invented new ways to use up the season's offerings, and eventually they began to write down and share those recipes, first with their friends, then their churches and communities, then by publishing them in flyers, newspapers and cookbooks.

But the 20th century changed everything. Industrial innovation and wars brought us processed and frozen food. Advances in home appliances and cooking technology allowed home cooks (mostly women) to work less in the kitchen and more elsewhere. Fast food was invented and quickly evolved from novelty to epidemic. Americans started cooking less for basic sustenance and more for pleasure and entertainment.

That was a terribly condensed history, but it leads us right back to ingredient-driven cooking. Many of today's cooks—amateur and professional—have gone back to the old ways, letting the seasons and local ingredients drive their appetites and creativity. Allowing ingredients to be the guide makes us better (and usually healthier) cooks. When you focus on a recipe, you master that one recipe. But when you get a deep understanding of one ingredient, you can broaden your horizons. The more ingredients you master, the more intuitively you can cook. And the more enjoyable, magical and romantic the process of cooking becomes.

THE BIRTH OF SHORT STACK EDITIONS

• • •

This idea was one of the driving forces behind Short Stack Editions, our series of miniature cookbooks that each showcases a single ingredient. By focusing a set of recipes around one ingredient, we hoped to capture everything we loved about cooking: the reliability and consistency of a great recipe and the intuitive, freewheeling confidence that ingredients help us develop as cooks. We wanted to celebrate the things that had led us to make careers out of this passion.

It also came out of feeling that those very things were increasingly under attack.

We spent the first years of our careers working in New York City at food-centric magazines, where every published recipe was the product of a team of highly skilled professionals. By the time a recipe hit the newsstand, it had been passed through multiple recipe testers, editors, proofreaders, fact-checkers and so on.

But then the Internet happened. We'd come of journalistic age during what we know now as the high-water mark of print publishing. Then, as advertising dollars moved to the Web in the late aughts, and magazines and newspapers began to shrink or fold as a result, we followed the money over to the digital side of publishing, taking with us the ideology we inherited from print: If you're going to proudly share recipes with the world, they'd sure better work.

But the Internet wasn't playing by the same rules. Remember the first time you discovered that a quick Web search for, say, "apple pie recipe," could offer you thousands of options in an instant? We do. It seemed magical. But do you also remember the first time you got burned (figuratively or literally) by a recipe you pulled from an unfamiliar website? Same here. We can't count the number of times someone has complained to us about a flawed recipe they found online. The same thing that makes the Internet so democratizing and liberating—anonymity and access—is the same thing that offers us so many broken apple pie recipes.

Of course, some great sources for recipes emerged on the Web—professionally run websites like Serious Eats and Food52, hundreds of talented food bloggers, the online versions of print publications and many food blogs among them—but beyond the safety net of accountability, it was (and still is) a culinary minefield.

As the Internet continued to consume our lives, we found ourselves revisiting our cookbook collections and stashes of old food magazines more than ever before. We not only missed the reliability of printed recipes, but we also longed to produce something we could hold in our hands again.

So we set out to make ourselves a creative outlet, a little side project to work out some of these frustrations while we continued to make websites, apps and other digital content. We considered everything that we loved about cookbooks, magazines and newspapers—well-tested, dependable recipes created by professionals—and everything that frustrated us about the Internet and how it was changing our lives.

Our little publication would also be a business experiment. Like our future authors, we can feel the food-publishing world shifting under our feet. Magazine budgets and cookbook advances are shrinking, book royalty pay-outs are as rare as hen's teeth and everyone is talking about how the value of the recipe is trending toward zero. But what if we created a publishing model that put the author first? We wanted to find a sustainable way to cele-brate the individuals who are responsible for driving the conversation about food and guiding the way we cook. We'd pay them for every one of their books that we print, forever and ever, and keep their issues in perpetual cir-culation. The author is rewarded for doing her or his job—creating awesome recipes that actually work—and the payoff continues as long as the publisher is doing its job by selling the books and printing more. It sounds obvious, but nobody (that we know of) does it this way.

Our plan wasn't an easy sell to potential authors, at least at first. We had no idea how many books we'd be printing, and therefore no real guess as to how much money they'd be making. It all depended on if we could find an audience.

At the same time, we were lucky enough to meet a very talented designer, Rotem Raffe, who shared our aesthetic admiration for the single-subject recipe pamphlets published by food and appliance brands in the mid-20th century. We decided that our booklets would be utilitarian, like magazines, but highly design-driven—little objects you'd want to display in your kitchen. We'd print the books on fancy paper and bind them by hand with baker's twine (still a questionable idea, but people seem to like it).

With all the pieces in place, we lined up three authors and their chosen ingredients—eggs, tomatoes and strawberries—and raised funds on Kickstarter (yes, we used the Internet! Fight fire with fire!) to publish their books under the name Short Stack Editions. The publication's name is an allusion to its diminutive size, yes, but also to its collectability—and, of course, pancakes.

We couldn't have predicted how quickly the concept would resonate. Within a few days, we'd met our Kickstarter goal, and by the end of the month-long fundraising period, we'd almost doubled it. Just a few weeks later, we were up to our necks in boxes of our first three volumes and learning, through trial and lots of error, the ins and outs of offset printing, the postal system, e-commerce and how long it takes to sew the spines of 9,000 books by hand.

We've figured a few things out since then. Now, some four years and 24 volumes later (and counting), we've applied our ingredient-forward ethos to the hardcover.

THE BIG BOOK

• • •

Initially, we didn't anticipate ever making a regular-size cookbook. Our small editions had exceeded all of our hopes and expectations. With every new manuscript, we're reminded of what we love about cooking: that we can still learn new things about ingredients we thought we knew so well and that there's always more to discover, always another dinner to successfully orchestrate.

But something else came out of Short Stack that we weren't expecting. We've started to see our approach as a framework for exploring the current state of American home cooking: a hugely expansive and amoebic food culture, developed over the past few decades by appropriating the world's many cuisines, borrowing and bending ingredients from hither and yon, then merging them with our increasingly evanescent regional traditions.

Promoting a specific ingredient embraces these broad, geographical influences on what and how we cook and invites questions about our broken agricultural and food systems. It taps into the zeitgeist of the country's current food obsessions, with its weird push-pulls of excess and restriction, entertainment and sanctity. The ingredient lens also helps us tackle some of our deepest frustrations with American cooking, most notably waste: The more you understand how to use an ingredient, the easier it is to use *all* of it. So it dawned on us that this discussion deserved a bigger platform than our small format allowed.

This is hardly the first—nor the 1001st—ingredient-driven cookbook. And, based on the 18 ingredients we've selected to feature here, it might seem as though we put on blindfolds, ran through the supermarket and

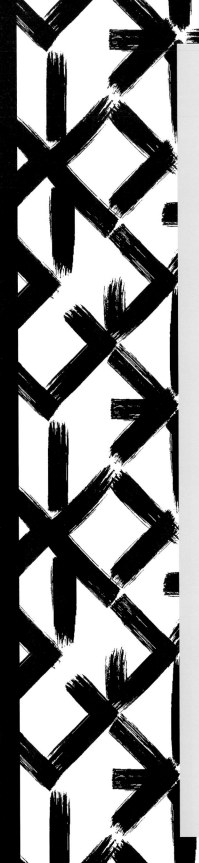

knocked random items into our shopping cart. But choosing the ingredients to highlight in the following recipes wasn't an easy task. We started with a list of about 100 items—fresh produce, pantry and refrigerator staples, meat and diary—and narrowed it down to the stuff we always keep stocked in our kitchen, as well as the fresh ingredients we crave and covet most. There were earnest, hours-long discussions about brussels sprouts and unnecessarily heated arguments about celery (which, alas, didn't make the cut). We researched which ingredients are popular with home cooks right now, while trying to separate the fads from the foundations. The ingredients that we landed on are the ones that, viewed as a group, paint a panoramic picture of our current relationship with cooking. Taken individually, each of these ingredients operates like a new vantage point in the kitchen, providing insightful discoveries about cooking that lead to new sets of skills.

The recipes in this book were developed by Nick, Kaitlyn and 27 of America's best food writers, recipe developers, cookbook authors, food stylists and chefs—all of whom have either authored Short Stack Editions in the past or are writing one in the near future. These are all new recipes, appearing in print for the first time, but many have been part of our personal repertoires for years. Some were invented in spontaneous fits of ingenuity; others have roots in our favorite restaurants, cookbooks and food mentors. They all evoke the feelings that we love most about cooking: that sense of wonder, excitement and satisfaction that occurs when watching a chemical process result in something altogether new and delicious. And they all make great springboards, offering up a lesson about an ingredient that can be taken and improvised on until a new recipe-less creation forms.

The recipes also reflect our many shared "cooking moods." Some of these recipes are extremely easy and can be cooked with one hand dribbling a basketball; others take extra care and attention to get just right—just like some nights you want to cook an ambitious spread, while others all you can think about is a grilled cheese sandwich.

You'll notice that many of the recipes in this book aren't hyper-seasonal. Yes, we love filling up our canvas totes at the farmers' market each week as much as you do, but we're not strict, unwavering locavores, as much as we'd love to be. Although fresh produce such as apples, tomatoes, brussels sprouts and squash are at their best in season, we can find decent specimens at the grocery store throughout the year. This book is meant to inform the way most of us cook on a day-to-day basis; cooking with the seasons is a huge part of that, to be sure, but not everything.

We who binge and purge hundreds of cookbooks over the years have a term for the volumes we'll never throw or give away: keepers. And it's not a bit surprising that many of us share the same favorites. They're full of recipes that inspire, that inform, that *work*. Eventually they became part of our subconcious cooking minds.

Our goal when we set out to write this cookbook was to create a keeper. We hope this book earns a place in your kitchen for years to come.

—Nick Fauchald and Kaitlyn Goalen, November 2015

THE SHORT STACK KITCHEN: SOME NOTES ON STAPLES AND EQUIPMENT

Butter. In our recipes, butter is identified as unsalted or salted. Traditionally, butter contained salt because it extended its shelf life, but now we have refrigerators for that. There's not much reason to use salted butter these days, and we prefer unsalted because it gives us more control over the seasoning process. Using salted butter is totally fine; just use less salt elsewhere in the recipe and adjust accordingly. One thing to keep in mind: Salted butter tends to contain more water, and therefore less butterfat, and therefore less flavor.

Eggs. Our recipes are made with "large" chicken eggs unless otherwise noted, but this really matters only in precise baking recipes. Otherwise, use whatever you have.

Flour. We prefer unbleached, all-purpose flour over the more common bleached variety, not because it's more "authentic" nor because it's free of the chemicals used to bleach flour, which haven't been proven to cause any harm (though some folks swear they can taste the difference between the two). From our experience, we've found that unbleached flour gives baked goods a little better structure. In short, use whatever you have on hand, but look for unbleached flour next time you need to stock up.

Pepper. If there's one ingredient about which we're going to be extra particular (at risk of sounding like snobs), it's pepper. Freshly ground pepper is so superior to the pre-ground stuff, and it's so easy to keep a pepper grinder on hand, that there's simply no use for that stuff in the tin box, ever. When it comes to measuring pepper, we find that it takes about 35 cranks of the mill to get 1 teaspoon of medium-coarse pepper. If we need a bunch of pepper, we'll grind a tablespoon of peppercorns in a spice mill before we start cooking. But the best thing you can do when it comes to this (or any) seasoning is let your taste buds be your measuring spoon.

Oil. We typically rotate among three types of cooking oil: neutral oil (which includes canola, vegetable and grapeseed, among others), olive oil and, less often, peanut oil. Canola and vegetable are interchangeable (canola is lower in saturated fat). For olive oil, we use a mild-flavored oil for cooking and, if we have it, a more flavorful and fancy extra-virgin for dressings and drizzling. Peanut oil is our favorite for frying.

Parmesan. In some recipes we call for Parmigiano-Reggiano cheese; in others Parmesan. This inconsistency is deliberate: Sometimes a recipe really highlights the highly regulated and consistently flavored DOC Parmigiano-Reggiano. Other times a more generic Parmesan works just as well—or even better, as there are some fantastic domestic Parms out there now.

Salt. We call for three types of salt in our recipes: fine sea salt, kosher salt and coarse or flaky sea salt. If a recipe calls for a specific measurement, we signify which of these three to use. Otherwise, use whatever you like, as long as it's not iodized. When we cook, we taste our food before seasoning it, often many times over the course of a recipe. You should do the same. Understanding how to—or not being afraid to—season food is the glass ceiling of cooking. Break through it!

Spices. Ground spices lose their potency more quickly than whole, so we usually buy the smallest amount of whole spices possible and grind them as needed (see **Mortar and pestle**). Unless you're one of those people who dates store-bought jars of spices and throws them away at the recommended time (we've never met), give your spices a sniff before you cook with them—most ground spices stay fresh for up to six months, while whole spices are good for one to two years. If they smell weak, you may need to use more than the recipe calls for.

Stock. Yes, we've heard you, every food writer and chef: Homemade stock is better than store-bought. Assume that any time you see stock listed—be it chicken, beef, vegetable, whatever—we're recommending homemade. However, decent canned stock is better than no stock at all, and there are many more passable options on the shelf now than when the stock truthers started their campaign.

Vinegar. You've probably heard that you should only cook with wine that you'd be happy to drink. The same goes for vinegar. Be it made from red wine, white wine, cider or some other beverage, the vinegar you cook with should be tasty enough on its own that you almost want to drink it. There's too much gross vinegar in this world, but luckily the good stuff is about the same price. We tend to go for the middle-of-the-road price point—not the cheapest thing on the shelf, but nothing more than $20 either. Keep trying different brands until you find some you like.

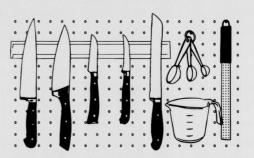

EQUIPMENT

Ovens. We'd guess that about half of all cooking snafus can be blamed on ovens. (Doesn't that make you feel better?) Most home ovens are wildly erratic, inaccurate and terrible at maintaining a constant temperature. It pays to get to know yours: Buy a couple of oven thermometers and place them in the front and back of your oven. Keep an eye on the actual temperature next time you bake (especially compared to whatever number you set your oven to), and you'll soon have a handle on how your oven behaves and how to calibrate it accordingly. That's why we usually offer a range—sometimes an absurdly wide range—of cooking times when using the oven, and why we include visual, temperature and tactile cues whenever possible. This is also a gentle reminder to employ all of your senses while cooking and rely less on the timer.

Stovetops.

Everything we said about ovens applies to stovetops and ranges as well, and then some. "High" heat on your average rented apartment stove is "medium" on one of those fancy commercial-type ranges that we covet. And while electric stovetops are inherently evil, plenty of us cooks have no other choice.

Knives.

Every chef pounds this into his or her staff: Keep your knives sharp or go home. But it's worth repeating here. We've actually seen cooking lives changed when someone switched from using dull knives to sharp ones. And yet we're all guilty of letting our blades go dull more often than we'll admit. A steel helps a sharp blade maintain its edge, but it doesn't do any actual sharpening (a diamond steel is slightly better, but it still won't rescue a dull blade). If you don't want to learn how to use a sharpening stone (that's what YouTube is for!), dump your knives into a box and take it to a kitchen shop or hardware store a couple times a year. There are three knives every cook should have: a small paring knife, a large chef's knife or santoku and a long serrated knife. Everything else is just gravy.

Measuring cups and spoons.

Except when we're baking or testing recipes, we don't use measuring spoons and cups much, yet we write and publish recipes that include very specific measurements. What's up with that? We (and the majority of modern recipe writers) have decided that it's better to be too specific than not specific enough, even though this encourages home cooks to lean too heavily on spoons and cups and not on their own intuition and personal preference. It takes only a small amount of practice to learn how to eyeball a tablespoon of salt or a cup of water, and most of the recipes in this book should be cooked with this in mind: It's very liberating when you realize that you don't have to precisely measure every ingredient in every recipe.

Kitchen scales.

We also don't call for ingredients to be weighed nearly as often as some current cookbooks. But sometimes it's easier to measure an ingredient by weight or essential to weigh out a very specific amount; for these two reasons, having an accurate kitchen scale around can be a lifesaver when you need it. That said, you can get by cooking the recipes in this book with the usual measuring cups and spoons.

Graters. A lot of our recipes call for finely zested ingredients, usually citrus peel or cheese. We're working under the assumption that you have a razor-sharp, rasp-style grater popularized by Microplane. The small holes on a box grater or its handheld equivalent work fine for cheese and nuts, but not so much for citrus. A sturdy box grater is nice to have around for everything else.

Mixers and blenders. If you don't own a stand mixer, an inexpensive handheld electric mixer can be used any time one is called for, whether or not the recipe says so. Even fewer of us are lucky enough to own a high-powered blender like the ones made by Vitamix, so any time we call for a blender, we're assuming you have a standard one. These are fine for pureeing and liquefying stuff, but food processors can do those tasks as well as chop and grind.

Mortar and pestle. Primitive-looking hand tools are so much more fun to cook with. The mortar and pestle makes us feel like an Aztec tribesman and an Italian grandmother all at once, but it's also more delicate than a food processor or spice grinder, making it easier to control the texture of sauces and spices.

Pots and pans. Heavy-bottomed pots and pans are always recommended, as they retain more heat and distribute it more evenly. Cooking with thin, flimsy pans is only going to cause you pain, and these days you can buy a set of decent heavy pans for the cost of a nice meal out.

For the purposes of this book, "large" saucepans hold 4 quarts (3.8 L) or more; "medium," 2 to 3 quarts (2 to 2.8 L); "small," 1 to 1.5 quarts (960 ml to 1.4 L). Dutch ovens are 5½-quart enameled cast-iron with a tight-fitting lid (unless otherwise noted). Likewise, "large" skillets are 12 to 14 inches (30.5 to 35.5 cm) across; "medium" are about 10 inches (25 cm); and "small" are 7 to 8 inches (17 to 20 cm).

Cast-iron skillets.
These are great because they're cheap, naturally nonstick and retain heat well (and they're "rustic," which is still cool at the time of publication). We call for them specifically in many recipes, but if you don't have one, don't sweat it: A heavy-bottomed skillet will work almost as well. One little-discussed drawback to cast-iron pans is that most are actually terrible at distributing heat evenly. If you're cooking a piece of meat or something that benefits from an evenly heated cooking surface, move your cast-iron pan around the burner as it heats (or, even better, heat it inside a hot oven first for 10 minutes).

Strainers.
Everyone should have at least one fine-mesh sieve or strainer in the kitchen—preferably two: one large and one small. You can use these to drain pasta and blanched vegetables, sift flour, strain stocks and sauces, fry stuff, etc., etc. Sorry, there's really no substitution or a MacGyver workaround for a mesh strainer.

Tongs.
Because no equipment-recommendation section is complete without an endorsement for spring-loaded tongs! Buy a pair in every size!

Thermometers.
The best meal-saving investment you can make is a high-quality instant digital thermometer. Learn to use one and you'll never overcook a piece of meat again. It can also replace that clunky candy/deep-fry thermometer. ThermoWorks makes the best thermometers we've used.

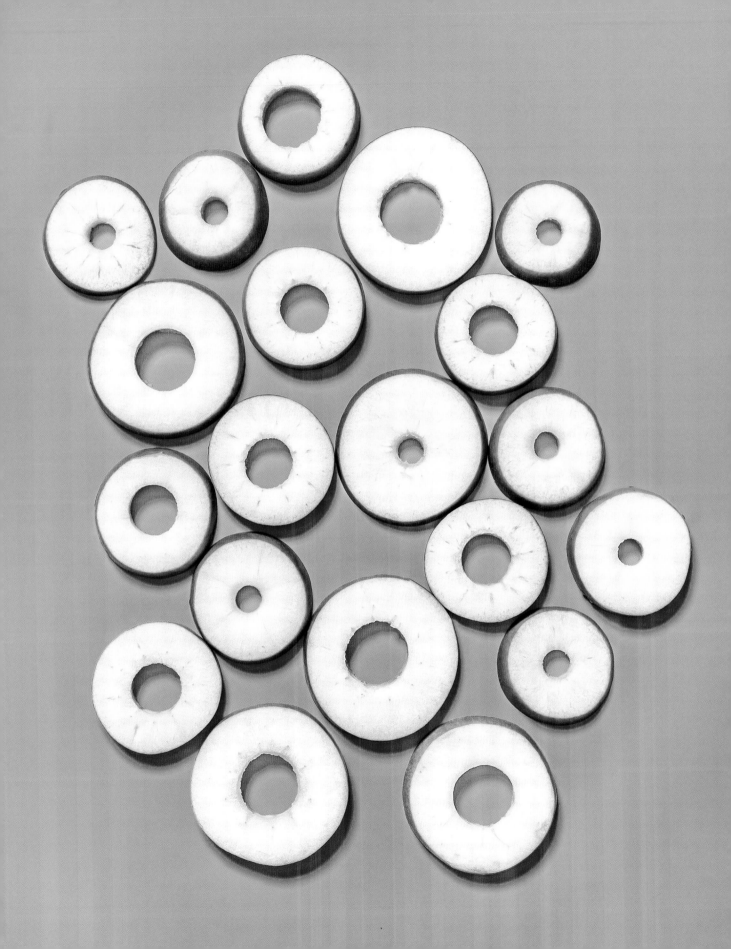

APPLES

Most ingredients gain their loyal devotees through cooking. But not apples, which seduce us long before they enter our kitchens. From the time we're young, the fruit embeds itself into our eating consciousness through myths, literature, maxims and the brown-bag lunch. Given apples' cultural weight and widespread accessibility, it's surprising they aren't even more of a cooking muse. Apple pie aside, the fruit sees a fraction of the excitement that other crops receive. It's almost as if all that early exposure we get leads to tedium in the kitchen.

But the beauty of apples is that they come in countless varieties, each offering different flavors, textures and nuances. Some, such as the Fuji, have a great crunch and delicate perfume that make them best for eating raw. Others, like the McIntosh, are a bit too mealy for eating out of hand but cook down into the most luxurious applesauce. Amazingly, many varieties are versatile workhorses that shine in all preparations. Used raw, they add crunch, acidity, sweetness and juiciness to their companions. When cooked, they can retain their crispness and personality, morph into tender caramelized morsels or melt into a thick, luscious puree. Best of all, apples lend themselves equally well to both sweet and savory preparations; they are as comfortable next to pork as they are in a cake or cocktail.

Apple, Sweet Potato & Smoked Trout Hash with Soft-Boiled Eggs

MAKES 4 SERVINGS

12 ounces (335 g) slender sweet potatoes (2 to 3), peeled and cut into ¾-inch cubes (3 cups/405 g)

2 tablespoons bacon drippings or butter

1 medium yellow onion, diced

1 celery stalk, diced

1 red bell pepper, cored and diced

Kosher salt

2 firm, tart apples, cored and cut into ¾-inch cubes

4 eggs

1 tablespoon chopped dill or thyme leaves

2 tablespoons chopped parsley

Finely grated zest and juice of 1 lemon

6 to 8 ounces (170 to 225 g) skinless hot-smoked trout, crumbled

Freshly ground black pepper

Lemon wedges, for serving

This hash pays homage to the traditional Appalachian breakfast of sautéed apples and smoky pork sausage or bacon, a favorite of author Sheri Castle (Vol. 20: Rhubarb), who grew up in the region. In her version, Sheri swaps in smoked trout for the pork and tops the hash with an oozing soft-boiled egg. You can also bake eggs right into the pan: Make four indentations in the top of the finished hash with a spoon and crack an egg into each, then broil the hash until the whites have set.

Bring a medium saucepan of salted water to a boil. Add the sweet potato cubes and blanch until barely tender, about 4 minutes. Drain well, transfer to a plate and set aside.

Heat the bacon drippings or butter in a large skillet over medium-high heat. Add the onion, celery, bell pepper and a pinch of salt. Cook, stirring occasionally, until almost tender, about 5 minutes. Add the apples and reserved sweet potato. Cook, stirring occasionally, until tender and beginning to brown in spots, about 12 minutes. Keep warm over low heat.

Place the eggs in single layer in a medium saucepan and cover with water. Cover the pan and bring the water to a boil over high heat. As soon as the water boils, remove the pan from the heat and let stand for 4 minutes. Drain and rinse the eggs under cold running water until cool enough to handle. Peel the eggs.

Fold the dill, parsley, lemon zest and juice and trout into the sweet potato mixture. Season with salt and pepper. Divide among 4 serving plates. Top each serving with a split egg sprinkled with salt and pepper. Serve immediately with lemon wedges.

Bruised Apple Quick Bread with Brown Butter Frosting

MAKES 1 LOAF

Our food system produces a shameful, environmentally disastrous, mind-blowing amount of waste. About a third of the American retail food supply gets thrown away each year, leaving behind landfills that produce a high percentage of our methane emissions, as well as hundreds of billions of dollars in lost revenue and millions of hungry people.

We've all been guilty of pushing aside imperfect ingredients at the market or discarding them long before they're actually unusable. This recipe is one small way to back off on your food waste, and your rewards will make the effort totally worthwhile. It begins by making a simple applesauce, for which bruised apples are essential. They're usually as sweet and flavorful as apples come, having hung on the tree long enough to become overripe (and, as a result, softer and more prone to blemishes). With this base, the cake-y bread requires less sugar and fat than most; in fact, the apples provide enough moisture to render additional butter extraneous.

4	bruised apples—peeled, cored and cut into quarters
2	teaspoons ground cinnamon, divided
2	cups (250 g) all-purpose flour
¼	teaspoon ground allspice
1½	teaspoons baking powder
½	teaspoon kosher salt
¼	cup (½ stick/55 g) unsalted butter, softened
¾	cup (165 g) tightly packed brown sugar
2	eggs, at room temperature
1	teaspoon vanilla paste or vanilla extract
	Brown Butter Frosting (recipe at right)
	Flaky sea salt, for garnish (optional)

Preheat the oven to 350°F (175°C). Spray a 9-by-5-inch loaf pan with nonstick cooking spray or coat with butter and set aside.

In a food processor, puree the apple quarters and 1 teaspoon of cinnamon until the mixture reaches the consistency of applesauce. Set aside. In a medium mixing bowl, whisk together the flour, the remaining teaspoon of cinnamon, allspice, baking powder and salt. Set aside.

In a stand mixer with a paddle attachment (or in a large mixing bowl with a handheld mixer), cream the butter and sugar at medium speed until light and fluffy. Beat in the eggs, one at a time, until fully incorporated. Add the flour mixture and beat until just incorporated, scraping down the bowl as needed. Remove the bowl from the stand and stir in the apple mixture and vanilla until evenly combined.

Pour the batter into the prepared pan and bake for 1 hour, or until the bread is a rich golden brown and a toothpick inserted into the center comes out clean.

Transfer the pan to a wire rack and let the bread cool for 15 minutes. Remove the bread from the pan and let cool completely before spreading with the Brown Butter Frosting (you might not need all of the frosting). Sprinkle with flaky salt, if desired. Slice and serve.

Brown Butter Frosting

MAKES ½ CUP (120 ML)

¼	cup (½ stick/55 g) unsalted butter
1	cup (125 g) confectioners' sugar
1	tablespoon plus 2 teaspoons whole milk

In a small skillet, heat the butter over low heat. Cook, stirring often, until the butter is melted and milk solids at the bottom of the pan turn dark amber and smell nutty. Remove the pan from the heat and skim off any foam. Set the butter aside and let cool to room temperature.

In a small mixing bowl, whisk together the cooled brown butter, sugar and milk until smooth.

Skillet Apple-Oat Cake

MAKES 6 SERVINGS

This recipe is the apple dessert of Alison Roman's dreams—literally. One night, the author of Short Stack Editions Vol. 13: Lemons imagined a cake that looked like a pancake, had the texture of a *cannelé* and tasted like a bowl of oatmeal with cinnamon apples in it. And after a few rounds of trial and error, Alison realized her vision: a cake that cooks like a Dutch baby, has a custardy texture (but with pieces of al dente apples, like a great pie) and tastes as good as the best bowl of oatmeal you've ever had.

½   cup (45 g) rolled oats

½   cup (65 g) all-purpose flour

2   tablespoons light brown sugar

½   teaspoon kosher salt

4   large eggs

½   cup (120 ml) buttermilk, shaken well

½   cup (120 ml) whole milk

4   tablespoons (½ stick/55 g) unsalted butter

2   large tart baking apples, such as Pink Lady or Granny Smith, cored and cut into ½-inch (12-mm) wedges

¼   cup (50 g) granulated sugar

¼   teaspoon ground cinnamon

     Honey, for serving

     Vanilla ice cream, for serving

Preheat the oven to 425°F (220°C).

In a medium cast-iron skillet, toast the oats over medium heat until they're lightly browned and have a toasty aroma. Transfer to a medium bowl and add the flour, brown sugar and salt and stir to blend. Whisk in the eggs, buttermilk and milk; set aside.

Add the butter to the same skillet and cook until it's foaming and starting to brown, about 2 minutes or so. Add the apples, sugar and cinnamon and stir to coat. Cook, stirring occasionally, until the apples are soft and the liquid in the skillet has reduced (the apples will release lots of juice, but it'll evaporate as they cook), 5 to 8 minutes.

Add the cake batter to the skillet (it will puff and start to set slightly around the edges from the heat of the skillet) and transfer to the oven. Bake the cake until the top is golden brown and the edges start to pull away from the sides of the skillet, 15 to 20 minutes.

Remove the skillet from the oven and drizzle honey over the top. Serve warm, preferably with some really good vanilla ice cream. Leftover cake can be refrigerated for up to 2 days.

Our Favorite Apples for:

COOKING: Empire, Golden Delicious, Granny Smith, Jonathan, Macoun, McIntosh, Northern Spy
NOT COOKING (AND JUICING): Braeburn, Orange Pippin, Fuji, Gala, Honeycrisp, Jonagold

Braised Duck Legs with Apples Three Ways

MAKES 4 SERVINGS

4   fresh duck legs (3 to 4 pounds/1.4 to 1.8 kg total)

Kosher salt and freshly ground black pepper

2   medium onions, thinly sliced, divided

2   rosemary sprigs

1   cup (240 ml) apple cider

1   cup (240 ml) apple cider vinegar

2   cups (480 ml) chicken stock

3   large tart apples, such as Granny Smith—peeled, cored and sliced ½ inch thick

As the name implies, this dish showcases apples in three forms: whole fruit, cider and vinegar. But it also shows us a trio of ways that apples can be used in cooking: as seasoning, sweetener and starch (or thickener).

Cooking duck successfully comes down to dealing with fat. Because ducks carry much more external fat than most poultry, you have to render some of it so it doesn't overwhelm the dish (bonus: you'll have a nice supply of rendered fat for cooking potatoes, vegetables and other stuff). At the same time, duck meat is rich enough to stand up to big flavors and long, slow cooking. We borrowed this method of braising duck uncovered from the English chef Fergus Henderson; the exposure lets the duck skin crisp up above the surface as the meat below slowly braises into submission. (For extra-crispy skin, place the pot under the broiler for a couple of minutes just before serving.)

Preheat the oven to 350°F (175°C). Trim the excess fat and skin from the sides of the duck legs, leaving the tops of the legs covered with skin. Score the skin on the legs in a ½-inch crosshatch pattern, cutting through the fat but not into the meat. Season both sides with salt and pepper.

Coarsely chop the excess duck fat. Place the fat in a large heavy skillet and cook over medium heat, stirring occasionally, until rendered. Using a slotted spoon, transfer any solids to paper towels to drain, then season with salt and eat the duck cracklings as a snack or save for garnish.

Carefully strain the rendered fat into a measuring cup and wipe out the skillet. Spoon 2 tablespoons of the rendered fat into a large heavy pot or enameled cast-iron casserole and heat over medium-high heat. Add 2 of the duck legs, skin-side down, and cook until the skin is well browned, 4 to 5 minutes. Flip and cook until browned on the other side, about 2 minutes longer. Transfer to a plate. Spoon off all but 2 tablespoons of the fat (reserve the fat for later) and brown the remaining 2 duck legs, then transfer to the plate.

Add half of the onions to the pot and cook, until browned, about 10 minutes. Add the rosemary and cook until fragrant, about 1 minute. Add the apple cider and vinegar and simmer vigorously, scraping up any browned bits on the bottom of the pan, until syrupy, about 10 minutes. Return the duck legs to the pot, skin-side up, arranging them into as close of a single layer as possible. Pour in enough stock to submerge the legs up to the skin, then bring to a boil. Transfer to the oven and braise, uncovered, until the meat is very tender, about 2 hours.

Meanwhile, in the large skillet, heat 2 tablespoons of reserved duck fat over medium-high heat. Add the remaining onion and cook until browned and soft, about 10 minutes. Add the apples and cook, stirring, until crisp-tender, about 6 minutes.

Transfer the braised duck legs to a platter. Strain the juices into a fat separator and return the juices to the pot, stopping when you reach the fat. Discard the solids. (Alternatively, strain the juices into a measuring cup and spoon off the fat.) Bring the liquid to a simmer and reduce until thickened slightly. Add the apple-onion mixture to the juices and heat through. Season to taste with salt, pepper and more vinegar, if needed. Spoon the juices around the duck legs and serve. The cooked duck legs can be refrigerated in the juices overnight. Reheat gently and serve.

Apple Margarita

MAKES 1 DRINK

We bought our first high-powered juicer with apples in mind; the vast majority of store-bought apple juice is nowhere near as aromatic and complex as the fresh stuff. After a few (mostly failed) attempts at making homemade hard cider, we turned to more immediate ways to enjoy fresh apple juice in a boozy environment.

Apple juice is amazingly versatile as a cocktail mixer: It gets along with both clear (gin, vodka) and aged (whiskey, brandy, rum, tequila) spirits; can be used in both shaken and stirred drinks; and works both as a sweetener and an acid. In this extra-refreshing margarita, for instance, it adds sugar to the cocktail and pairs with lime juice to provide another layer of bright, lightly floral flavor. Swap the tequila for gin and top with soda and you've got yourself an apple rickey; replace it with vodka and you have an actually good apple martini, and so on. We think the best varieties for juicing are Fuji and Honeycrisp, but try a bunch of apples to find your favorites.

2   ounces (60 ml) reposado tequila

2   ounces (60 ml) fresh sweet-tart apple juice (or high-quality bottled apple juice)

1   ounce fresh lime juice

     Ice

     Thinly sliced apple, for garnish

In a cocktail shaker, combine the tequila, apple juice and lime juice. Fill the shaker with ice and shake vigorously until the shaker is very cold. Strain the margarita into a glass, garnish with a slice of apple and serve.

Apple, Cabbage & Pork Sausage Hand Pies

MAKES 8 HAND PIES

In many savory apple recipes, the apples are just another form of sweetness. But here, the fruit's texture is its essential contribution: It helps bind the other ingredients into a cohesive filling and adds a bright, tart flavor to that favorite cold-weather trio of apples, cabbage and pork. We've learned from experience that it's worth making extra pies: Bake and serve four pies right away, and freeze four more for later. They can go from the freezer to the oven to happy hands in less than an hour.

1   large leek, roots and dark green leaves discarded

1   tablespoon olive oil

     Kosher salt and freshly ground black pepper

2   semi-tart apples, such as Braeburn or Fuji (about 1 pound/455 g total)—peeled, cored and cut into ¼-inch dice (about 4 cups/640 g)

½   teaspoon chopped thyme leaves

½   pound (225 g) pork sausage, such as sweet Italian

2   cups (140 g) lightly packed finely shredded Savoy cabbage (from a 4-ounce/115-g chunk of cabbage)

½   cup (240 ml) crème fraîche or heavy cream

¼   cup (25 g) freshly grated Parmigiano-Reggiano cheese

     Hot sauce

     Fresh lemon juice, to taste

1   batch The Best, Flakiest Pastry Dough (page 81)

Halve the leek lengthwise, then slice it into ¼-inch half-moons. Rinse well in a colander, then drain very well (a salad spinner works great).

Heat the oil in a large skillet over medium heat. Add the leek, season lightly with salt and pepper and cook, stirring, until very soft and fragrant, about 13 minutes. (If the leeks seem dry, cover the pan to capture steam; add a spoonful of water if you need more moisture.) Scrape the leek into a large bowl.

If the pan looks dry, add another splash of oil, increase the heat to medium-high and add the apples. Season with salt, pepper and the thyme. Cook, stirring occasionally, until the apples are lightly browned on the outside and tender but not yet mushy, about 5 minutes. Add them to the bowl with the leek.

Add the sausage to the pan and cook over medium-high heat, breaking it up with a spatula so there are no chunks larger than a peanut, until it's no longer pink, about 6 minutes. Add the sausage to the bowl.

Add the cabbage to the skillet, season with salt and pepper, and add about ¼ cup (60 ml) of water. Cover the skillet and cook over medium heat until the cabbage has wilted, about 5 minutes. Uncover and continue cooking the cabbage, tossing frequently, until it's very tender and starting to turn golden, about 8 minutes longer. Add the crème fraîche or cream and cook until the cream has reduced to a glossy coating, about 4 minutes. Add the cheese and scrape everything from the skillet into the bowl with the apples. Toss to combine, then season to taste with salt, pepper, hot sauce, and lemon juice until the mixture is highly savory and delicious. Let the filling cool completely, preferably in the refrigerator (you can't assemble the pies if the filling is warm).

To assemble the hand pies: Cut the dough into 8 even pieces. Gently shape each piece into a circle. Flatten the circle by pressing with your fingertips until you have a disk that's about 3 inches across. If the dough is sticking as you're doing this, dust it or your hands with flour.

Lightly flour the work surface and roll the disk into a circle about 7 inches in diameter. Scoop out one-eighth of the filling and pile it onto the lower half of the circle, leaving a 1-inch border.

Brush the border lightly with water. Fold over the top half of the dough circle, tucking it around the filling, and press gently around the edges to seal the two layers of dough. Starting on one end, fold the edge over in small pleats, pressing firmly to seal. Work your way around the edge until the pie is fully sealed. Repeat with the rest of the dough and filling. If your kitchen is warm, place the assembled pies in the refrigerator as you work on the rest. Chill for at least 30 minutes. (If you want to make the pies ahead of time, you can chill them well and freeze them for up to 1 month. Bake the frozen pies without thawing them, but lower the oven temperature to 350°F/175°C and bake for closer to 1 hour.)

To bake the pies, preheat the oven to 375°F (190°C). Cut three ½-inch slits into the top of each pie, arrange the pies on a heavy baking sheet and bake until the pies are light brown all over (be sure to check the underside of the pies), 30 to 40 minutes. Some juices from the filling may bubble through the seams or slits; that's fine. Transfer the pies to a rack to cool slightly before serving warm. The pies can be baked a few hours ahead of time and reheated for 10 minutes or so in a 375°F (190°C) oven.

Apple Cider Molasses

MAKES ABOUT ¾ CUP (180 ML)

Recipes for apple molasses (aka boiled cider) in America date back to the 17th century. Back then, it was a quotidian sweetener, as was maple syrup, because it could be produced using local ingredients and didn't rely on processed sugar or molasses, which had to be imported. But we don't encounter much apple molasses these days, which is a shame: This stuff, especially when it's made with really good, unpasteurized cider—the kind you buy on that annual fall pilgrimage to the pick-your-own orchard—is apple flavor in a very pure, concentrated form.

Cider molasses can impart the tart fruit's flavor anywhere regular molasses is called for—hell, anywhere sugar is needed. Use it to sweeten an apple pie or crumble. Add a little to your tea. Swap it for simple syrup in cocktails (especially hot toddies); use it in salad dressing to glaze pork or ham. It loves roasted vegetables as well. Drizzle it over pancakes or waffles, blend it with cream cheese and use it to stuff French toast, or mix it into frosting for carrot cake.

The goal here is to slowly cook apple cider down to one-tenth of its volume. If you're starting with a half-gallon (about 2 L) of cider, for example, you'll end up with 6.4 ounces (195 ml) of molasses, which is a little more than ¾ cup (180 ml). If you like, infuse your syrup with spices (cinnamon, cloves, etc.) while it cooks down. This is very much a by-feel kind of recipe. The timing will change based on the size of the batch you're making, the size of your pot and what "simmer" means to you. You can reduce it a little less and leave it loose, like maple syrup, or go all the way down to dark, intense molasses.

½   gallon (2 L) apple cider

Salt

Pour 1 cup (180 ml) of water into a saucepan. Stand a wooden skewer in the pot. Take it out, and mark the line where the water hit on the skewer. Set it aside, pour out the water and dry the pot. Add the cider and a pinch of salt. Bring the cider to a boil, then reduce the heat until it's simmering briskly. Check on it every 10 minutes or so and give it a stir with a heatproof spatula or wooden spoon. It will take a while to fully reduce (an hour or longer), depending on the size of your pot. Resist the urge to cook the cider higher than a brisk simmer because it can burn easily, especially toward the end. When it starts to thicken, stay close and keep stirring. When you think it's almost finished, use the skewer to guide you. If the cider starts to thicken to molasses consistency before it hits the level the one-tenth the mark the skewer, feel free to pull it off the heat.

When the molasses is done, pour it into a nonreactive bowl and let it cool, then transfer it to a lidded jar. Use a sterilized jar if you want to store it at room temperature (it will keep for up to 4 months). A nonsterilized jar is fine as long as you refrigerate the molasses (up to 2 months). It will thicken in the fridge, but it's easily thinned by warming it gently.

Salted Apple Jam

MAKES 2 CUPS (480 ML)

3 pounds (1.4 kg) apples, such as Granny Smith, Cortland, or Gala (use a mix!)—peeled, cored, and cut into ½-inch pieces

1 cup (200 g) sugar, divided

1 vanilla bean, split and seeds scraped

2 cinnamon sticks

1 whole star anise

1 tablespoon apple cider vinegar

Coarse sea salt

This is another great way to use up blemished apples or the spoils from an overly enthusiastic trip to the orchard. It falls somewhere between a jam and a chunky compote. Most apple-based condiments become muddy and brown when you cook them, but this recipe begins with making a caramel, which helps lock in the apples' color and adds extra depth. This technique works great with other light-fleshed fruit as well, such as pears and peaches. In addition to topping morning toast, the jam can be dressed up as a dessert (spread on toasted brioche and top with vanilla ice cream) or used as a cheese-plate accompaniment.

In a large bowl, combine the apples, ¼ cup (50 g) of sugar, the vanilla bean and seeds, cinnamon sticks and star anise. Stir until well mixed, then let sit for about 30 minutes; the apples will release some of their juices.

Combine the remaining ¾ cup (150 g) of sugar and ¼ cup (60 ml) of water in a saucepan. Bring to a simmer over medium heat and cook until the mixture is a light-amber color (do not let it get too dark), 5 to 8 minutes. Add the apples to the caramel and stir to coat (the caramel will seize up momentarily—this is okay; it will melt back down).

Lower the heat to medium-low and cook, stirring occasionally at first, then more frequently as the mixture cooks down. The apples will break down and turn into a chunky applesauce-like texture; the total cooking time will range from 25 to 40 minutes, depending on the size of the pot and the types of apples you're using.

Stir in the vinegar and a hearty pinch of salt and taste the mixture; it should be pleasantly salty and a little tangy. Adjust with more vinegar and salt as needed. Remove the cinnamon stick, vanilla pod and star anise before transferring the mixture to an airtight container or jar; refrigerate until ready to use, up to 2 weeks.

BACON

Our relationship with bacon is complicated. We came of food-writing age just as America's favorite breakfast meat became a celebrity. This must have been a product of the Internet; imagine such a thing happening anytime before 2000. One day, bacon was America's modest, enduring breakfast meat, and then, suddenly, it was omnipresent. We don't need to recap the whole bacon explosion—not to be confused with the monstrosity that is the Bacon Explosion™, the protein's shark-jumping moment—with its bacon-covered apparel, bacon-themed memes, bacon-flavored, -scented and -infused everything, everywhere, in every store, on every menu. At some point, we got baconed out. We avoided dishes at restaurants *because* they contained bacon; we ceased wrapping our scallops and Thanksgiving turkeys in the stuff. We moved on to other cured and smoked meats: country ham, chorizo, 'nduja, etc.

But this over-adored, overexposed burnout wasn't bacon's fault. Bacon is a delicious preserved pork product—one of the few foods that deserves the word "delicious"—and it's one of the most generous ingredients we've met. When cooked, it surrenders up its sweet, porky fat, a gift that we can use again to cook something else or, hell, spread over a piece of bread like butter. It leaves behind rich, smoky, umami-flavored meat that really does "make everything better," as the T-shirts, mugs and so on say.

So we're here, bacon, with our backlash to the backlash. And we're not leaving you again. Just don't forget where you came from.

Bacon Jam-Crusted Sticky Ribs

MAKES 4 SERVINGS

1   pound (455 g) sliced bacon, cut crosswise into ½-inch pieces

1   12-rib rack of St. Louis–style pork spare ribs (about 4 pounds/1.8 kg)

1   yellow onion, quartered

4   garlic cloves

¼   cup (55 g) packed brown sugar

¼   cup (60 ml) pure maple syrup

¼   cup (60 ml) apple cider vinegar

2   tablespoons tomato paste or ¼ cup (60 ml) ketchup

12   ounces (360 ml) non-hoppy beer

Now here's some pig-on-pig-on-pig action: pork ribs braised in bacon fat and their own juices, then covered with bacon jam and broiled. This is definitely a Sunday recipe, but more due to total time than active labor, and you can always split up the project by making the bacon jam on its own (serving instruction: Spread. On. Everything.).

Buy the smokiest bacon you can find: Generally speaking, hickory-smoked bacon will be more pronounced than applewood-smoked, though double-smoked bacon, which you'll find at Polish butchers, is especially great in this recipe.

Preheat the oven to 225°F (110°C). In a large cast-iron skillet, cook the bacon over medium heat until crispy and well browned. Using a slotted spoon, transfer the bacon to paper towels to drain; leave the remaining fat in the pan.

Cut the rack of ribs in half and place the halves, meaty-side down, in the skillet. Cover with foil and bake in the oven for 3 hours, or until very tender and cooked through.

Make the bacon jam: Place the rendered bacon pieces, onion, garlic, brown sugar, maple syrup, cider vinegar and tomato paste in a food processor. Pulse until finely chopped. Transfer to a saucepan and add the beer. Bring to a boil, then lower the heat and simmer until reduced to a jammy consistency, about 45 minutes. Let cool.

When the ribs are cooked, uncover the pan and pour off any fat and juice (save this delicious cooking liquid for other uses if you like). Flip the ribs over so they're meaty-side up. Evenly spread the bacon jam over the top of the ribs and bake, uncovered, for 1 hour. Remove from the oven and let cool for 10 minutes.

Preheat the broiler. Broil the ribs until the top is bubbling and golden brown, 1 to 2 minutes. Let the ribs rest for 5 minutes before slicing and serving.

Pappardelle with Bacon & Root Vegetable Ragu

MAKES 4 TO 6 SERVINGS

1 pound (455 g) thick-cut bacon slices, cut crosswise into 1/4-inch pieces

1 large onion, diced

3 garlic cloves, thinly sliced

1 8-ounce (225-g) piece celery root, peeled and cut into 1/4-inch dice

8 ounces (225 g) carrots (about 4 medium), peeled and cut into 1/4-inch dice

8 ounces (225 g) parsnips (about 2 medium), peeled and cut into 1/4-inch dice

1 sprig rosemary

1 sprig thyme

1/4 cup (60 ml) tomato paste

1/2 cup (120 ml) dry white wine

1 cup (240 ml) chicken stock or low-sodium broth

12 ounces (340 g) pappardelle pasta

Salt and freshly ground black pepper

Freshly grated Parmigiano-Reggiano cheese, for serving

We love the combination of smoky bacon and sweet, earthy root vegetables, especially parsnips and celery root. When simmered, bacon gives up most of its flavor to the cooking liquid, and the meat left behind is more porky than bacon-y. To avoid this and keep the flavor focused, we pull the bacon from the pan while it's still crisp and use the rendered fat to sauté the vegetables for the sauce, then add the bacon bits to the finished dish as a crunchy garnish.

In a large heavy saucepan, cook the bacon over medium heat, stirring frequently, until most of the fat has rendered, about 15 minutes. Increase the heat to medium-high and cook until the bacon is lightly browned and crisp, 3 to 5 minutes. Using a slotted spoon, transfer the bacon to a paper towel–lined plate to drain.

Pour out all but about 3 tablespoons of the bacon fat (reserve the rest for another use). Add the onion, garlic, celery root, carrots and parsnips to the pan and cook over medium heat, stirring to loosen as many browned bits from the bottom of the pan as possible, until the onion is softened, about 6 minutes. Add the rosemary and thyme and cook until fragrant, about 1 minute. Add the tomato paste and cook until it coats the vegetables and glazes the bottom of the pan, about 2 minutes.

Add the wine and simmer, stirring to loosen the browned bits from the bottom of the pan, until reduced by half, about 2 minutes. Add the stock and bring to a boil, then reduce the heat to medium-low, cover the pan and simmer until the vegetables are tender, about 15 minutes.

Meanwhile, bring a pot of salted water to a boil and cook the pappardelle until al dente. Reserve at least 1 cup (240 ml) of the cooking water, then drain the pasta.

Discard the herb sprigs from the sauce and stir in half of the bacon. Season with salt and pepper. Add the pasta and some of the cooking water and toss until the sauce coats the pasta, adding more cooking water as necessary.

Transfer the pasta and ragu to bowls, garnish with the remaining bacon and the cheese and serve.

Cider-Braised Bacon

MAKES 4 TO 6 SERVINGS

We sometimes forget that before bacon is sliced, it's just a slab of meat. It takes to a braise as well as anything else, and does more to flavor its cooking liquid than other cuts (making it all the better for reducing it into a pan sauce). The step of reducing the cooking liquid is vital: We've tried this dish both with and without the thickened sauce, and it's well worth the extra reduction. The extra effort will elevate the dish from bacon to BACON!!!

1   1½-pound (680-g) piece slab bacon

3   cups (720 ml) apple cider

¼   cup (60 ml) apple cider vinegar

¼   cup (60 ml) honey (clover, apple or orange blossom honey work especially well)

1   bay leaf

1   tablespoon whole black peppercorns

Preheat the oven to 325°F (165°C). In a Dutch oven or baking dish, combine the bacon, apple cider, vinegar, honey, bay leaf and peppercorns. Cover the dish tightly with a lid or aluminum foil and place in the oven. Braise for 1 hour; turn the bacon over, recover and continue to braise for 1 hour longer. Remove the Dutch oven from the oven and let the bacon cool, uncovered, in the liquid for 1 hour.

Transfer the cooled bacon to a cutting board and cut into ¼- to ½-inch-thick slices. Strain the braising liquid through a fine-mesh sieve into a saucepan. Bring to a boil over medium-high heat and cook until the liquid is reduced to about ½ cup (120 ml), 18 to 20 minutes. Heat a skillet over medium-high heat and fry the bacon slices, turning once, until they're browned and caramelized all over, 2 to 3 minutes a side. Add the reduced sauce, tilt the pan to coat the bacon slices and serve.

Leftovers?

Rebekah Peppler (Vol. 8: Honey), who created this recipe, suggests re-crisping leftover slices of bacon and using them in BLTs (or BLATs, or whatever acronym-based sandwiches you're into). We couldn't agree more with her.

Dark Chocolate Chunk-Bacon Cookies

MAKES 5 TO 6 DOZEN

We love this recipe from Beth Lipton (Vol. 16: Peaches) because it brings together two beloved-but-pedestrian things—bacon and chocolate chip cookies—and breathes a little new life into both. It's also a tidy lesson on using bacon fat in baking: You can swap it in for some of the butter, shortening or, of course, lard, as long as the total amount of fat remains the same. In these cookies, bacon fat accounts for about a third of the total fat, which is plenty to give the cookies a sweet-smoky flavor but without bacon stealing the show (which happens all too often when adding bacon to sweets). This is a good occasion to use a less-intense applewood-smoked bacon.

8	ounces (225 g) thick-cut bacon (about 4 slices), cut into 1/2-inch pieces
2 1/4	cups (280 g) all-purpose flour
1	teaspoon baking soda
1/2	teaspoon salt
11	tablespoons (155 g) unsalted butter, at room temperature
3/4	cup (150 g) granulated sugar
3/4	cup (165 g) packed dark brown sugar
2	large eggs
2	teaspoons pure vanilla extract
10	ounces (280 g) dark chocolate (at least 70% cacao), chopped into 1/2-inch pieces

Cured vs. "Uncured" Bacon

When shopping for bacon, you've probably noticed that some packages contain "uncured" bacon. This is a misnomer: All of the "uncured" bacon we've encountered has actually been cured, though without the use of sodium nitrate (saltpeter) or sodium nitrite (pink salt), two compounds commonly used in meat preservation. Because these additives have been linked to bad side effects, some folks avoid meats cured with them. Instead, manufacturers use celery salt or extra sea salt to make up the difference. For this reason, you can usually spot "uncured" bacon by its grayish color. It will probably also be saltier than cured bacon, so back off on your seasoning a bit when cooking with it.

Place a fine-mesh sieve over a bowl. In a large skillet, cook the bacon over medium heat, stirring occasionally, about 10 minutes. Pour the contents of the skillet into the sieve, collecting the fat in the bowl. Refrigerate the fat until it's firm, at least 20 minutes. If you want smaller pieces of bacon in your cookies, chop it again (you should have about 1/2 cup/115 g); place the bacon in a bowl and set aside.

In a small bowl, whisk together the flour, baking soda and salt. Using a tablespoon measure, spoon 5 tablespoons (75 ml) of the bacon fat into the bowl of a stand mixer fitted with the paddle attachment (if you don't have 5 tablespoons/75 ml of fat, you can make up the difference with more butter as long as you use a total of 1 cup/240 ml of fat). Add the butter and both sugars and mix at medium-high speed until light and fluffy, about 3 minutes. Add the eggs, one at a time, mixing well after each addition. Beat in the vanilla. Scrape down the side of the bowl with a spatula.

Turn the mixer speed to low and beat in the flour mixture until just combined. Using a wooden spoon, stir in the chocolate and reserved bacon pieces. Form the dough into a ball, wrap in plastic and refrigerate for at least 1 and up to 12 hours.

Place racks on the top and bottom thirds of the oven and preheat to 375°F (190°C). Line two large baking sheets with parchment paper or silicone baking mats. Using a tablespoon, portion the dough into individual balls. Arrange the dough balls on the baking sheets about 2 inches (5 cm) apart. Bake for 10 to 12 minutes, until golden and firm, rotating the baking sheets from top to bottom and front to back halfway through.

Transfer the baking sheets to wire racks and let cool for 5 minutes, then transfer the cookies to the racks and let cool completely. Repeat with the remaining dough. (You can also portion the dough into balls and freeze them for up to 1 month. Bake the cookie dough from its frozen state; it may need an extra minute or two and the cookies will not spread as much.)

Smoky Whipped Bacon Fat

MAKES ABOUT 1½ CUPS (360 ML)

1   cup (240 ml) cold rendered bacon fat

1   small shallot, finely grated

1   teaspoon finely grated lemon zest

1   tablespoon fresh lemon juice

1   teaspoon smoked paprika

2   tablespoons finely chopped cilantro

Fine sea salt and freshly ground black pepper

This recipe takes a brunch byproduct and makes it a star. If you're not saving every drop of leftover fat when you cook bacon, perhaps this smoky spread will convince you to do so. At first it sounds insane to eat whipped bacon fat, but it's a sign of how intimate we've become with this ingredient.

Use this as a butter alternative for spreading on breads and rolls, or serve a small bowl of it with radishes and other raw vegetables for dipping.

Place the fat, shallot, zest, juice, paprika, cilantro, 1½ teaspoons of salt and ½ teaspoon of pepper in the bowl of a stand mixer fitted with a whisk attachment (or use a bowl and a handheld electric mixer). Beat the fat until fluffy, about 3 minutes. Season with salt and pepper to taste and serve. Refrigerate the fat in an airtight container or jar for up to 1 week.

Saving Bacon Fat

As easy as it sounds, there are a couple of things to remember when storing leftover bacon fat. First, strain the fat through a fine-mesh sieve to remove any solids. Save your fat in a glass container (hot fat can melt plastic, and grease-coated plastic is tough to clean) and store it in the refrigerator. Discard unused fat after a month or two; you'll be able to smell it if it begins to go rancid. You can also freeze bacon fat; it should keep for several months, if not longer.

Bacon-Fried Steaks with Pan Gravy

MAKES 2 SERVINGS

Country-fried (or chicken-fried) steak—the American South's answer to Wiener schnitzel—has always been as welcome on the breakfast table as it is at dinner, and the addition of bacon and gravy make it even more so. But we've broken a couple of rules: First, CFS is traditionally made with a tough, cheap cut of beef that's been beaten to mush with a meat tenderizer. You could certainly follow suit, but we prefer the sirloin tip, which is lean, tender and still inexpensive compared to other steak cuts. (You might also see sirloin tip sold under its less-appealing moniker, "flap meat.")

Second, we've put bacon all over this thing: ground bacon in the crust and bacon fat in the cooking oil and gravy. And if you have any leftover slices of uncooked bacon handy when you've finished cooking the steaks, you can batter and fry those, too.

FOR THE STEAKS:

8 to 10 strips (8 ounces/225 g) thinly sliced bacon

1 cup (125 g) all-purpose flour

½ teaspoon baking powder

1 teaspoon kosher salt

1 teaspoon freshly ground black pepper

¼ teaspoon cayenne pepper

¼ cup (30 g) cornstarch

1 large egg

⅔ cup (165 ml) buttermilk, well shaken

2 8-ounce (225-g) sirloin tip steaks (about ¾ inch thick)

Peanut or vegetable oil, for frying

FOR THE GRAVY:

2 tablespoons all-purpose flour

1 cup (240 ml) warm whole milk

Kosher salt and freshly ground black pepper

Tabasco hot sauce (optional)

Make the steaks: Preheat the oven to 375°F (190°C) and place a wire rack in a rimmed baking sheet.

Arrange the bacon slices on top of the rack and bake, turning the bacon over once or twice, until very crisp, about 30 minutes. Carefully pour the fat from the pan into a measuring cup and reserve. Transfer the bacon to a cutting board and chop it very finely; you should have about ½ cup (115 g).

In a shallow bowl, whisk together the flour, baking powder, salt, pepper and cayenne pepper. Add the bacon pieces and work them into the flour with your hands; the flour should dampen slightly and the bacon should be completely coated. Place the cornstarch in a separate shallow bowl. In a third shallow bowl, beat the egg, then beat in the buttermilk.

Place the steaks on a cutting board and pound them with a meat hammer or some other heavy object until about they're ¼ to ½ inch thick. Season with salt and pepper. Dredge one of the steaks in the cornstarch until coated, then shake off any excess. Slide the steak into the egg mixture and turn to coat well. Lift the steak and let any excess egg drip off, then dredge in the bacon-flour mixture, pressing it into the steak until completely coated. Transfer the meat to a wire rack and repeat with the remaining steak.

In a large cast-iron or nonstick skillet, heat 1 inch of oil and all but 2 tablespoons of the bacon fat until it reaches 375°F (190°C) on a deep-fry thermometer. Carefully slide one of the steaks into the oil and cook, turning once, until browned and crisp on both sides, 2 to 3 minutes per side. Transfer the meat to a plate and repeat with the other steak.

Make the gravy: Pour out all of the frying oil and add the remaining 2 tablespoons of bacon fat; place the skillet over medium-high heat. Add the flour and cook, whisking constantly, until it turns light brown, 1 to 2 minutes. Slowly add the milk, whisking constantly. Bring the milk to a boil, then simmer until thickened to a gravy-like consistency, about 5 minutes. Remove the gravy from the heat and season to taste with salt, lots of pepper and Tabasco sauce, if using.

Transfer the steaks to plates, spoon some of the gravy over the top and serve.

Bacon-Chile Relish

MAKES ABOUT 1 CUP (240 ML)

This relish is loosely based on *nam prik pao*, a Thai condiment made with fried or roasted chiles and dried shrimp. In Thailand, this sweet-salty-tangy-funky relish is often served with *tom yum* (a hot-and-sour soup) and stir-fries or as a snack-like dip for pork rinds. It was actually this last application that gave us the idea for substituting crispy bacon for the shrimp. You end up with two condiments in one, really: a crunchy paste and a gently spicy chile oil. (If you really love heat, make this with the Salted Chiles on page 120 or a spicier jarred pepper.)

The relish also contains two Thai pantry staples that have become indispensable in our own kitchen: fried garlic and shallots. These thinly sliced alliums have been fried into a feathery crispiness and lend a desirable crunch. If you can't find them at an Asian market or in the (potentially xenophobic) "ethnic" or "international" section of your supermarket, they're easy to make at home: Fry paper-thin slices in 365°F (185°C) oil for a couple of minutes. But these are two ingredients—like ketchup or Oreos—where store-bought is actually better.

5	slices bacon (not thick cut)
⅓	cup (75 g) jarred pickled red chiles in oil (we love Mama Lil's brand or Peppadew)
2	tablespoons chile oil from the jar
1	tablespoon fried garlic (available at Asian markets)
1	tablespoon fried shallots (available at Asian markets)
1	tablespoon palm sugar or light brown sugar
1	tablespoon Asian fish sauce, or more to taste
1	tablespoon fresh lime juice, or more to taste

Preheat the oven to 300°F (150°C) and place a wire rack in a rimmed baking sheet. Arrange the bacon on the rack and bake, turning once or twice, until dark brown (but not burnt) and crispy, about 1 hour. Transfer the bacon to paper towels and blot away any excess fat. Let cool completely, then chop very finely; you should be left with a coarse meal. Transfer to a small bowl.

Finely chop the pickled chiles, then add them to the bacon along with the chile oil, fried garlic and shallots. In a separate small bowl, whisk together the sugar, fish sauce and lime juice until the sugar has dissolved. Pour this mixture into the bacon-chile mixture and stir well with a fork to break up the garlic and shallots. Season to taste with more fish sauce and/or lime juice. Refrigerate in an airtight container or jar until ready to use, up to 1 week.

Dirty Devils

MAKES 3 DOZEN

½ pound (225 g) organic chicken livers

1 cup (240 ml) whole milk

4 tablespoons (½ stick/55 g) butter, divided

1 tablespoon canola oil

2 thyme sprigs, plus 1 teaspoon leaves for garnish

2 garlic cloves

1 tablespoon honey

Salt and freshly ground black pepper

12 slices thin-cut bacon

36 pitted Deglet dates

Long before the Internet wrapped everything from tacos to hot dogs in bacon, the most common gifts befitting this meaty wrapping paper were chicken livers, known as *rumaki*, and dates, aka devils on horseback. This recipe combines these two trailblazers in one rich, savory bite. Deglet dates are a bit smaller and less sticky than Medjool dates, which make them easier to wrap tightly—but either will work fine.

Combine the chicken livers and milk in a small bowl, cover, and refrigerate overnight. Strain and rinse the chicken livers, then pat dry.

In a medium skillet, melt 1 tablespoon of butter in the canola oil over medium heat. Add the thyme sprigs and garlic and cook until fragrant, about 1 minute. Add the chicken livers and cook, turning occasionally, until browned all over but still pink in the center, about 6 minutes total. Transfer the contents of the pan to a bowl and refrigerate for 1 hour.

Transfer the liver mixture to a food processor. Add the honey and process until the mixture forms a thick paste. Cut the remaining 3 tablespoons of butter into small cubes and, with the machine running, add the cubes one at a time, waiting until each one is completely incorporated before adding more. Season to taste with salt and pepper. Cover and place the filling in the refrigerator for 30 minutes.

Preheat the oven to 400°F (205°C) and place a wire rack in a rimmed baking sheet. When the liver mixture is cool, place in a quart-size (960-ml) plastic bag and seal. Snip one corner of the bag to form a small opening and set aside. Cut each slice of bacon into 3 equal pieces.

On a clean work surface, cut each date lengthwise along one side. Pipe just enough liver puree inside each date to fill it without overstuffing, then tightly roll 1 piece of bacon around the date so that it is completely wrapped. Place it seam-side down on the prepared baking sheet. Repeat with the remaining dates.

Roast the dates for 15 to 18 minutes, or until the bacon is golden brown and crispy. Let cool slightly, then garnish with thyme leaves and serve.

BRUSSELS SPROUTS

At this point, can we stop referring to brussels sprouts as that ingredient we hated as kids but have come to cherish as grown-ups? Sprouts deserve neither blame nor credit in this about-face; we've simply learned how to cook them better than our progenitors did. Any would-be converts have already been converted, so anyone who still doesn't like sprouts can be left alone. Cool?

Previous generations mostly boiled or steamed their brussels sprouts, but we've learned the positive effects that other cooking methods, be they hot oil, dry heat, simmering liquid—or no cooking at all—can have on the sprouts' flavor. And we've accepted that the brussels sprout is an alpha ingredient whose funky, brassica-family flavor needs other assertive flavors to help it find peace and harmony on the plate. This can make dreaming up new ways to showcase sprouts difficult, which is why you see ingredients like bacon, apples, nuts and cheese invited to the party so often.

In the recipes that follow, we'll expand your sprouts skillset by introducing some new cooking techniques and flavor buddies. Think of the sprout as a mini cabbage, and your mind goes to thinly shredded slaws and fermented kimchi; combine steam and dry heat for optimal caramelization; or plunge it into hot oil for an entirely new experience.

Brussels Sprouts Slaw with Herbs & Peanuts

MAKES 4 SERVINGS

¾ pound (340 g) brussels sprouts

2 tablespoons fresh lime juice, plus more to taste

2 tablespoons unseasoned rice wine vinegar

1 tablespoon Asian fish sauce

2 large shallots, thinly sliced into rings

2 red chiles, such as Fresno or red jalapeño, thinly sliced into rings (with seeds if you like heat)

Kosher salt and freshly ground black pepper

2 tablespoons vegetable oil

1 cup (50 g) coarsely chopped parsley

1 cup (40 g) coarsely chopped cilantro

½ cup (25 g) mint leaves, torn

2 tablespoons toasted sesame seeds

½ cup (70 g) chopped salted, roasted peanuts, plus more to taste

We'll take thinly shaved brussels sprouts over shredded cabbage any day. The tiny vegetables pack more flavor and less water, so they absorb dressings more quickly in slaws and quick sautés (the key is to shave them as thinly as possible.) This aggressively flavored dressing is a nod to the fact that the magical combination of funky fish sauce and tart lime juice is a match made in heaven with brussels sprouts—or other brassicas, such as broccoli and cauliflower.

Holding each brussels sprout by the stem end, shave the sprouts cross-wise as thinly as possible (use a mandoline if you have one), discarding the stems as you go.

In a large bowl, combine the lime juice, vinegar, fish sauce, shallots and chiles. Season with salt and pepper and let sit for 5 minutes.

Add the shaved sprouts and oil to the bowl and toss to coat. Season with salt, pepper and more lime juice if you like. Just before serving, add the parsley, cilantro, mint, sesame seeds and peanuts and toss. Top with more peanuts, if desired, and serve.

Steam-Roasted Brussels Sprouts

MAKES 4 SERVINGS

Roasted brussels sprouts are pretty much unassailable, but they want to dry out in the oven before they're tender enough to eat (which is why most recipes call for dousing them with some kind of liquid or sauce after roasting). But we learned how to solve the problem with this technique we read in *Cook's Illustrated* magazine, which has been the source of many other tricks we've picked up over the years. Covering and steaming the sprouts with a splash of liquid as they roast results in a juicy, tender vegetable with lots of external caramelization.

This is a fine, low-maintenance side dish on its own, but you can also add to the roasted sprouts before serving. To start: toasted nuts, crumbled or grated cheese, a squirt of hot sauce or a shower of herbs.

1   pound (455 g) brussels sprouts, halved lengthwise

1   large or 2 medium shallots, cut into ¼-inch rings

3   tablespoons olive oil

1   teaspoon kosher salt

¼   teaspoon freshly ground pepper

2   tablespoons dry white wine

Preheat the oven to 475°F (245°C) and position a rack in the top third of the oven.

In a bowl, toss the sprouts and shallot with the oil, salt and pepper. Add the wine and toss again, then dump the contents of the bowl onto a rimmed baking sheet. Arrange the sprouts, cut-side down, and scatter the shallots over the sprouts.

Cover the baking sheet tightly with aluminum foil and roast in the top third of the oven for 10 minutes. Remove the foil and continue roasting until the sprouts are tender and browned and the shallots are softened and lightly caramelized, about 10 to 12 minutes longer. Transfer the sprouts to a bowl and serve.

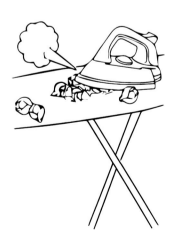

Brussels Sprouts Colcannon

MAKES 4 SERVINGS

This recipe is based on the classic Irish colcannon, a creamy starch that started as a way to use up left-over—what else?—potatoes and cabbage. But this humble mash has a surprise in the center: a little pond of melted butter, into which one dips each bite.

Here, shredded brussels sprouts stand in (once again) for their cruciferous cousin, and the recipe offers a built-in lesson on making great mashed potatoes: Don't overcook the spuds, and let the excess steam escape before ricing them into creamy perfection. Double the recipe and add it to your Thanksgiving repertoire, as the dish fills both the sprouts and potatoes slots, and it's one of the rare sides that reheats well in the microwave.

2	pounds (910 g) russet potatoes, peeled and cut into 3-inch chunks
	Kosher salt
5	tablespoons (70 g) unsalted butter (preferably grass-fed), at room temperature, divided
2	medium leeks, white and light-green parts thinly sliced (1 cup/90 g)
6	ounces (170 g) small brussels sprouts, trimmed and shredded (3 cups/525 g)
2	ounces (55 g) cream cheese, at room temperature
¼	to ⅓ cup (60 to 75 ml) whole milk, warmed
¼	teaspoon freshly grated nutmeg
	Freshly ground black pepper

Place the potatoes and 1 tablespoon of salt in a large pot and cover with water. Bring to a boil, reduce the heat and cook just until tender when pierced with a knife, about 20 minutes.

Meanwhile, melt 1 tablespoon of butter in a large skillet over medium-high heat. Add the leeks, sprouts and a pinch of salt and stir to coat. Cook, stirring often, until the vegetables are just tender, 4 to 5 minutes. Remove from heat.

Drain the potatoes and let stand until they steam dry and their edges look chalky, about 3 minutes. Pass the warm potatoes through a food mill or ricer into a large bowl. Add 2 tablespoons of butter and the cream cheese; stir until melted. Stir in enough warm milk to make a thick puree. Season with salt, nutmeg and pepper. Fold in the sprouts mixture and top with the remaining 2 tablespoons of butter, which will melt into a lovely little pool. Serve warm.

Make Ahead: Spoon the warm mixture into a generously buttered baking dish and let cool, then dot the top with butter. Cover with foil and refrigerate for up to 2 days. Heat through in a 350°F (175°C) oven, about 45 minutes. This recipe can also be reheated in a microwave.

Quick Brussels Sprouts & Pear Kimchi

MAKES 4 CUPS (425 G)

2	Asian pears, quartered and cored, divided
4	garlic cloves, chopped
1	2-inch piece of ginger, peeled and chopped (about 2 ounces/55 g)
2	tablespoons *gochugaru* (Korean chile flakes; available at Asian markets); can substitute crushed Aleppo pepper or chile de àrbol
1	tablespoon plus 1½ teaspoons kosher salt
2	pounds (910 g) brussels sprouts, ends trimmed, quartered
4	scallions, thinly sliced on the bias

As we've become more familiar with kimchi—which was inevitable, as it's seemingly *everywhere* these days—we've learned that the word, like "pickle," is as much a verb as it is a noun. You can kimchi all sorts of vegetables, and even a few sturdy fruits. And, just as pickles range from slow-fermented to almost-instant, kimchi is also made in a variety of speeds. This quick version can be eaten right away, but it definitely improves with each passing day. We'll re-emphasize here: You should massage the sprouts with vim and vigor to work the spice paste deep between the leaves.

Gochugaru is worth seeking out for this recipe. For the uninitiated, this coarse spice powder is made from sun-dried chiles and is essential to Korean cooking. It has a more robust, earthy flavor than those generic red pepper flakes in your spice drawer, but Aleppo pepper and chile de àrbol flakes come pretty close. Speaking of substitutions, tart, firm apples (like Granny Smith) are marvelous in this kimchi in place of the pear.

In a food processor, combine 1 pear, the garlic, ginger, *gochugaru* and salt. Pulse until the mixture forms a paste. Add the sprouts and the chile-pear paste to a large bowl and massage thoroughly with your hands for at least a couple of minutes. Some of the leaves will fall away from the cores of the sprouts; keep massaging and massaging until the paste is coating everything and worked between the leaves of any intact sprouts.

Thinly slice the remaining pear and add it to the sprouts along with the scallions. Toss everything well. You can eat the kimchi right away, but its flavor will improve if you pack it into jars and store in the refrigerator; it will get funkier and more flavorful the longer you wait. Discard after a few weeks.

Brussels Sprouts Chips

MAKES 4 SERVINGS

1   pound (455 g) brussels sprouts

3   tablespoons extra-virgin olive oil

½   teaspoon fine sea salt

This recipe was the result of a happy accident. After over-roasting some brussels sprouts, we noticed that the outermost leaves were deeply caramelized and tasted extra toasty. Separating the leaves changes the entire character of the sprout. As a whole, it's a hearty vegetable, but breaking the sprout up into its individual leaves yields a delicate, petal-like ingredient. Use these crispy chips as a garnish, mix them into salads or pack as a crunchy, healthy snack.

Preheat the oven to 400°F (205°C) and line a baking sheet with aluminum foil. Cut off the bottom from one sprout so that the leaves can be pulled away, then peel away the leaves, trimming the bottom of the sprout as you go to peel off more layers of leaves. Repeat with the remaining sprouts.

In a large bowl, toss the leaves with the oil and salt, then spread in a single layer on the baking sheet.

Bake the chips until they're crisp and well browned. After about 8 minutes, check the chips frequently, removing any finished chips with tongs and transferring them to a bowl. Store the chips in an airtight container until ready to use; they'll begin to lose their crispness after a couple of days.

Salt-Roasted Brussels Sprouts with Maple & Blue Cheese Dressing

MAKES 4 SERVINGS

Brussels sprouts, particularly those bite-size baby ones that show up at the farmers' market in the fall, have a design flaw. We love the idea of serving them whole, since they're basically nature's fun-size version of cabbage. But brussels are dense, which makes it difficult to season them properly without cutting them open. The solution? Roast your whole sprouts in salt.

Salt roasting is a popular technique with fish because it creates an environment that keeps the protein moist while also imparting seasoning. The same effect applies with vegetables, particularly dense ones like root vegetables and brussels sprouts. Captured steam tenderizes the sprouts while the salt crust seasons each sprout to its core.

1½ pounds (680 g) baby brussels sprouts

9 cups (2.4 kg) flaked kosher salt

12 egg whites

2 tablespoons pure maple syrup

2 tablespoons cider vinegar

2 ounces (55 g) creamy blue cheese, such as Gorgonzola

⅓ cup (75 ml) neutral vegetable oil

Preheat the oven to 400°F (205°C). Trim the woody ends off the sprouts and remove any discolored or blemished leaves.

In a large bowl, combine the salt and egg whites with your hands until the mixture resembles wet sand. Layer the surface of a large baking sheet with about a third of the salt mixture. Arrange the sprouts on the salt, then pack the remaining salt over the sprouts so that they are completely covered. Transfer the baking sheet to the oven and cook for 20 minutes. Let cool for 5 minutes.

Meanwhile, in a food processor, combine the syrup, vinegar and blue cheese and process until smooth and no chunks remain. With the motor running, add the oil in a slow, thin stream until the mixture is emulsified.

Use the butt of your knife to crack the salt shell and carefully unearth the sprouts. Transfer them to a bowl and toss with the vinaigrette. Serve immediately.

Baked Salmon with Curry-Mustard Brussels Sprouts Hash

MAKES 4 SERVINGS

We've flagged this hash as a frequent rerun in our kitchen, pulled out whenever we want to start the week with something light. As a three-in-one side dish, it's juicy and flavorful enough to act like a sauce, especially when it catches the juices of the meat above; it's substantial enough that you don't need anything else to make this a meal; and it's a healthy vegetable. Pair it with the protein of your choice (it's also delicious with chicken and pork) to bulk it up.

1   tablespoon extra-virgin olive oil, plus more for brushing

    Zest of 1 lemon plus 1 teaspoon juice

4   6-ounce (170-g) salmon fillets (with or without skin)

    Salt and freshly ground black pepper

3   tablespoons unsalted butter

1   large shallot, halved and thinly sliced (about ½ cup/60 g)

1   tablespoon minced fresh ginger

1   teaspoon mild curry powder

1   pound (455 g) brussels sprouts, halved and very thinly shredded crosswise

1   tablespoon whole-grain mustard

Preheat the oven to 300°F (150°C). Line a rimmed baking sheet with parchment paper or foil and lightly brush with oil. In a small bowl, mix 1 tablespoon of oil with the lemon zest.

Rub the salmon fillets with the lemon zest oil and season well with salt and pepper. Arrange the salmon on the baking sheet and bake for about 12 minutes, or until just opaque in the center (use a paring knife to take a peek; you won't hurt the fish).

Meanwhile, in a deep skillet, melt the butter over moderately high heat. Add the shallot and a pinch of salt and cook, stirring, until softened, about 2 minutes. Add the ginger and cook, stirring, until softened, about 1 minute. Add the curry powder and cook until fragrant, about 30 seconds. Add the brussels sprouts, mustard and ½ cup (120 ml) of water and cook, stirring frequently, until the sprouts are wilted and tender, about 5 minutes. Add the lemon juice and toss, then season with salt and pepper and serve with the salmon. The sprouts hash can be refrigerated overnight. Reheat gently or serve at room temperature.

Deep-Fried Brussels Sprouts with Ranch Dressing

MAKES 4 SERVINGS

The truth: Deep-frying is a pain in the ass. First, we rarely have enough oil on hand, and we cringe at the idea of using a giant container of the stuff once and then throwing it away (yes, you can cool and strain your oil and store it in the refrigerator, but unless you're a frequent fryer, it'll go off by the time you next need it). Then there's the messy splattering and those tiny red burns that appear on your hands a few minutes after frying. Plus, it's obviously not the healthiest way to cook.

That said, there are a handful of frying recipes that are worth the fuss, and this is undoubtedly one of them. Deep-frying the sprouts yields a surprisingly light, ultra-crispy texture that you can't replicate with other cooking techniques. We like to treat them like miniature fried artichokes and serve them with a creamy dip or sauce, such as the ranch dressing (aka "the ketchup of the future") here.

Make sure you use plenty of oil for frying. If you're short, use a smaller saucepan and divide the sprouts into more batches.

2 pounds (910 g) brussels sprouts

2 quarts (2 L) vegetable, canola or peanut oil

   Kosher salt

   Buttermilk Ranch Dressing (recipe follows)

2 tablespoons finely chopped chives, for garnish

Remove any dark, tough leaves from the sprouts and trim the very end of the stems. Cut the sprouts in half lengthwise. If the sprouts are wet, pat them dry with paper towels.

Line a platter with a couple layers of paper towels and set aside. Heat the oil in a Dutch oven or wok until it reaches 375°F (190°C) on a deep-fry thermometer. Add half of the brussels sprouts and fry, stirring frequently with a slotted spoon or mesh strainer, until the sprouts are deep golden brown, about 3 to 4 minutes. Transfer the sprouts to the paper towel–lined platter to drain and sprinkle with salt. Return the oil to 375°F (190°C) and repeat with the remaining sprouts.

Transfer the sprouts to a serving bowl and drizzle with the ranch dressing. Sprinkle with chives and serve with more dressing on the side.

Buttermilk Ranch Dressing

MAKES 1 CUP (240 ML)

¼ cup (60 ml) buttermilk, shaken

¼ cup (60 ml) mayonnaise

¼ cup (60 ml) sour cream

½ large garlic clove, finely grated

½ teaspoon Dijon mustard

1 teaspoon white wine vinegar

½ teaspoon Worcestershire sauce

2 teaspoons finely chopped parsley

2 teaspoons finely chopped chives

1 teaspoon finely chopped dill

¼ teaspoon onion powder

¼ teaspoon salt

¼ teaspoon freshly ground pepper

Combine all ingredients in a Mason jar and shake well. Taste and adjust the seasoning to your liking. The dressing can be made up to 1 day ahead; refrigerate until ready to use.

BUTTER

Butter is the ultimate fat. It adds structure and richness to baked goods; it begins and finishes most sauces. Strip it of its milk solids and it becomes an excellent cooking fat; brown those milk solids and it takes on an entirely new spectrum of flavor. Add salt and treat it like spreadable cheese; add sugar and make the best imaginable cake topping. Butter really can do it all. Butter *leans in*.

Although it's been a staple of many food cultures for millennia, butter's throne has not always been safe. In the 1950s, Americans began consuming more margarine than butter, a trend that continued, amazingly, until 2005. Butter is, in oversimplified terms, the very-whipped form of milk, which is the second-most important beverage in the world. Margarine is essentially whipped vegetable oil and some chemicals. What were we thinking?

Imagine, for a moment, a world of food without butter—and rejoice that we don't live in it. And now that we trust cows more than chemists once again, let's celebrate what the poet Seamus Heaney called "coagulated sunlight" and revisit all the things it can do in the following recipes.

Black Pepper Butter Crackers

MAKES 4 DOZEN

10 tablespoons (1¼ sticks/140 g) unsalted butter, divided

1 cup (125 g) all-purpose flour

1 cup (125 g) whole-wheat flour

2 teaspoons baking powder

1 tablespoon sugar

½ teaspoon kosher salt

Freshly ground black pepper

½ to ⅔ cup (120 to 165 ml) ice-cold water

Flaky sea salt, such as Maldon

At first, homemade crackers sound like more trouble than they're worth. But once you look at the ingredient list on a box of commercial crackers (or the price tag on a package of "artisanal" ones), you might change your mind. No? What if the crackers you made were better than both, and took about 15 minutes of effort to pull together? What if you could tweak the recipe a thousand ways (by adding good cheese or other kinds of flours or spices)? What if you could use leftover crackers as breading for chicken or fish? What if we told you just to trust us on this one?

Cut 8 tablespoons (1 stick/115 g) of the butter into small pieces, place on a baking sheet and place in the freezer for 10 minutes to chill. In a food processor, combine both flours, baking powder, sugar and salt; pulse to mix well. Grind a few turns from a pepper mill into the processor; pulse once to mix. Add the chilled butter pieces and pulse until well combined. With the machine running, slowly add the water just until a dough begins to form (you may not use it all). Form the dough into a disk, wrap in plastic wrap and refrigerate for at least 1 hour or up to overnight.

Place racks on top and bottom thirds of the oven and preheat to 400°F (205°C). Line two large baking sheets with parchment paper or silicone baking mats. On a lightly floured surface using a lightly floured rolling pin, roll the dough to about ¹⁄₁₆ inch (2 mm; as thin as you can get it). Cut shapes with a cookie or biscuit cutter, or use a knife or pizza wheel to cut squares or other shapes. Transfer the crackers to the baking sheets. (You will have some extra dough.) Hold the pepper grinder high over the baking sheets and grind enough pepper over the crackers to give them a light dusting. Prick each cracker 3 or 4 times with a fork.

Bake for 10 to 12 minutes, or until the crackers are light golden brown and firm, rotating the pans between top and bottom racks halfway through baking (if any crackers brown before the others, remove them with a spatula as you go). Place the pans on wire racks and let cool for 5 minutes, then transfer the crackers to racks to cool completely. Melt the remaining 2 tablespoons of butter. Very lightly brush the crackers with butter and sprinkle with a little bit of coarse salt.

Repeat with the remaining dough scraps to make another batch of crackers. Serve the crackers right away, or store in an airtight container at room temperature. These are best the day they're made or the following day, but they'll keep for up to 4 days.

Butter-Poached Scallops with Grapefruit-Butter Sauce

MAKES 4 SERVINGS

Not all seafood is at its best when seared in a hot pan. Poaching in butter is an excellent way to cook delicate seafood—such as scallops, shrimp or lobster—because it's such a mild cooking method. There are different schools of thought on this technique, but we took the absolute gentlest approach: keeping the butter close to 120°F (50°C) (which is also the optimum internal temperature for cooked scallops) ensures that the scallops won't overcook. An instant-read thermometer is crucial to nailing this recipe.

1   large grapefruit (about 1 pound/455 g)

12   large (U15) dry-packed sea scallops (about 1 pound/455 g)

       Kosher salt and freshly ground black pepper

1½   cups (3 sticks/340 g) unsalted butter, cut into cubes

       Flaky sea salt, such as Maldon

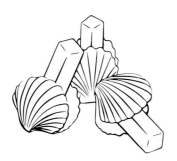

Cut off just enough of the top and bottom of the grapefruit to reveal the flesh. Stand the grapefruit on a cutting board and follow the contour of the fruit with a knife to cut away the rind and white pith. Trim away any white membrane with a paring knife. Holding the grapefruit over a bowl to catch the juice, cut sections from between the membranes and place in the bowl. Discard the white membrane and set the bowl of sections and juice aside.

Pat the scallops dry with a paper towel and season lightly with salt and pepper.

In a large skillet, melt the butter over low heat until it reaches 120°F (50°C) on an instant-read thermometer. Add the scallops to the pan in a single layer and let the butter return to 120°F (50°C) to 125°F (52°C) (it's fine if the butter doesn't cover the scallops completely). Cook the scallops, flipping them once halfway through, for 20 minutes, or until they're opaque in the center and firm to the touch. You may have to adjust the heat or remove the skillet from the heat to maintain a steady temperature.

Place the scallops on a warm serving plate. Pour all but about ¼ cup (60 ml) of the butter out of the skillet and set aside (the extra scallop butter is great stirred into seafood-based soups and sauces). Add the grapefruit sections and juice to the skillet. Cook the grapefruit gently over low heat for 3 minutes; you want to just warm them through. Spoon the grapefruit butter over the scallops, sprinkle generously with the flaky salt and serve immediately.

Nori Butter-Braised Radishes

MAKES 4 SERVINGS

For a couple of decades now, French chefs have incorporated Japanese ingredients into their food and, lately, some of the best chefs in Paris are Japanese. This recipe speaks to the affinity between the two cultures. To add another dimension to the classic French dish of braised radishes, we infuse the butter first with nori (a sheet of toasted seaweed).

If you've never braised radishes in butter before, now's the time: The technique, which also works well with baby turnips, transforms the snappy, peppery vegetable into something succulent and mellow.

1	sheet toasted nori (about 8 inches square)
3	tablespoons unsalted butter
	Kosher salt
1	large bunch red radishes with greens (about 12 radishes)
1	teaspoon rice vinegar
	Toasted sesame seeds, for garnish (optional)

Cut the nori in half crosswise.

In a deep skillet with a tight-fitting lid, melt the butter over medium-low heat. Add 1 piece of the nori, turn off the heat and let stand for 15 minutes, until the butter is infused with the flavor. Using tongs, remove the nori, squeezing out as much butter as possible. Discard the nori and season the butter with salt.

Meanwhile, use tongs to hold the other piece of nori over a medium flame and toast until it's crisp and fragrant, 5 to 10 seconds. (If you have an electric stovetop, you can toast the nori briefly in a hot, dry skillet). Snip or slice the nori into small strips and reserve for garnish.

Separate the radishes from the greens. If the greens look healthy, wash them well and roughly chop; otherwise, discard them. Scrub the radishes and, if they're large, cut into halves or quarters.

Reheat the nori-infused butter over medium heat. Add the radishes and stir to coat. Add 2 tablespoons of water, cover and cook, stirring a few times, until the radishes are just tender when pierced with a fork, about 7 minutes.

Stir in the radish greens, if using, and cover and cook over medium heat until wilted, about 1 minute. Uncover and cook until the greens are tender, 1 to 2 minutes longer. Stir in the vinegar and season with more salt, if desired. Transfer the radishes to a bowl and let cool slightly. Garnish with the nori strips and sesame seeds and serve.

Butter Lettuce Salad with Brown Butter Vinaigrette, Crispy Mushrooms & Roasted Hazelnuts

MAKES 2 TO 4 SERVINGS

½ pound (225 g) fresh maitake mushrooms, brushed clean

1 to 2 tablespoons olive oil

Kosher salt and freshly ground black pepper

½ cup (70 g) hazelnuts, with skin

2 tablespoons unsalted butter

1 tablespoon balsamic vinegar

Juice of half a lemon

1 large head of butter lettuce

This salad is an ode to ingredients that have butter-envy: butter lettuce is so named for its tender, melt-in-your-mouth texture; toasted hazelnuts smell like browned butter (and vice versa); and maitake mushrooms take on a deep, buttery flavored when roasted. Don't be surprised if the brown butter vinaigrette used here becomes a dressing you return to again and again. It's luscious and bright enough for any salad but with a big flavor that can stand up to the full spectrum of proteins, from fish to red meat.

Preheat the oven to 350°F (175°C). Trim the bottom end of each mushroom and separate each cap from the cluster. Arrange the mushrooms in a single layer in a large oven-safe skillet. Add 1 tablespoon of olive oil and toss; add the additional tablespoon if needed to coat the mushrooms well. Season with salt and pepper.

Place the hazelnuts in a small oven-safe skillet and transfer both skillets to the oven. Roast the hazelnuts until golden brown and fragrant, 15 to 20 minutes. Remove and transfer to a bowl to let cool. Once the nuts are cool, rub the skins off by placing them in a kitchen towel or paper towels and rubbing them together. Continue roasting the mushrooms until dark brown and crisp, about 45 minutes total. Remove from the oven and set aside.

Cut the butter into pieces and place them in a skillet. Cook the butter over medium heat until it turns golden brown and smells nutty, about 4 to 5 minutes.

Remove from the heat and add the balsamic vinegar (stand back; the vinegar will bubble and release a strong aroma). Stir in the lemon juice and transfer the mixture to a measuring cup. Let cool slightly, then season to taste with salt and pepper.

Trim the stem of the lettuce head and separate the leaves. Arrange the leaves in a bowl and add the hazelnuts. Drizzle with vinaigrette to taste and toss gently. Top with the roasted mushrooms and serve.

Butter-Roasted Lamb

MAKES 8 SERVINGS

There aren't many contexts in which we'd be excited about the term "fat blanket," but this is an exception. Here, an herb-flecked butter acts as both marinade and shield for a lamb shoulder, slowly melting into the crevices of the meat as it roasts. The effect of this butter-soaked slow roast is almost like a confit, yielding extra-tender meat. The mixture of fennel seeds, red pepper, rosemary and anchovies gives it a Tuscan edge, but the technique can be used with any combination of spices.

1	5- to 6-pound (2.3- to 2.7-kg) bone-in lamb shoulder
1	tablespoon fennel seeds
1	teaspoon red pepper flakes
6	garlic cloves
¼	cup (20 g) fresh rosemary needles
4	anchovies
½	teaspoon kosher salt
1	teaspoon sugar
½	cup (1 stick/115 g) unsalted butter, at room temperature

Trim the lamb shoulder, cutting off any excess fat or membranes to leave just a thin layer of fat across the surface. With a paring knife, make shallow ½-inch incisions all over the shoulder.

In a small skillet, toast the fennel seeds and red pepper flakes over high heat until fragrant, about 1 minute. Using a mortar and pestle, crush the toasted fennel and pepper flakes with the garlic, rosemary, anchovies, salt and sugar into a paste. Place in a mixing bowl with the butter and mash together with a fork until fully incorporated.

Spread the butter all over the lamb shoulder, creating a thick coating. Use all of the butter, and make sure to push butter into the incisions. Set the shoulder in a baking dish, cover in foil and refrigerate overnight (or up to 2 days).

Preheat the oven to 500°F (260°C). Remove the lamb from the refrigerator 1 hour before cooking so it can come to room temperature.

Place the lamb in the oven and immediately reduce the temperature to 325°F (165°C). Cook for 3½ to 4 hours, until the lamb pulls apart easily and a meat thermometer inserted into the thickest part of the shoulder registers between 170°F (70°C) and 180°F (82°C). Let the lamb rest for 30 minutes before carving and serving.

Asparagus with Miso Beurre Blanc

MAKES 4 SERVINGS

Practically every sauce benefits from a tablespoon or two of butter stirred in at the end, from wine reductions and gravies to heartier pasta sauces. Butter adds extra richness in both flavor and texture. Beurre blanc begins where these sauces end: a mostly butter emulsification that can be served by itself or augmented with myriad ingredients. Although they come from wildly different culinary traditions, miso and butter are incredible when paired. Here, miso's salty, umami-heavy flavor wakes up the silky sauce. We paired this beurre blanc with asparagus, but keep this recipe handy when you're cooking other green vegetables, chicken, fish (especially salmon) or shellfish.

   As with most emulsions, this sauce is somewhat unstable. Be careful not to overcook the sauce or it can break, and be ready to serve it right away. If your sauce does break, don't panic: Either whisk in a small ice cube or little bit of cold cream (this is why many beurre blanc recipes contain cream), or throw the sauce in a blender and use the power of electricity to re-emulsify it.

1   pound (455 g) asparagus, ends trimmed

¼   cup plus 2 tablespoons (90 ml) sake or dry white wine

1   tablespoon fresh lemon juice

1   tablespoon white miso paste (see Note)

½   cup (1 stick/115 g) cold unsalted butter, cut into small pieces

If the asparagus stems are thicker than ½ inch, peel the bottom third of the stalks with a vegetable peeler. In a medium saucepan, bring 1 cup (240 ml) of water to a rapid simmer over medium-high and add the asparagus. Cover and steam the asparagus until the thickest parts of the stalks are just tender and bright green, about 3 minutes. Drain the water from the pan, return the asparagus to the pot and cover to keep warm.

In a small heavy saucepan, combine the white wine or sake, lemon juice and miso and bring to a boil over medium-high heat, whisking to dissolve the miso. Reduce the heat to medium and simmer, uncovered, whisking occasionally, until reduced by three quarters, about 5 minutes. There should be about 2 tablespoons of liquid left in the pan and the sauce should have a butterscotch-like color. If you don't let the liquid reduce enough, the sauce will be too thin.

Remove the pan from the heat and add the butter, one piece at a time, whisking slowly and constantly until the sauce is creamy and pale and all the butter is incorporated. You can add the next piece before the previous one has completely melted. If you need a bit more heat to soften the butter, set the pan briefly over very low heat. Do not let the sauce sit over the heat for long or it may separate.

Arrange the asparagus on a serving plate and pour the beurre blanc over the top. Serve immediately.

> **NOTE** Some brands of miso are very smooth, while others are a bit chunky. If you want a very smooth sauce, buy a visibly smooth Japanese miso. If you use miso that's not as smooth as you desire, you can strain the sauce through a fine-mesh sieve at the end of cooking.

Kentucky Butter Cake with Walnut Frosting

MAKES 10 SERVINGS

Kentucky butter cake is a staple of church picnics and cakewalks across the Bluegrass State. Our upgraded version—created by native daughter Sarah Baird (Vol. 15: Summer Squash)—gets an over-the-top butter frosting and adds the nuttiness of walnuts for a deeper dimension. This is the cake you want when you think about Bundt cake: It's a sturdy, sweet, contact-high dessert.

FOR THE CAKE:

3   cups (375 g) all-purpose flour

1½   teaspoons baking powder

1   teaspoon baking soda

⅛   teaspoon fine sea salt

1   cup (2 sticks/225 g) unsalted butter, melted and cooled slightly

2   cups (440 g) packed light brown sugar

1   tablespoon walnut extract

4   large eggs, at room temperature

1   cup (240 ml) half-and-half

1   cup (120 g) chopped walnuts

FOR THE FROSTING:

1   cup (2 sticks/225 g) unsalted butter, softened

3   cups (375 g) confectioners' sugar

2   tablespoons walnut extract

1   teaspoon aged rum

⅓   cup (40 g) chopped walnuts; plus more walnut halves to decorate the cake

Make the cake: Preheat the oven to 325°F (165°C) and grease a 10-inch Bundt pan.

In a medium bowl, combine the flour, baking powder, baking soda and salt and whisk until combined. In the bowl of a stand mixer (or use a large bowl and a handheld electric mixer), combine the butter, sugar and walnut extract. Beat at medium-low speed until combined, then beat in the eggs, one at a time, until combined. Add a third of the flour mixture, followed by a third of the half-and-half, mixing for about 30 seconds for each addition and scraping down the bowl as needed. Repeat with the remaining flour mixture and half-and-half, alternating until completely incorporated. Use a rubber spatula to fold in the chopped walnuts.

Pour the batter into the pan and bake for 1 hour, or until a toothpick inserted in the center comes out clean. Let the cake cool in the pan for 20 minutes, then turn over onto a wire rack and let cool completely, about 1 hour.

Make the frosting: In the bowl of a stand mixer (or use a large bowl and a handheld electric mixer), beat the butter at medium-low speed until creamy. Beat in the confectioners' sugar, ½ cup (65 g) at a time, until all the sugar is incorporated. Add the walnut extract and rum, increase the mixer speed to medium-high and continue beating until the frosting is thick and glossy, about 2 minutes. Fold in the chopped walnuts.

With an offset spatula or thin rubber spatula, completely cover the cake with the frosting. Garnish the top of the cake with walnut halves and let set at room temperature for at least 1 hour before slicing and serving. The cake can be covered in an airtight container and stored at room temperature for up to 4 days.

The Best, Flakiest Pastry Dough

MAKES ONE 9-INCH CRUST

There are a million pastry dough recipes out there—and the never-ending debate about the best fat for the task: lard, shortening, butter or some combination thereof. But if a flaky piecrust is your goal, this recipe will allow you to achieve it. The biggest secret behind pastry dough is temperature: The butter needs to stay cold in order to form the many tiny layers that yield a flaky crust. Although we like the romance of making pastry dough by hand, using a food processor makes quick work of the process, ensuring your butter doesn't melt into the flour. We also add a bit of acid to slow down the formation of gluten, which prevents the dough from getting tough. If you have a big food processor, you can double this recipe, but in a smaller machine, producing successive batches makes it easier to keep the butter cold and ends up being faster in the long run.

---

2   cups (250 g) all-purpose flour

1   teaspoon sugar

1   teaspoon kosher salt

14   tablespoons (1¾ sticks/200 g) cold unsalted butter, cut into pieces

2   teaspoons fresh lemon juice or apple cider vinegar

     Ice water

In a food processor, combine the flour, sugar and salt and pulse to combine. Add the butter and continue pulsing until the largest pieces of butter are the size of marbles and peas.

Combine the lemon juice or vinegar with enough ice water to make ¼ cup (60 ml), then pour it in through the feed tube while pulsing the machine. Continue pulsing until the dough starts to clump together. Transfer the mixture to a large bowl and work into a rough mass with your hands, but do it quickly so as not to soften the butter. Gather the dough into a disk and place on a sheet of plastic wrap. Fold the edges in and press down lightly to make a tight package. Chill until firm, at least 30 minutes. The dough can be refrigerated for 2 days or frozen for a month or two.

When you're ready to use the dough, remove it from the refrigerator and let soften slightly, 15 to 30 minutes. Generously dust the work surface, the rolling pin and the surface of the dough with some flour. Whack the dough a few times with the rolling pin soften it up. Starting from the center, roll the dough outward, rotating it a quarter turn as you roll. Carefully flip the dough over from time to time by rolling it onto the pin to pick it up, then laying it down on the opposite side. Keep both sides lightly floured to prevent sticking. Aim for an even thickness throughout. Roll the dough out into a round of the desired size and thickness.

Brush off any loose flour using a dry pastry brush, and loosely roll the crust around the rolling pin.

Transfer to a 9-inch pie plate by unrolling the dough over the top. Trim the edges with scissors to leave a 1½-inch overhang. If you're making a single-crust pie, crimp, chill and proceed with the rest of the pie recipe. If you're making a double-crust pie, make two batches of dough and repeat the rolling procedure with the second dough. Top the filled pie with the second piece of dough. Seal the two pieces using a little cold water to adhere the edges. Trim the overhang to 1½ inches, roll it underneath itself and crimp the edges as desired.

Cultured Butter with Bonus Buttermilk

MAKES 1 POUND (455 G) BUTTER PLUS 2 CUPS (480 ML) BUTTERMILK

There are many reasons to make your own butter. Here are three: 1. For the experience: Making butter always feels a little bit like magic, no matter how often we do it. 2. Because you've gotten your hands on some amazing cream—from a farm you just visited, the local farmers' market, your illegal raw milk delivery service, wherever. Because you're washing the butter and extracting a lot of liquid, the butterfat content will be higher than commercial butter, meaning there will be more butterfat in your cookies, in your pan sauces, in your everything. 3. It leaves you with a gift of bonus buttermilk, which can be used to make Frozen Greek Yogurt (page 155), Skillet Apple-Oat Cake (page 31) or Buttermilk Ranch Dressing (page 66). For even more ideas, pick up our Buttermilk Short Stack (Vol. 4), written by Angie Mosier.

4½ cups (1 L) of the absolute best heavy cream you can find

½ cup (120 ml) crème fraîche

2 to 2¼ cups (480 to 600 ml) filtered ice water

1 teaspoon fine sea salt

In a medium bowl, whisk together the cream and crème fraîche. Cover with a clean towel and let sit at room temperature for at least 12 and up to 48 hours.

Remove the towel and refrigerate the mixture for 45 minutes, then pour it into the bowl of a stand mixer fitted with the whisk attachment (you can also use a handheld mixer or a food processor). Whip the mixture at medium-high speed until the fat separates from the liquid, 1 to 2 minutes. Reduce the speed to low and continue to beat (use a splash guard, aluminum foil or towel to loosely cover the top of the bowl, as the mixture tends to slosh around) until the butter rides up the whisk, about 45 seconds longer. Turn off the mixer.

Set a fine-mesh strainer over a large bowl and transfer the butter and buttermilk to the sieve. Lightly knead and fold the butter to create a semisolid mass (don't knead it so hard that it starts to go through the strainer). When the butter is solid enough to remove, line the strainer with a double layer of cheesecloth and place the butter on top. Gather the corners of the cheesecloth and gently squeeze more buttermilk out of the butter. Transfer the buttermilk to a container and refrigerate; it will keep for up to 2 weeks.

Place the butter in a medium bowl. Pour about ½ cup (120 ml) of ice water over the butter and knead it to extract more liquid. Discard the liquid and use paper towels to pat the butter dry. Repeat until the liquid coming out from the butter is clear, 3 to 4 more times, discarding the liquid pooling in the bowl and patting the butter dry after each addition of water. Using a rubber spatula, fold the salt into the butter.

Divide the butter in half and set each piece on a large sheet of parchment paper or plastic wrap. Shape the butter into a log, wrap and refrigerate up to 3 weeks (or freeze for up to 3 months).

Better the Butter

There are countless ways to flavor your just-made butter by adding an ingredient or two. Some of our favorite mix-ins are smoked salt, harissa, anchovies, Meyer lemons and blue cheese.

CHEDDAR

We're a curds-loving culture with an appetite for variety that ranges from imported specialty cheeses to squares of cellophane-wrapped singles. But if we had to pick just one cheese, it'd be Cheddar. Not because it's America's most popular cheese—that honor, since 2006, has been held by mozzarella, thanks to our vehement consumption of pizza. We choose Cheddar because it encapsulates the paradox of our country's cooking habits with more elegance than almost any ingredient we can think of. First, there's versatility. Cheddar checks all of the boxes for a cook's needs: easily melted over a burger, delicious when layered into a sandwich or ideal for grating into a sauce or soup.

But then there's the value proposition: Cheddar is an affordable cheese. There's a danger to espousing a cooking philosophy ruled by "inspiring ingredients." It's easy to praise the farmers' market heirlooms or the artisan meats that are far out of reach for many cooks. The version of an ingredient that cookbooks frequently trumpet is often different, sometimes vastly so, from the version that that can be purchased on a budget.

In fact, Cheddar was invented as a way to make cheese more accessible. In the 15th century, cheesemakers in the Cheddar village of England discovered that pressing the moisture (whey) from cheese curds created a product that lasted much longer and was easier to transport and distribute without refrigeration.

Cheddar may have its roots across the pond, but in our minds, it's distinctly American—the perfect blend of versatility, accessibility, craft and commodity.

Broccoli & Cheddar French Dip

MAKES 4 LARGE SANDWICHES

Cheddar is a superior sandwich cheese. It slices well, melts well and has just the right amount of sharpness to make it versatile. But we never knew just how brilliant a Cheddar sandwich could be until this creation from our sandwich guru, Tyler Kord, owner of No. 7 Sub shops in New York and author of Vol. 7: Broccoli.

In Tyler's reimagined French dip, Cheddar and broccoli take the place of roast beef. But as with the original, the real clincher is in the "au jus." Tyler figured out how to make a stock flavored with melted Cheddar and thickened with a roux made of Cheddar fat in place of butter. The result has all the flavor of Cheddar in broth form. Beyond the obvious dipping applications for the sandwich, leftover broth would be brilliant for cooking a pot of beans or as the base of a vegetable soup. One caveat: The melted cheese tends to stick to the stockpot and the strainer, which makes cleaning up a challenge. But a little elbow grease is worth it for this masterpiece.

---

2   large heads broccoli (1½ to 2 pounds/680 to 910 g)

1   large white onion, quartered

8   ounces (225 g) shredded sharp Cheddar cheese (about 2 cups/230 g), plus ¼ pound (225 g) sliced sharp Cheddar

1   tablespoon plus 1 teaspoon all-purpose flour

3   garlic cloves, smashed

1   tablespoon pure maple syrup

½   teaspoon dried thyme

¼   teaspoon dried rosemary

⅛   teaspoon red pepper flakes

Kosher salt

2   tablespoons olive oil

4   hero-style loaves that have a decent amount of crust, split lengthwise, lightly toasted

Mustard and prepared horseradish, for serving

Preheat the broiler.

Cut the broccoli stems from the heads. Slice the stems into ½-inch coins, and cut the florets into 2-inch pieces; set the florets aside.

On a rimmed baking sheet lined with foil, spread the broccoli stems and onion and broil, turning occasionally, until everything is a little bit burnt around the edges, 12 to 14 minutes. Remove the vegetables from the oven and set aside. Lower the oven temperature to 400°F (205°C).

Meanwhile, spread half (1 cup/115 g) of the shredded Cheddar in an even layer in a medium nonstick skillet and place over medium heat. Cook until the cheese is melted and caramelized on the bottom, 5 to 7 minutes. Using tongs or a spatula, transfer the cheese to a medium stockpot, leaving the cheese fat behind in the pan. Repeat with the remaining shredded Cheddar.

Add the flour to the skillet and use a rubber spatula to stir the flour into the leftover cheese fat. Cook over medium heat, stirring constantly, for 2 to 3 minutes, or until the flour has browned slightly. Add the mixture to the pot with the caramelized Cheddar, followed by the broccoli stems and onions, garlic, maple syrup, thyme, rosemary, pepper flakes, 1 teaspoon salt and 4 cups (960 ml) of water. Bring to a boil over high heat, stirring occasionally. Reduce the heat and simmer, continuing to stir occasionally, and making sure to scrape the bottom of the pan so the cheese won't settle and burn, for 40 minutes. Turn off the heat and let the stock sit for 10 minutes. Strain the broth into a clean saucepan and season to taste; cover and keep warm.

Meanwhile, spread the broccoli florets on the rimmed baking sheet and toss with the olive oil and 1 teaspoon salt. Roast for 12 to 15 minutes, or until the broccoli is cooked and dark in places but still a little crunchy and bright green in other places. Transfer the broccoli to a bowl. Turn the broiler back on. Lay the hero halves on the baking sheet cut-side up, ladle about ¼ cup (60 ml) of broth over each half and top with a slice of Cheddar. Broil until the cheese is melted, about 3 to 5 minutes.

Divide the broccoli evenly among the bottom halves, then top with the remaining halves and cut the sandwiches in half. Serve with mustard, horseradish and some extra broth on the side for dipping.

Cheddar-Walnut Shortbread

MAKES ABOUT 6 DOZEN

Keeping a roll of this dough in your freezer is like having money in the bank—it makes on-the-fly entertaining effortless. This recipe has roots in a classic hors d'oeuvre of the American South: Cheddar pennies, a homemade precursor to the Cheez-It. Here, the ratio of Cheddar is cranked up so that each bite is undeniably cheesy but retains that crumbly butter-laden shortbread texture. The egg wash is optional and its purpose entirely aesthetic, like an Instagram filter for baked goods. Brush it on the surface of the shortbread before baking for a shiny gloss; omit it for a matte look.

½   cup (60 g) walnut pieces

3   cups (345 g) coarsely grated extra-sharp Cheddar cheese (orange or white)

½   cup (1 stick/115 g) unsalted butter, cut into 8 pieces and softened

1   large egg, separated

1   tablespoon minced rosemary

2   teaspoons sweet paprika (preferably smoked, such as Pimentón de la Vera dulce)

¾   teaspoon salt

¼   to ½ teaspoon cayenne pepper

1¼   cups (155 g) all-purpose flour

     Black sesame seeds, for garnish

Preheat the oven to 350°F (175°C). Toast the walnuts on a rimmed baking sheet until they smell fragrant and the skins are deep golden, 10 to 12 minutes. Chill the walnuts in the freezer until cooled completely, about 20 minutes. Transfer the walnuts to a food processor and pulse until finely chopped, then transfer to a small bowl (do not clean the processor).

Add the Cheddar, butter and egg yolk to the food processor and blend, stopping and scraping down occasionally, until smooth. Add the rosemary, paprika, salt and cayenne pepper and blend well. Add the flour and walnuts and pulse until just combined.

Gather the dough into a ball and divide it in half. Place each half on a large sheet of waxed paper and form each into 10-inch logs. Roll each log in the waxed paper—like forming snakes from clay—to make it as round and even as possible (if the dough is too soft to work with, chill the wrapped log until firmer but still malleable, 1 to 1½ hours).

Refrigerate the logs until very firm, at least 3 hours or overnight. If chilling overnight, wrap the waxed-paper roll tightly in foil or plastic wrap.

Preheat the oven to 350°F (175°C). If the dough has been previously frozen, let it thaw slightly, about 30 minutes (it should still be pretty firm). Cut one roll of dough crosswise into ¼-inch-thick rounds and arrange them, 1 inch apart, on a parchment-lined baking sheet (if the dough becomes too soft at any point, quick-chill in the freezer for several minutes). If desired, lightly brush the rounds with beaten egg white before sprinkling the center of each round with a few sesame seeds, gently pushing them into the dough with your fingers (you can add the seeds without using the egg white).

Bake the shortbread until the edges of the rounds are golden and the tops are set when lightly touched, 12 to 14 minutes. Slide the parchment with rounds onto a large rack to cool. Continue slicing and baking rounds from the remaining chilled dough log.

(The rolls, wrapped in waxed paper and foil or plastic wrap, can be frozen for 3 months. For entertaining, shortbread rounds can be baked 2 days ahead, cooled completely and stored in an airtight container at room temperature. Leftovers will keep 5 days if you manage not to devour them before then.)

Cheddar Obatzda

MAKES 2½ CUPS (500 G)

This recipe comes with a built-in beverage pairing. After you've measured out the beer that this Bavarian-style beer cheese requires, there's the bulk of a bottle left for sipping while you quickly whip this spread together.

Obatzda packs plenty of punch to be so simple. A close relative of Liptauer cheese, an Eastern-European spread spiked with paprika and caraway, this German interpretation, frequently found on Biergarten menus, takes its cues and flavor from the beverage with which it's often paired.

Make sure your butter and cream are at room temperature before you begin so that everything incorporates nicely. The finished product is great with pretzels or as part of a ploughman's lunch with a few slices of hearty smoked sausage and pickles.

¼ cup (½ stick/55 g) unsalted butter, at room temperature

6 ounces (170 g) cream cheese, at room temperature

1 tablespoon finely grated shallot

1 tablespoon smoked paprika

Salt and freshly ground black pepper

8 ounces (225 g) sharp Cheddar cheese, finely grated

8 ounces (225 g) mild Cheddar cheese, finely grated

4 to 6 tablespoons (60 to 90 ml) dark beer (such as brown ale)

1 small red onion, thinly sliced

Rye bread and/or soft pretzels, for serving

In a stand mixer fitted with the paddle attachment, cream the butter and cream cheese at medium-low speed until smooth. Add the grated shallot and paprika; season with salt and pepper. Add the cheeses, mixing until combined, then the beer, 1 tablespoon at a time, until the mixture is spreadable. Serve at room temperature with red onion, rye bread and/or soft pretzels.

Kimcheese

MAKES ABOUT 2 CUPS (480 ML)

The history of pimento cheese isn't very romantic. At the beginning of the industrial food movement in the late 19th century, two new products came to market around the same time: a Neufchatel-style cheese that would later become cream cheese, and canned sweet red peppers imported from Spain. The coincidental appearance of these two ingredients quickly bore the earliest version of what we now know as pimento cheese. Timing, in this case, was everything.

The popularity of this creamy spread waned over the decades, and its geographical orbit moved from the factories of the North to the pepper fields of the South, from cream cheese to hoop cheese (a mild, easy-to-make farmer cheese) bound with mayonnaise. It was relegated to a regional Southern food and forgotten about everywhere else.

Recently, pimento cheese has broken back into the mainstream, appearing with regularity across the country and across highbrow and lowbrow demarcations. And what other ingredient has its star rising from genre-specific cooking to all-out pantry staple? Kimchi, Korea's funky fermented pride. The bite and heat of kimchi is an easily defended substitute for the peppers in pimento cheese; it provides an extra layer of texture and an umami-rich sharpness that gives the spread character. So here we are, with a new version of pimento cheese that is once again a cause of good timing. Like it was fated. (Maybe this is a romantic story, after all.)

---

8   ounces (225 g) extra-sharp Cheddar cheese, coarsely shredded

1   cup (230 g) finely chopped and drained kimchi

1   teaspoon sugar

3   to 4 tablespoons (45 to 60 ml) mayonnaise

    Sriracha sauce or chile paste, to taste (optional)

In a medium bowl, stir together the Cheddar, kimchi and sugar.

Fold in enough mayonnaise just to bind the mixture together. Add Sriracha to taste, if needed. (The heat level of kimchi varies from brand to brand. This spread should have a noticeable kick, but not be so spicy that it overwhelms the Cheddar.)

For the best flavor, cover and refrigerate for 1 day before serving. Store for up to 2 weeks.

Grilled Kimcheese Sandwich

This was inevitable, right? Spread ¼ cup (60 ml) of kimcheese on a slice of white bread and top with a second slice of bread. Spread 1½ teaspoons of mayonnaise on each face of the sandwich. Heat a skillet over medium heat. Add the sandwich and cook until the cheese in the center is melty and the bread is golden brown, about 4 minutes a side. Serve with a cold beer.

Cheddar-Stout Bitterballen

MAKES 30; SERVES 8 AS AN APPETIZER

1¼ pounds (570 g) boneless chuck roast, halved

Kosher salt and freshly ground black pepper

¼ cup (½ stick/55 g) unsalted butter

¼ cup (30 g) all-purpose flour

½ cup (120 ml) stout beer, such as Guinness

1½ cups (170 g) shredded sharp Cheddar cheese, plus about 1 ounce cut into ¼-inch dice

½ teaspoon freshly grated nutmeg

2 tablespoons finely chopped parsley

2 scallions, finely chopped

2½ cups (250 g) dried bread crumbs

3 large eggs, beaten

Vegetable or peanut oil, for frying

Dijon mustard, for serving

It's hard to believe that these breaded meatballs of Dutch origin don't traditionally have cheese in them. The addition of Cheddar improves on the recipe in great ways, like a cover that you listen to more than the original song. Each bite shape-shifts between meatball, croquette and arancini, a triumvirate of the world's best bite-size snacks.

These bitterballen also illustrate Cheddar's worth in the kitchen more than many dishes with longer, stronger ties to the cheese. It picks up on Cheddar's affinity with beer in a mornay sauce that uses Guinness instead of milk. Then it reminds us, by way of an advertisement-worthy molten, gooey center, that nothing beats melty, oozy cheese.

Place the chuck in a medium pot and add water to cover it halfway. Add 1½ teaspoons salt and a few grinds of pepper and bring to a boil over medium-high heat. Reduce the heat to maintain a gentle simmer and cook, covered, flipping the meat occasionally, until very tender and the meat pulls apart easily with a fork, about 3 hours. Transfer the meat to a cutting board to cool. Reserve ½ cup (120 ml) of the cooking liquid and discard the rest.

Use your fingers to shred the meat into small pieces, then evenly chop the shredded pieces. Transfer to a medium bowl.

Melt the butter in a medium saucepan over medium heat. Add the flour and cook, stirring, 1 minute. While whisking, add the reserved cooking liquid and the stout. Continue to cook, whisking often, until the mixture starts to boil, then cook for 1 minute longer; the mixture will thicken considerably. Turn off the heat and whisk in the shredded cheese and nutmeg until the cheese melts completely. Cool to room temperature.

Stir the cheese mixture into the meat along with the parsley and scallions. Season with salt and pepper. Line a baking sheet with parchment paper. Spoon out about 1 tablespoon of the meat mixture. Flatten it slightly in your hands and place one piece of the diced Cheddar in the center. Gather the mixture around the cheese and roll it into a ball. Place it on the baking sheet and continue with the remaining meat and cheese.

Place the bread crumbs in one shallow bowl and the eggs in another. Working with one meatball at a time, roll a ball in bread crumbs then roll it to coat in the egg. Let the excess egg drip off and return it to the bread crumbs, rolling to coat thoroughly. Return the breaded meatball to the baking sheet and repeat with the remaining meatballs.

In a wide shallow pot, heat about 2 inches (5 cm) of oil until it reaches 350°F (175°C) on a deep-fry thermometer. Fry half of the meatballs, stirring occasionally, until deep golden brown, about 2 minutes.

Transfer to a paper towel–lined plate to drain and fry the remaining meatballs. Serve immediately with Dijon mustard for dipping.

Cheddar & Rye Gougères

MAKES ABOUT 4 DOZEN

Most gougères we come across are dainty little numbers, where cheese is more of a suggestion than a driving force. They're undeniably French, from the *pâte à choux* base down to the Comté cheese that traditional recipes call for.

Here, gougères get an American makeover that allows them to move seamlessly between the worlds of high tea and Miller High Life. Rye flour adds an edgy weight to the light-as-air dough, but the driving flavor is the sharp Cheddar, which imbues each buttery bite with undeniable cheesiness. It's the everyman's cheese puff.

½ cup (65 g) all-purpose flour

½ cup (50 g) rye flour

¼ teaspoon freshly ground black pepper

¼ teaspoon salt

2 teaspoons thyme leaves or finely chopped chives

1 cup (240 ml) water or beer (preferably a lager or stout), poured and settled

½ cup (1 stick/115 g) unsalted butter, cut into cubes

4 large eggs, at room temperature

1½ cups (170 g) grated sharp Cheddar cheese, divided

Preheat the oven to 400°F (205°C). Place racks in the top and bottom thirds of the oven.

In a medium bowl, combine the all-purpose flour, rye flour, pepper, salt and thyme and set aside.

In a large saucepan, combine the water or beer and butter and bring the mixture to a boil over high heat. Once the butter has melted, add the flour mixture all at once and stir vigorously with a wooden spoon. The mixture will look rough at first, but it will suddenly become smooth. Reduce the heat to medium and continue to stir for about 1 minute, until the dough pulls away from the sides of the pan. Transfer the dough to a bowl or to the bowl of a stand mixer fitted with the paddle attachment and let cool for 10 minutes, occasionally stirring or turning the mixer on briefly to help the cooling process. (Don't leave the mixer running or you risk overworking the dough.)

With the mixer running, add the eggs, one at a time, beating vigorously after each addition and stopping to scrape down the bowl before adding the next egg. Each egg should be fully incorporated before the next is added. Do not worry if the mixture looks curdled; that's normal. Simply continue beating until the dough is smooth. When the last of the eggs is incorporated, beat in 1 cup (115 g) of the Cheddar. The dough should be smooth, shiny and sticky. At this point, you can wrap the dough in plastic and refrigerate for up to 4 hours before using it.

Scoop the dough into a pastry bag fitted with a ½-inch tip and pipe small (about 1 inch wide and 1 inch high) balls onto parchment-lined baking sheets, spacing them a couple inches apart. (You can also use two spoons to drop the dough onto the baking sheet.)

Sprinkle the gougères with the remaining ½ cup (55 g) of Cheddar. Bake for 15 minutes. Reduce the heat to 350°F (175°C), rotate the baking sheets between the top and bottom racks and bake until brown and firm, 10 to 15 minutes longer. Transfer the gougères to a wire rack to cool. These are best the day they're made, but can be made a day ahead and rewarmed in the oven.

Celery-Cheddar Salad with Horseradish-Cider Vinaigrette

MAKES 4 SERVINGS

One of our favorite styles of Cheddar is the mature stuff, aged for a couple years or longer. These senior citizens have a crystalline bite to their texture (they crumble quite easily) with every bit of concentrated, nutty flavor as a chunk of Parmigiano-Reggiano. Cheddar doesn't melt as well in its old age, but it's unbeatable on a salad or a cheese plate. Here, we've coupled it with some of its most reliable playmates: celery, apples, olives and horseradish.

2	bunches celery
1	tablespoon fresh lemon juice
2	tablespoons apple cider vinegar
2	tablespoons honey (or Apple Cider Molasses, page 37)
2	teaspoons Dijon mustard
2	teaspoons prepared horseradish
1	cup (240 ml) neutral vegetable oil
	Salt and freshly ground black pepper
¼	cup (13 g) chopped parsley
20	pitted green olives, roughly chopped (mild, buttery versions such as Castelvetrano work best)
2	ounces (55 g) two-year-aged white Cheddar cheese

Remove the base and tips of each celery bunch and separate all of the stalks. Thinly slice the stalks on a bias (a mandoline is great for this) and place in a medium bowl. Toss with the lemon juice and set aside.

In a small bowl, whisk together the vinegar, honey, mustard and horseradish. While whisking, add the oil in a slow, thin stream until the vinaigrette emulsifies and thickens. Season to taste with salt and pepper.

Drain the celery and return it to the bowl. Add the parsley and olives and toss with your hands. Drizzle with ¼ cup (60 ml) of the vinaigrette and toss well to coat. Season generously with pepper.

Using a Y-shaped vegetable peeler, cut the Cheddar into thin strips. Crumble the strips into craggy pieces and sprinkle them over the salad. Toss the salad to incorporate the Cheddar, season with additional salt and pepper, if needed, and serve.

Mornay Macaroni & Cheese

MAKES 4 SERVINGS

This mac and cheese isn't going to revolutionize the way you think about the dish. In fact, the opposite is true: It's the recipe we can rely on to deliver exactly what we want out of this comfort-food institution. Under a molten cap of melted cheese and bread crumbs, the noodles are clad in creamy, cheesy sauce. It's the mac that every boxed and frozen TV dinner version tries so hard to re-create.

To maximize the perfect crust-to-creamy ratio, be stingy with the oven time, and cook the dish in a shallow, wide pan (such as a skillet). Since the mornay is already cooked through, you're simply using the broiler to melt and caramelize the cheese crust. And using a wide vessel creates more surface area for that crispy topping.

12 ounces (340 g) dried elbow macaroni

2 cups (480 ml) Mornay Sauce (recipe follows)

Kosher salt and freshly ground black pepper

½ cup (55 g) grated Cheddar cheese (your preference of sharpness)

½ cup (45 g) coarse Bread Crumbs (see page 232), optional

Cook the macaroni in salted water until al dente. Drain and return to the pot. Add the Mornay sauce, stirring to coat the macaroni. Season to taste with salt and pepper.

Transfer the macaroni to a large skillet or shallow casserole dish and spread the grated cheese evenly over the top. Top with bread crumbs, if using. Preheat the broiler and arrange a rack about 4 inches from the heating element. Broil the macaroni and cheese until the cheese on top is melted and the crumbs are deeply browned, about 4 minutes (watch carefully, as broiler intensity varies). Serve hot.

Mornay Sauce

MAKES 2 CUPS (480 ML)

Mornay sauce (along with its cheese-free sibling, béchamel) is a first-week-of-cooking-school recipe, essential and classic. Melted cheese is delicious when it covers a plate of fries or nachos, but it needs the presence of milk to become the creamy, velvety sauce that defines so many cheesy recipes. Mac and cheese is first on that list (see above), but lasagna, *croque-madames* and any vegetable gratin strengthen the argument for Mornay's induction in the cooking hall of fame. We prefer sharp Cheddar in Mornay because it has enough lactic tang (the characteristic often defined as "sharpness") to help create contours of flavor within the sweet, mild combination of milk and butter.

2 cups (480 ml) milk

2 tablespoons unsalted butter

3 tablespoons all-purpose flour

1½ cups (170 g) grated Cheddar cheese

Kosher salt and freshly ground black pepper

Ground nutmeg

In a small saucepan, heat the milk over medium heat until it just begins to bubble at the edges. While the milk heats, melt the butter in a medium saucepan over medium heat. When the butter stops foaming, whisk in the flour. Cook, whisking, for 30 seconds. Gradually whisk in the hot milk and let the mixture come to a boil over high heat, whisking occasionally. Let the milk boil for 1 minute, at which point the mixture will thicken visibly.

Remove the pan from the heat and add the cheese, whisking until smooth. Season to taste with salt, pepper and nutmeg. If you won't be using the sauce immediately, transfer it to a bowl and press a sheet of plastic wrap directly onto the surface of the sauce to prevent a skin from forming. Refrigerate until ready to use, up to 2 days.

Bedazzle Your Mac

Although there's a strong argument for going the purist route, there are endless ways to customize mac and cheese. With this recipe, just make sure that any ingredient you add to the mix is already cooked through since the dish doesn't spend much time in the oven. Here are some of our favorite mix-ins:

- Roasted mushrooms
- Roasted broccoli
- Crispy bacon lardons
- Roasted tomatoes

CHICKEN

Chicken is an excellent microcosm for what we have come to want out of our ingredients. We are returning to an older way of thinking about feeding ourselves, as our obsession with the provenance and honesty of our ingredients can show. But meat, in particular, poses a roadblock. Many cooks are just not ready to pull back the curtain on the reality of life and death that surrounds meat; we're far more comfortable thinking of our meat as born in a butcher case than something that once had skin, eyes and, perhaps, a soul. The closest we can come to eating meat with a clear conscience is making sure that we're purchasing humanely raised meat, and only in small amounts.

We see chicken as a bridge to the reality of our food system. Its status as a bland, familiar comfort food is a Trojan horse. Where we were once content to pick up packaged cuts divorced from any reminders of biology or farms, we've been eased into using the whole animal, cunningly indoctrinated into a comfortable space where carving and cutting through bones doesn't seem to bother us. When we prepare whole chicken, there's no way to deny its history because we're literally up to our elbows (well, wrists) in a carcass. It's a baby step, but one that's helping us reawaken ourselves to a deeply flawed relationship with food.

So here's to chicken, which fooled us all into thinking it was boring while secretly inspiring a revolution.

Crispy Chicken-Skin Tacos

MAKES 4 SERVINGS

1 pound (455 g) chicken skins (from about 2 to 3 chickens), cut into 3-inch pieces

Salt and freshly ground black pepper

1 serrano chile, seeded and finely chopped

1 large shallot, finely chopped (about ¼ cup/35 g)

¼ cup (60 ml) fresh lime juice, plus lime wedges for serving

¼ cup (10 g) chopped cilantro, plus a few sprigs for garnish

1½ cups (270 g) finely chopped ripe heirloom tomatoes (about 1 large tomato)

12 to 16 small corn tortillas

1 head little gem lettuce—washed, dried and broken down into individual leaves

¼ cup (60 ml) crème fraîche

Chicken skins are a cook's reward. As the first responder to the beep of an oven timer, the cook gets the privilege of pulling a tile of golden chicken skin from the side of the bird to snack on while going about the business of carving. Sara Jenkins (Vol. 14: Prosciutto di Parma) has taken our guilty pleasure and maxed it out like a Las Vegas light bulb in this recipe, and we're forever thankful. To procure the chicken skin, you'll need about 3 chickens; better yet, make friends with the guy behind the meat counter and hit him up for the invaluable dermis.

Preheat the oven to 375°F (190°C) and line a large rimmed baking sheet with parchment paper. Spread the chicken skins flat on the prepared baking sheet and season lightly with salt and pepper; they might crowd a bit but will shrink during baking. Top with another sheet of parchment paper and another rimmed baking sheet to weigh the skin down. Bake for about 40 minutes, until the skins have shrunk significantly and are starting to crisp. Remove the top baking sheet and parchment and separate any overlapping pieces. Continue baking until the skins are browned and crisp, about 10 minutes longer. Transfer the skins to a wire rack until ready to use

Place the chile and shallot in a bowl and sprinkle with salt and lime juice. Let the mixture wilt for 10 minutes or so, then add the chopped cilantro and tomatoes.

Toast the tortillas on both sides in a cast-iron pan or directly over a gas burner and stack them together wrapped in a clean dishtowel.

When all the tortillas are toasted, assemble the tacos with a leaf of lettuce, a spoonful of the tomato salsa and a teaspoon of the crème fraîche. Crumble the crispy chicken skin in shards over the top. Garnish with the cilantro sprigs and lime wedges. Eat immediately.

Chicken-Skin Chips

These crispy baked chicken skins are also delicious served as a snack. Toss them with a squeeze of lime and some chopped cilantro and serve with hot sauce and a margarita. Or pile on the toppings for chicken-skin nachos.

Pan-Roasted Chicken Breasts with Lemon Pan Sauce

MAKES 2 SERVINGS

This recipe started with a simple goal: to turn the chicken's simplest, most-ubiquitous cut—boneless breasts—into a show-stopping dish that can be cooked in a single pan on a moment's notice. We wanted juicy meat, very crisp skin and a simple pan sauce—nothing more, nothing less. There are lots of hacks for boosting chicken's moisture content (wet and dry brines) and achieving crackling skin (extensive air drying), but these all require a day or two of advanced prep.

After many experiments, we landed on this method. The breasts get a gentle pounding to flatten them just enough so that all of the skin can make contact with the pan during the searing stage. We also rub the skin with baking powder, which pulls moisture to the surface and then evaporates as the chicken cooks, creating an extra-crispy exterior. After that, it all comes down to patience: When searing the breasts, don't move them until the skin releases from the pan, and watch the meat's internal temperature carefully as it roasts. We recommend pulling the chicken out when it reaches 150°F (68°C), which is 15 degrees less than the USDA's recommended temperature, but the temperature will continue to rise as the chicken rests.

2	boneless chicken breast halves with skin, about 8 ounces (225 g) each
2	teaspoons baking powder
2	tablespoons clarified butter (see Note) or canola oil
	Kosher salt and freshly ground black pepper
2	tablespoons finely chopped shallot
¼	cup (60 ml) white wine or dry vermouth
½	cup (120 ml) chicken stock
1	tablespoon fresh lemon juice
1	tablespoon unsalted butter
1	tablespoon finely chopped tarragon and/or parsley

Preheat the oven to 450°F (230°C) and place a rack in the center position. Cover a cutting board with paper towels and place the chicken breasts, skin side down, on top. Using the heel of your hand, pound the thickest part of the breasts until the entire breast is a uniform thickness (about ½ to ¾ inch thick). Turn the breasts over and pat the skin very dry with paper towels. Sprinkle the baking powder over the skin and rub until it's evenly coated; lift the breasts and pat off any excess baking powder.

Heat the butter or oil in a large heavy-bottomed skillet over high heat until it shimmers. Season the breasts generously with salt and pepper and gently lay them, skin-side down, in the skillet. Lower the heat to medium-high and cook the chicken, pressing down on the top of the breasts occasionally with a spatula to ensure that all of the skin comes in contact with the skillet. After about 4 minutes, the skin should release from the skillet and allow you to peek underneath by lifting the chicken with a spatula (if the chicken sticks, wait another minute). When the skin is a deep golden brown, flip the chicken over and place the skillet in the oven. Roast the chicken until an instant-read thermometer inserted into the thickest part of the breast reads 150°F (68°C), about 5 to 10 minutes (cooking time will vary based on the thickness of your breasts and the temperature of the chicken when you place it in the skillet.)

Remove the skillet from the oven and transfer the chicken breasts to a plate to rest, skin-side up. Pour out all but about 1 tablespoon of the oil and place the skillet over medium heat. Add the shallot and cook, stirring, until translucent, about 2 minutes. Add the wine and stir with a wooden spoon, scraping up any browned bits from the bottom of the pan. Add the stock and bring to a boil; reduce the sauce for a couple of minutes until it reaches a syrupy consistency. Turn off the heat and whisk in the lemon juice and butter. Once the butter has completely melted, stir in the herbs. Taste the sauce and season with salt and pepper as needed.

Transfer the chicken to plates, spoon the sauce around the breasts and serve.

NOTE: To make clarified butter, cut ½ cup (1 stick/ 115 g) of butter into small pieces and place in a saucepan over low heat. When the butter has completely melted, remove it from the heat and let stand for a few minutes. Skim any foam floating on top of the butter with a fine-mesh strainer or spoon, then slowly pour the butter into a measuring cup, leaving the milky solids on the bottom the saucepan behind. The clarified butter can be refrigerated for up to 1 week.

Six Ways to Soup

USE THIS CHICKEN STOCK AS THE BASE OF ANY OF THE FOLLOWING SOUPS:
- Egg drop soup
- Pasta e fagioli
- Kale, sausage and lentil
- Chicken tortilla
- Matzo ball soup
- Rice, lemon and herb soup

Rotisserie Chicken Broth

MAKES 1½ QUARTS (1.4 L)

If we had to cop to one dirty grocery store convenience secret, it'd be rotisserie chicken. When we learned how quick and easy it is to repurpose the carcasses into homemade stock, we felt a little bit less guilty about our habit, and we've been known to turn our freezer into a chicken bone yard, each carcass awaiting its chance for karmic redemption as homemade stock. The pressure-cooking method extracts the most flavor from the chicken in the least amount of time, but you could certainly do this on the stovetop, too.

1   picked-over carcass from a roast chicken

1   large onion, halved

2   celery stalks, cut into 3-inch pieces

2   garlic cloves, smashed

1   bay leaf

1   teaspoon black peppercorns

5   thyme sprigs

    Kosher salt

Prepare the chicken: Remove any skin and tear the carcass into 3 or 4 pieces so that it will fit better in the pan.

Place all of the ingredients in pressure cooker with 6 cups (1.4 L) water. Cover and secure (or lock) the lid. Bring to high pressure and cook for 30 minutes. Turn off the pressure cooker and let rest until the pressure indicator has gone all the way down, 20 to 30 minutes. Strain the stock through a fine-mesh sieve. Stir in 1 tablespoon of salt and let cool to room temperature before transferring it to containers and storing in the refrigerator or freezer.

(To make the stock on the stovetop, combine the ingredients in a stockpot with 9 cups (2.2 L) water. Bring to a boil, then reduce to a gentle simmer and cook for 3 hours, until the stock has reduced by a third. Strain the stock through a fine-mesh sieve. Stir in 1 tablespoon of salt and let cool to room temperature before transferring it to containers and storing in the refrigerator or freezer.)

Michelada Chicken

MAKES 4 SERVINGS

A few summers ago, our minds were blown when a friend made us a michelada cocktail by mixing the ingredients directly in a can of beer. She took a healthy sip, then added to the can a squirt of lime juice, a squirt of Worcestershire sauce and a healthy sequence of hot sauce dashes. She then littered the rim with salt and pepper and left us to admire the creation as we gulped it down.

The simplicity of that canned cocktail informed this approach to beer-can chicken, a technique in which a can of beer acts as hat stand to a whole bird, allowing it to sit vertically on the grill or in the oven while absorbing the beer's malty steam. Lime juice informs a chimichurri-like sauce, while the fiery kick of hot sauce is reduced down to a rich concentrated base for a brine. A note to beer aficionados: Resist the urge to use anything but very basic beer here, lest it overpower the other flavors at play.

FOR THE BRINE:

1 cup (240 ml) Tabasco hot sauce

1 12-ounce (360 ml) can lager beer (nothing too hoppy)

¼ cup (67 g) kosher salt

FOR THE CHICKEN:

1 whole 3- to 4-pound (1.4- to 1.8-kg) chicken

1 12-ounce (360 ml) can lager beer (same as you used above)

1 bunch parsley

1 bunch cilantro

Juice and finely grated zest of 1 lime

1 garlic clove

Kosher salt

1 teaspoon dark brown sugar

¾ cup extra-virgin olive oil

Make the brine: In a medium saucepan, bring the hot sauce and beer to a boil over high heat, then reduce to a simmer and cook until the mixture reduces to a quarter of its original volume, about 15 to 20 minutes. Let cool.

In a large nonreactive container or stockpot, combine the kosher salt and 4 cups (960 ml) of water; stir until the salt dissolves. Stir in the hot sauce–beer reduction, 4 more cups (960 ml) of water and 2 cups of ice. Submerge the chicken in the brine and refrigerate for at least 4 and up to 8 hours.

Make the chicken: Drain the chicken, discarding the brine, and pat completely dry.

Remove all but the bottom rack from the oven and preheat to 400°F (205°C). Open the remaining can of beer and pour out (or drink) about a third from the can. Place the can in the center of a roasting pan and carefully position the chicken on top of the can so that the can is resting inside the chicken's cavity (you know, beer-can chicken). Carefully transfer the roasting pan to the oven and roast for 50 minutes to 1 hour, until the juices run clear and a thermometer inserted into the thigh reaches 165°F (75°C). Transfer the chicken to a cutting board and let it rest for 15 minutes.

Meanwhile, in a food processor, combine the parsley, cilantro, lime juice and zest, garlic, 2 teaspoons of salt and the sugar. With the motor running, drizzle in the oil until the mixture comes together in a rich sauce.

Carve the chicken into 8 pieces and drizzle with the sauce. Serve with any additional sauce on the side.

Salt & Szechuan Pepper-Roasted Chicken

MAKES 4 SERVINGS

In the Flushing neighborhood of Queens, New York, there are dozens of Szechuan-style Chinese restaurants that serve skewers of dark chicken meat finished in a combination of Szechuan pepper and salt. For whatever reason, the seasoning has a hold over us like a love-struck teenager; neither the threat of high blood pressure nor the numbness of our tongues can stop us from picking the skewers clean. Even then, we're always left wishing that we had a whole chicken with this spice treatment waiting for us at home. So high fives to this recipe for making those dreams come true. By cooking the chicken slowly, the bird retains all of its moisture and the meat pulls easily from the bones (it's the way we prefer to roast chicken when using the meat for a salad or as a filling). The skin doesn't crisp up as much as it would if cooked over high heat, but the spice rub adds that elusive textural crunch.

1   3½- to 4-pound (1.6- to 1.8-kg) whole chicken

2   tablespoons Szechuan peppercorns

1   teaspoon black peppercorns

1   teaspoon red pepper flakes

2   whole star anise

4   teaspoons kosher salt

2   tablespoons canola oil

    White rice, for serving

    Chile oil, for serving (optional)

Set the chicken breast-side down on a cutting board and, using kitchen shears or a cleaver, separate the backbone from the ribs (save the backbone for your next batch of chicken stock). Turn the chicken breast-side up, place both your hands in the center of the breastplate and press down hard until you hear the breastbone snap; the chicken should be flattened at this point.

In a spice grinder (or mortar and pestle), finely grind the Szechuan peppercorns, black peppercorns, pepper flakes and star anise. Dump the mixture into a small bowl and stir in the salt. Rub oil all over the chicken and season with the spice blend all over the skin and the chicken's underside (you should use all of the spice blend). Let the chicken sit at least 1 hour, or refrigerate up to overnight (let the chicken come to room temperature before cooking).

Preheat the oven to 325°F (165°C).

Place the chicken on a rimmed baking sheet, skin side up, and roast until it's falling-apart tender, 2 to 2½ hours.

Pull the meat from the bones and serve with rice. Top with chile oil, if desired.

Chicken Rillettes

MAKES 2 CUPS (255 G); SERVES 8 AS AN APPETIZER

2   whole chicken legs, with skin

1   tablespoon kosher salt

1   teaspoon freshly ground black pepper

10   garlic cloves, smashed and peeled

1   tablespoon thyme leaves

2   cups (480 ml) rendered chicken, duck or goose fat (see box)

2   tablespoons Dijon mustard

Crostini and cornichons, for serving

Rillettes are a pâté-like spread made by slowly cooking meat in fat (aka confit), then mixing the cooked meat with some of that fat and other flavorings. Pork- and duck-based variations are common in France and elsewhere, but chicken makes a less-gamy version that works both as a snack spread and filling for sandwiches or ravioli. This recipe will leave you with a few pieces of bonus chicken skin, which you can crisp up in a 350°F (175°C) oven or use to make Crispy Chicken-Skin Tacos (page 100).

Season the chicken legs all over with the salt and pepper. Place one leg, skin-side down, on top of a piece of plastic wrap and scatter the garlic and thyme leaves evenly over the top. Place the other chicken leg, skin-side up, on top, then wrap the two legs together tightly and refrigerate overnight to let the chicken cure.

Preheat the oven to 275°F (135°C). Unwrap the chicken and place it, along with the garlic, in a pan small enough to fit both legs snugly in an even layer (a 4-quart/3.8-L saucepan will work well).

In another saucepan, melt the fat over low heat. Pour enough melted fat over the chicken to completely cover it (if you're a little short, you can add olive oil to cover). Heat the pan over medium heat until the first bubbles appear, then transfer it to the oven and cook, uncovered, until the meat is very tender and separates easily from the bone, about 3 hours. (While the chicken bakes, the fat should bubble ever so gently; adjust the oven heat as necessary.)

Remove the pan from the oven and let cool for 30 minutes, then remove the chicken from the fat, letting any excess drip back into the pan. Transfer the chicken to a cutting board. Pass the fat through a fine-mesh strainer and reserve; transfer the garlic cloves to a cutting board and mash into a paste with a fork.

When the chicken is cool enough to handle, remove the skin (save it!) and pull the meat from the bones. Discard the bones and transfer the meat to a bowl. At this point, you should have about 2 cups (390 g) of chicken meat. Add the mustard, garlic paste and ½ cup (120 ml) of the reserved fat and mix well with a fork. Season to taste with salt and pepper and divide between two small jars, packing the meat in tightly with a spoon. Pour enough of the reserved fat over the chicken to form a layer on top; refrigerate the remaining fat and use it for cooking. Serve the rillettes with crostini and cornichons.

Making Schmaltz

Chicken fat (aka schmaltz) isn't easy to find in stores unless you live near a kosher butcher. To make your own, freeze enough chunks of fat left over from trimming whole chickens or chicken parts until you have a couple cups of it. Place the fat and a pinch of salt in a saucepan and heat slowly over very low heat until all of the fat has rendered and any bits of skin are golden brown. Strain the fat, saving the cracklings for snacking or garnishing, and refrigerate the fat until ready to use.

Chicken Larb

MAKES 4 TO 6 SERVINGS

2 pounds (910 g) boneless chicken thighs (or any boneless cut of chicken), cut into 1-inch pieces

3 medium shallots, thinly sliced

2 garlic cloves, roughly chopped, divided

5 stalks lemongrass, rough exteriors removed

1 teaspoon finely chopped fresh ginger

2 Thai bird chiles, roughly chopped (with seeds), divided

4 tablespoons (60 ml) fish sauce, divided

1/3 cup plus 1 tablespoon (90 ml) fresh lime juice, divided

1 teaspoon finely grated lime zest

1 tablespoon chopped cilantro stems

2 tablespoons canola oil, divided

1/4 cup (55 g) packed dark brown sugar

1/2 cup (25 g) mint leaves

1/2 cup (20 g) cilantro leaves

Lettuce leaves, for serving

Every cook has an invisible line that divides what he or she is willing to make from scratch versus what gets outsourced to the grocery store. A lot goes into factoring this line, from personal preferences such as schedule or interest (do I really have time to make spaghetti from scratch?) to larger cultural and economic ones, including availability and affordability of ingredients.

Usually, grinding our own meat falls outside the line—most of the time, we'll just grab some ground beef from the store, even when the latest cheffy cookbook tells us how great it is to make your own burger blend. But chicken is an exception to that rule. Chicken doesn't hold up well under the meat grinder; it turns into a paste that, when cooked, lacks much texture. We prefer mincing chicken into a coarse crumble in a food processor, which offers a much more appealing bite. Be sure the chicken is very cold so that the meat is easier for the blade to cut cleanly through.

Arrange the chicken on a baking sheet and place in the freezer for 10 minutes. Transfer the chicken to the food processor along with the shallots, 1 clove of garlic, the lemongrass, ginger, 1 of the chiles, 1 tablespoon of fish sauce, 1 tablespoon of lime juice, the lime zest, cilantro stems and 1 tablespoon of oil. Pulse until the ingredients are combined and the chicken is roughly chopped into pieces about 1/2 inch in size.

Heat the remaining 1 tablespoon of oil in a skillet over medium heat. Add the chicken mixture and cook, stirring occasionally, until the chicken is cooked through and browned in spots, about 8 to 10 minutes. Transfer to a serving bowl.

In a small bowl, whisk together the remaining garlic, chile, 3 tablespoons of fish sauce, 1/3 cup (75 ml) of lime juice and the sugar. Serve the larb with the herbs, lettuce leaves and dressing on the side.

Spatchcocked Steakhouse Grilled Chicken

MAKES 4 SERVINGS

What happens when you treat a chicken like a steak? Only good things, if this recipe is any indication. From the Lawry's-inspired spice rub (don't judge—that stuff is delicious) to the high-heat grilling technique, this bird is juicy and highly flavorful. Spatchcocking the chicken, wherein the backbone is removed and the chicken is flattened, creates a shorter, more even cooking process; alternatively, you could also use this rub for cooking individual chicken pieces.

1   teaspoon cumin seeds

¾   teaspoon fennel seeds

½   teaspoon whole black peppercorns

2½   teaspoons sweet paprika

1½   teaspoons garlic powder

1   tablespoon plus ½ teaspoon kosher salt, divided

1   3- to 4-pound (1.4- to 1.8-kg) whole chicken

2   tablespoons canola oil

12   scallions

2   lemons, halved

2   teaspoons extra-virgin olive oil

In a small skillet, toast the cumin seeds, fennel seeds and peppercorns over medium heat until fragrant and the seeds become slightly golden, 2 to 3 minutes. Transfer the seeds and peppercorns to a spice grinder (or mortar and pestle) and add the paprika and garlic powder; pulverize until fine. Transfer the mixture to a small bowl and stir in 1 tablespoon of salt.

Rinse the chicken cavity and pat the inside and outside dry. Set it breast-side down on a cutting board and, using kitchen shears or a cleaver, separate the backbone from the ribs (save the backbone for your next batch of chicken stock). Turn the chicken breast-side up, place both your hands in the center of the breastplate and press down hard until you hear the breastbone snap; the chicken should be flattened at this point.

Wiggle your fingers between the skin and the breast meat to create a pocket. Do the same at the thigh junction, wiggling your fingers deep down to the leg. Generously season beneath the chicken skin with the spice rub. Season the underside of the chicken as well, and sprinkle the remaining rub over the top of the skin. Set the chicken on a plate and let marinate at room temperature for 1 hour or for up to 2 days in the fridge.

Prepare a charcoal or gas grill to medium-high heat with a medium-low zone. (For medium-high, you should be able to hold your hand a few inches above the grill grate for about 3 to 4 seconds; 6 to 7 seconds for medium-low).

Use grill tongs to dip a folded paper towel into the canola oil and wipe down the grill grate; repeat this a few times. Place the chicken on the hotter side of the grill, skin-side up. Cover the grill, open the vents in the top and bottom of the grill and cook until the underside of the chicken is deep brown, 12 to 15 minutes. Turn the chicken over and place it on the cooler side of the grill. Cover the grill and cook until the internal temperature in the leg-thigh joint registers 155°F (68°C) on an instant-read thermometer, about 10 to 15 minutes longer (depending on the size of the chicken and the intensity of your fire).

Transfer the chicken to a plate and let it rest for 10 minutes. Toss the scallions and lemon halves with the olive oil and remaining ½ teaspoon of salt and place them on the hot side of the grill, setting the lemons cut-side down. Grill until they're marked and browned, turning the scallions over halfway through cooking, 3 to 4 minutes for the lemons and

4 to 6 minutes for the scallions. Transfer the lemons and scallions to a platter.

Carve the chicken and arrange it on the platter with the lemons and scallions. Let guests squeeze the lemon over the chicken before eating.

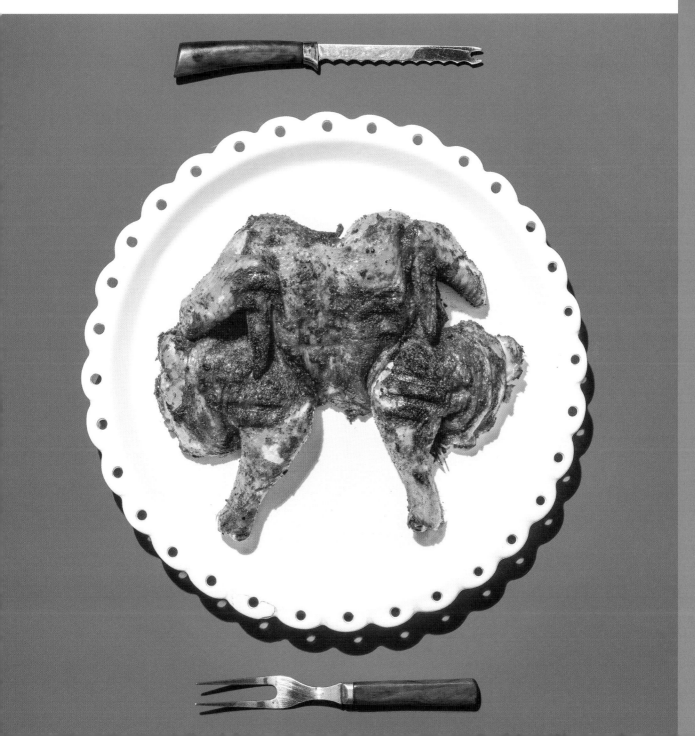

CHILE PEPPERS

Mad Dog. Satan's Rage. Toxic Waste. Ass Blaster. These are names of actual hot sauces. Notice a theme?

There's so much more to hot chile peppers than the gimmicks of hot sauce companies, which have encouraged chile consumption to take the form of culinary extremism with a scorched-earth approach to one's mouth (and other orifices).

Thankfully, almost every cuisine in the world has a healthy relationship with chiles, acknowledging their heat without freaking out over it. Thanks to our porous culinary borders and a growing diaspora of recipes, we too have gained balance in our approach. Yes, there are still the heat seekers who speak only in Scoville units. But the rest of us, who've started to follow in the footsteps of other cultures, are drowning them out.

By looking outward, we've been reminded to go back to our own canon of chile-based dishes, from jalapeño poppers (stop smirking, because you love them as much as we do) to New Mexican green chile–chicken stew.

Simultaneously, the chile market has diversified. In addition to stocking up on red pepper flakes (which now come in many different varieties), we load our baskets with shishitos, cherry hots, and Anaheims, as well as the gallant old reliable, jalapeños. There's Sriracha on every table, and we're still making our own sauce, too.

What better summation could there be for the push-pull of our global-local approach to eating?

Blistered Peppers with Lemon-Paprika Aioli

MAKES 4 SERVINGS

2 garlic cloves, chopped

Flaky sea salt

1 cup mayonnaise, homemade (page 204) or store-bought

Finely grated zest and juice of ½ lemon

¾ teaspoon hot smoked paprika

1 tablespoon canola or vegetable oil

8 ounces shishito or Padrón peppers

We imagine the shishito and Padrón are the envy of the chile-pepper world: They are a dish in their own, often eaten by the platter-ful with nothing more than a sprinkling of salt. The two varieties are interchangeable, though Padróns are slightly spicier and have a smokier flavor, while shishitos are mild (with the occasional extra-spicy outlier) and slightly sweeter. To make this quick appetizer a little more interesting, we like to serve it with a dipping sauce, like this smoky, citrusy aioli. And if you have any rendered bacon or duck fat sitting around, use it in place of the vegetable oil.

Place the garlic on a cutting board and sprinkle with a pinch of salt. Smash the garlic with the side of a knife until pureed. Place the mayonnaise in a bowl and add the garlic, lemon zest and juice and paprika. Stir to combine and set aside.

Heat a large, heavy skillet over medium-high heat. Add the oil and swirl to coat. When it begins to shimmer, add the peppers and a pinch of salt and cook, stirring frequently, until they're blistered all over, about 5 minutes. Transfer to a serving bowl, sprinkle with salt and serve with the aioli.

Kung Pao-Style Beef

MAKES 4 SERVINGS

The food of the Szechuan province of China, the original home of this now-Americanized dish, is distinguished by the intermingling of dried chiles and Szechuan peppercorns. Toasting the chiles in a skillet is one of those essential-yet-simple moves that defines an entire cuisine; it's the type of technique (if you can even call it that) that should be committed as a habit, like cooking pasta al dente. The quick sear activates the essential oils, scorching them to give off a toasty, complex flavor.

For the best results, it's worth making a trip to the nearest Asian market to snag Szechuan peppercorns, black vinegar and chile-bean paste. You'll also be able to stock up on Tien Tsin chiles, which come in giant bags and last forever in your pantry. These dried chiles have paper-thin skins, which makes them easy to toast. If you can't find Tien Tsins or the closely related *japones*, chiles de árbol will work in a pinch.

3   tablespoons light soy sauce, divided

2   tablespoons rice wine

1   tablespoon plus 1½ teaspoons cornstarch, divided

1   pound (455 g) flank steak

¼   cup (60 ml) peanut or canola oil

20   dried red chiles, such as Tien Tsin or *japones*, seeded

2   teaspoons Szechuan peppercorns

4   garlic cloves, thinly sliced

1   1-by-2-inch piece fresh ginger, peeled and cut into matchsticks

2   bunches scallions, root ends trimmed, cut into 2-inch pieces

1½   tablespoons Chinese black vinegar (available at Asian markets and online)

2   teaspoons chile-bean paste (also called *doubanjiang*; available at Asian markets and online)

2   teaspoons sugar

1   cup (150 g) unsalted roasted peanuts

Steamed white rice, for serving

In a medium bowl, whisk together 2 tablespoons of the soy sauce, the rice wine and 1 tablespoon of the cornstarch. With a sharp knife angled on the bias, slice the flank steak with the grain into 1-inch-thick slices, then cut each slice crosswise into ½-inch-thick pieces. Add the beef to the bowl with the marinade and toss to coat. Let stand at room temperature for 30 minutes.

In a wok or large cast-iron skillet, heat the oil. When you see a few wisps of smoke rising from the oil, add the chiles and peppercorns and fry just until fragrant and crisp, about 30 seconds, taking care not to scorch them. Remove the chiles and peppercorns from the oil with a fine-mesh skimmer and transfer to a bowl.

Add half of the beef to the oil and cook, stirring, until brown on the exterior but still rare within, about 3 minutes. Use a slotted spoon to transfer the beef to the bowl with the chiles and peppercorns. Let the pan and oil return to temperature, then cook the remaining beef. When the second batch of beef is cooked, add the garlic, ginger and scallions to the pan, along with the first batch of beef and the chiles and peppercorns and stir to combine.

In a small bowl, whisk together the remaining 1 tablespoon of soy sauce, remaining 1½ teaspoons of cornstarch, the vinegar, 1 tablespoon water, chile-bean paste and sugar. Pour the mixture over the beef and cook over high heat, stirring, until the scallions are tender and the sauce thickens slightly, coating the beef, about 2 minutes more. Add the peanuts and stir to combine, then transfer to a serving platter. Serve hot, accompanied by steamed white rice.

Fresh & Dried Chile Chili

MAKES 8 TO 12 SERVINGS

One of the biggest mysteries in food writing is the spelling and misspelling of chiles. Nobody can seem to agree on a standardized way: Does it end with an e or an i? As far as we're concerned, *chili* is the dish that comes in a bowl and is served during football games. *Chile* is the vegetable that's used fresh or dried as an ingredient. Chili powder is a spice blend meant for seasoning that aforementioned dish; chile powder and chile flakes refer to dried and ground chile peppers. Now that we've said our piece, feel free to argue.

Luckily, this recipe brings both the pepper and the stew together in one dish that everyone can agree on. This is a chili about chiles: It doesn't contain any tomatoes or beans, letting fresh and dry varietals of peppers operate as both the main source of flavor as well as the chief agent of texture. In picking dry chiles, we like to use 4 guajillo and 2 each of pasilla and ancho.

8	mild dried chiles, such as guajillo, pasilla and/or ancho
4	cups (960 ml) boiling water
2	poblano chiles
1	jalapeño chile
¼	cup (60 ml) extra-virgin olive oil, divided
2	pounds (910 g) beef stew meat, cut into 2-inch cubes
	Salt and freshly ground black pepper
2	large onions, finely chopped
4	large garlic cloves, thinly sliced
2	teaspoons ground cumin
¼	teaspoon ground cinnamon
1	tablespoon brown sugar
2	tablespoons sherry vinegar, divided
2	15-ounce (430-g) cans hominy, drained and rinsed
¼	cup (45 g) fine cornmeal
	Fresh sliced jalapeño and red chiles, avocado, sour cream and cilantro, for serving

In a large heavy pot, toast the dried chiles over medium-high heat, turning frequently, until they're pliable and fragrant, about 2 minutes. Transfer to a work surface. When cool enough to handle, snip off the stems and shake out all of the seeds, snipping the chiles into pieces. Transfer to a blender and cover with the boiling water; let stand until very soft, about 30 minutes.

Meanwhile, preheat the broiler. Arrange the poblanos and jalapeño on a foil-lined baking sheet and broil 2 to 4 inches from the heat, turning once, until the skin is blistered all over, about 8 minutes a side. Transfer the chiles to a bowl and cover with plastic wrap. Let steam for 10 minutes, then rub the skins off and stem and seed the chiles. Transfer the chile flesh to the water with the dried chiles. When the chile liquid is cooled to warm, puree the dried and fresh chiles with the liquid in a blender.

In the large pot, heat 2 tablespoons of the oil over medium-high heat. Pat the beef dry with paper towels and season with salt and pepper. Add enough meat to the pan so that the pieces fit in a single layer; cook the meat until it's nicely browned on all sides, about 6 minutes. Transfer to a plate and brown the remaining beef. Set the beef aside.

Add the remaining 2 tablespoons of oil to the pot. Add the onions and garlic and cook over moderate heat until softened, about 8 minutes. Add the cumin and cinnamon and cook for about 1 minute. Add the chile puree and cook, stirring, until the browned bits are loosened from the bottom of the pan. Return the beef to the pot and add the sugar and 1 tablespoon of the vinegar. Cover the pot and gently simmer the beef over medium-low heat until very tender, 1½ to 2 hours, depending on the size of the pieces.

Add the hominy and the remaining 1 tablespoon of vinegar and gradually stir in the cornmeal; cook until the liquid is thickened, about 5 minutes. Serve the chili in bowls with the garnishes.

Make ahead: The chili can be refrigerated for up to 4 days and frozen for up to 2 months.

Stuffed Cherry Hots

MAKES 4 PINTS (480-ML JARS)

3   pounds (1.4 kg) fresh red cherry hot chiles

2   cups (480 ml) white wine vinegar

2   tablespoons fine sea salt

½   pound (225 g) anchovy fillets in olive oil

¾   cup (85 g) salt-cured Sicilian capers, rinsed and drained

½   pound (225 g) pitted Sicilian green olives, such as Castelvetrano

2   quarts (2 L) extra-virgin olive oil

There's an Italian deli called Bay Cities in Santa Monica, California, that turns out the best sandwiches on the planet (as far as we're concerned). Most famous of all is the Godmother, a behemoth loaded with prosciutto, salami, mortadella and capicola. But the thing that brings the sandwich together and truly makes it shine is the briny heat of a cherry pepper salad.

This version of stuffed cherry hots, a classic pickle-bar accoutrement, has all the brine and dish-making pucker of that Bay Cities condiment in a single bite, thanks to the high-quality ingredients it's stuffed with and the punchy flavor of fresh peppers. We like to take these one step further by adding chunks of fresh Pecorino or Provolone to the mix, creating the ultimate antipasto—a bite-size cheese plate.

Using a small paring knife, remove the stems from the cherry hots and scrape out all the seeds inside while keeping the pepper whole (if you have sensitive skin, wear a pair of rubber gloves when you're preparing the chiles). In a large saucepan, combine 2 cups (480 ml) of water, the vinegar and salt and bring to a boil. Add half of the peppers. When the water returns to a boil, remove the peppers and drain them upside down on paper towels; repeat with the second half of the peppers. When they're cool enough to handle, pack each pepper with an anchovy fillet, a few capers and an olive.

Pack the stuffed peppers into four sterilized, pint-size (480-ml) Mason jars. Cover the peppers with the oil and let stand for 40 minutes or so. Top up with more oil. The peppers will keep for up to 1 month in the refrigerator, or you can process the jars in a boiling-water bath for 20 minutes and they'll keep for several months.

Salted Chiles

MAKES 1 CUP (100 G)

Chiles, like salt, are fundamental to proper seasoning. They bring light, not just fire, to a range of dishes. This two-ingredient recipe demands the best chiles. They should be unblemished and as fresh as possible. Serranos or Thai bird chiles from a grocery store work nicely if the chiles are in good shape. If you can snag an uncommon chile type from the farmers' market, all the better. Be sure to use a sterilized container, and toss any chiles that look like they're turning before you start the recipe, otherwise mold can creep (it's happened to us).

½   pound (225 g) fresh chiles

1   tablespoon kosher salt

Wash the chiles well and let them dry. (If you have sensitive skin, wear a pair of rubber gloves when you're preparing the chiles.) Remove the tops and tails from the chiles. Slice the chiles very thinly crosswise. In a small bowl, toss the sliced chiles well with the salt. Transfer the mixture to a sterilized glass container with a tight-fitting lid. Let the container sit at room temperature for a few days, shaking the contents a couple of times a day. The chiles are ready when they've collapsed slightly, are a bit translucent and are surrounded by a fair amount of liquid. (If mold forms on the chiles, it means either the chiles or the container were not clean enough and the chiles should be discarded.) Transfer to the refrigerator, where the chiles will keep for a few months.

Pickled Thai Chiles

MAKES 2 CUPS (480 ML)

Fish sauce, the fermented condiment made from dried anchovies, is the perfect base of a brine for Thai chiles. These pickles have way more flavor than that jar of store-bought jalapeños sitting in your fridge, and they can improve everything from scrambled eggs to a sandwich.

¾   pound (340 g) Thai bird chiles (preferably red and green), stemmed and thinly sliced crosswise

1   garlic clove, smashed

1   cilantro sprig

1   2-inch-long strip lime zest (removed with a vegetable peeler)

½   cup (120 ml) unseasoned rice wine vinegar

3   tablespoons Asian fish sauce

1   tablespoon soy sauce

1   teaspoon sugar

Put the chiles, garlic, cilantro and zest in a glass pint jar with a lid. In a small saucepan, combine the vinegar, ⅓ cup (75 ml) of water, the fish sauce, soy sauce and sugar. Bring the mixture to a simmer, then pour the hot brine into the jar. Let the brine cool to room temperature, then cover the jar and refrigerate it for 2 days. The pickled chiles can be refrigerated for up to 3 months.

What Should You Do With Your Salted Chiles?

HERE ARE A FEW IDEAS:
- **Toss in stir-fries.**
- **Add to vinaigrettes, especially those with Southeast Asian flavors or ingredients.**
- **Combine with the oil of your choosing to make a marinade for grilled or sautéed meats, fish or vegetables.**
- **Puree them with white vinegar to make a simple chile sauce.**

Green Chile Chicken Stew

MAKES 6 SERVINGS

New Mexico claims chiles like Maine claims lobster. They appear with regularity in the state's most beloved dishes, and "red, green or Christmas?" is a standard inquiry at restaurants, referring to the color of chile sauce you'd like ladled over your enchiladas or eggs. Green chile stew is a foundational dish, one that often sparks debate at family functions and potlucks. Purists call for Hatch chiles, indigenous to the state, but we're content to use a blend of jalapeños and poblanos. By roasting them prior to adding them to the stew, the chiles transform from bright and biting to concentrated and complex.

For Jessica Battilana (Vol. 10: Corn), New Mexican chiles are forever tied up in a traumatic breakup with her college girlfriend: "We'd driven across the country to her hometown, Albuquerque, and I'd been there for two weeks before she dropped the hammer. I'd tried my first *sopaipillas* and my first fresh flour tortillas. The actual scene of the dumping was Frontier restaurant, a sort of shabby but beloved spot near the university that serves, among other things, legendary sweet rolls. The night I was jilted, I was eating a green chile cheeseburger, which, as I recall, caught in my throat as the enormity of the situation dawned on me. But I still remember the green chile stew at Frontier, from the New Mexican section of the menu. This recipe is my homage."

---

1   3- to 4-pound (1.4- to 1.8-kg) whole chicken

1   tablespoon plus 1¼ teaspoons kosher salt, divided

1   pound (455 g) fresh tomatillos, husks removed and halved

3   poblano chiles

2   jalapeño chiles

2   tablespoons extra-virgin olive oil

1   large yellow onion, diced

2   garlic cloves, minced

1   teaspoon ground cumin

1   teaspoon ground coriander

2   cups (290 g) corn kernels (fresh or frozen)

1   cup (40 g) coarsely chopped cilantro

Flour tortillas or cornbread, for serving

Place the chicken in a large saucepan or stockpot and add enough cold water to cover it by 1 inch. Add 1 tablespoon of salt, then bring the water to a boil and skim any scum that rises to the surface. Reduce the heat so the liquid is barely simmering, then cover and simmer for 25 minutes. Carefully remove the chicken from the pot, transfer to a rimmed baking sheet and let stand until cool enough to handle. Shred the meat, discarding the skin and bones. Reserve 3 cups (585 g) of meat (a mixture of white and dark) and save the remaining meat for another use. Strain the cooking liquid through a fine-mesh sieve and set aside.

Preheat the oven to 400°F (205°C). Scatter the tomatillos on a rimmed baking sheet, cut-side down, and roast until they are very soft and beginning to brown on the edges, 20 minutes. Transfer to a blender or food processor and process until smooth. Set aside.

Preheat the broiler and arrange a rack 3 inches from the element. Arrange the poblanos and jalapeños on a foil-lined baking sheet and broil, turning once, until the skins are blistered all over, about 8 minutes a side. Transfer to a bowl and cover with plastic wrap. Let the chiles steam for 10 minutes, then rub the skins off and discard the stem and seeds. Cut the poblanos into long strips and finely dice the jalapeños.

In a large Dutch oven or heavy-bottomed saucepan, heat the oil over medium-high heat. Add the onion and cook, stirring occasionally, until softened and translucent, about 6 minutes. Add the garlic and cook, stirring, 2 minutes longer. Stir in the cumin and coriander and the remaining 1¼ teaspoons of salt and cook for 1 minute, then add the poblano strips, half of the diced jalapeños, the reserved tomatillo puree and 8 cups (2 L) of the reserved chicken cooking liquid. Bring to a simmer and cook for 10 minutes, then stir in the reserved chicken, corn and cilantro; cook until the chicken is heated through, about 5 minutes. Season to taste with additional salt and diced jalapeño. Serve hot with flour tortillas or cornbread.

Oysters Sugarman

MAKES 4 SERVINGS

Our friend Tyler Kord (Vol. 7: Broccoli) created these Rockefeller-inspired oysters and named them for a guy who doesn't care much for shellfish. All we can say is: Mr. Sugarman, you're missing out. Chiles operate in two departments here: Fresh pickled chiles help balance the richness, while smoky canned chipotles (and the adobo sauce they come with) give the pork a deep, round warmth. The DIY chorizo method described here is worth learning; we've turned back to the pretty genius invention a number of times in a pinch and used it to fill tacos and toss with pasta.

2	small serrano chiles, sliced very thin
½	small shallot, sliced very thin
4	tablespoons (60 ml) sherry vinegar
1	chipotle in adobo sauce, finely chopped
1	garlic clove, finely chopped
1	tablespoon white vinegar
1	tablespoon elderflower cordial or sweet Riesling
	Pinch ground cloves
	Pinch ground cinnamon
1	teaspoon *gochugaru* (Korean red chile powder)
¼	teaspoon sesame oil
1	pound (455 g) ground pork
	Kosher salt
1	tablespoon canola oil
4	tablespoons (60 ml) white wine
4	tablespoons (60 ml) tomato puree
1	tablespoon cornstarch
	Kosher salt
1	handful baby spinach
4	leaves basil, roughly chopped or torn into smaller pieces
½	cup (45 g) fresh bread crumbs
2	tablespoons grated Parmesan cheese
1	tablespoon olive oil
1	dozen oysters, shucked, on the half shell

In a small plastic container with a tight-fitting lid, combine the serrano chiles, shallot and sherry vinegar. Mix thoroughly and let sit for at least 15 minutes and up to overnight.

In a medium bowl, combine the chipotle with its sauce, the garlic, vinegar, cordial, cloves, cinnamon, chile powder, sesame oil, pork and 1 teaspoon of kosher salt. Mix very thoroughly.

Place a medium skillet over medium heat. Add the canola oil and swirl to coat the pan. Add the pork and cook, breaking it up into crumbles with the back of a wooden spoon, until it's lightly browned and no pink remains on the outside (you're not trying to cook the pork completely through; it will finish cooking in the oven).

In a small saucepan, combine the wine, tomato puree, cornstarch and a pinch of salt. Whisk thoroughly and cook over medium heat, whisking constantly, until hot and thick. Remove from the heat, stir in the spinach and basil and let cool completely.

In a small mixing bowl, combine the bread crumbs, cheese and oil. Mix thoroughly.

Preheat the oven to 400°F (205°C). Cover a rimmed baking sheet with a thin layer of rock salt (or, in a pinch, dried beans or rice) and spread the oysters out on the salt. Sprinkle 1 teaspoon of the crumbled pork on each oyster, then place two or three spinach leaves with some of the sauce on top of the oysters. Finally, top each oyster evenly with 1 teaspoon of the bread crumb mixture. Bake the oysters for 7 to 10 minutes, or until the bread crumbs are lightly browned and the oyster is just barely cooked through. Top each oyster with a slice of pickled serrano chile and serve warm.

Open-Faced Jalapeño Poppers

MAKES 2 DOZEN

There's a time and place for the cheesy, deep-fried, state fair–worthy style of jalapeño poppers. But it's not something we regularly want to make at home (we'll let our favorite bar do the work). In our kitchen, we go a different route, with a roasted, open-face version of the popper. Treated this way, the jalapeño is in the driver's seat, and it blooms from a catchall "hot pepper" into a varietal with special character—thin skin, grassy flesh and just the right amount of heat when roasted.

For the filling, tahini takes the role of cheese, binding together crumbled sausage (run-of-the-mill Jimmy Dean or Neese's brands are best...trust us), bits of diced lemon and tomatoes. For a vegan version, omit the sausage and add pickled carrots or kalekraut (page 182).

12   jalapeño chiles, stems removed

4   ounces (115 g) breakfast sausage, casings removed

1   cup (240 ml) tahini, well stirred

½   cup (90 g) diced tomatoes (about 1 small tomato)

½   cup (25 g) chopped parsley

½   cup (90 g) diced lemon (with rind)

     Salt and freshly ground black pepper

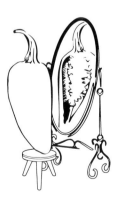

Preheat the oven to 425°F (220°C). Slice the jalapeños in half lengthwise and scoop out the seeds and inner fibers with a spoon.

In a skillet, cook the sausage over medium heat, stirring frequently and breaking it up into crumbles with a wooden spoon. When the sausage is browned throughout, about 6 to 8 minutes, transfer it to a paper towel–lined plate and let cool.

Place the tahini in a food processor and process for about 2 minutes, until it lightens in color. With the motor running, slowly add ¼ cup (60 ml) of water in a steady stream (the tahini will seize up momentarily, but then soften again) until the tahini has a light, whipped consistency. Transfer to a medium bowl.

Place the tomatoes in a colander or sieve and sprinkle with salt. Set the sieve over a bowl or the sink and let sit for 10 minutes to drain some of the juices. Add the tomatoes, parsley, lemon and reserved sausage to the bowl with the tahini and stir to combine. Season generously with salt and black pepper.

Set a wire rack in a baking sheet and arrange the peppers on the rack (this will keep them upright while baking). Spoon about 1 teaspoon of the tahini filling into each half pepper.

Transfer the jalapeños to the oven and cook for 15 minutes, until lightly browned on the tops. Remove from the oven, let cool for a few minutes, then serve.

Thai Coconut-Chile Macaroons

MAKES 2 DOZEN

3 cups (255 g) shredded unsweetened coconut

½ teaspoon kosher salt

1 tablespoon chopped Thai basil

Zest of 1 lime

1 Thai bird chile, seeded and minced (about 1 teaspoon)

1 cup (240 ml) sweetened condensed milk

2 large egg whites

½ teaspoon cream of tartar

It takes a delicate hand (and palate) to make desserts with chiles. The heat often overpowers sweet concoctions so that all you can taste is the pepper. But these macaroons are one of the few chile desserts we've ever tried that nail that incredibly fragile balance.

That said, it's crucial to taste a bit of the chile before proceeding with adding it to the batter. When shopping, buy two or three extra Thai bird chiles so that if one is exceedingly hot (or not hot at all), you can swap it out. Look for a chile with heat that is pronounced but not mouth-burning and overpowering.

If you can only find dried chiles, put 4 to 5 of them in a small bowl of water for a few minutes to soften, then chop aggressively to form a rough paste. The dried ones may be more intense, so make sure to test the heat. If the peppers are very hot, use ¼ teaspoon. If they are medium hot, go ahead and use ½ teaspoon or even 1 teaspoon, if you like heat.

Preheat the oven to 350°F (175°C) and place a rack in the top third of the oven. Line two baking sheets with parchment paper.

In a medium mixing bowl, combine the coconut, salt, basil, zest and half of the minced chile and work the ingredients together with your fingers, making sure to incorporate the basil, zest and chile evenly. Check the spice level and add the remaining chile to taste. Stir in the sweetened condensed milk to form a thick paste.

In a separate bowl, beat the egg whites and cream of tartar together until stiff peaks form. Fold the egg whites into the coconut mixture. Working in batches, use a small or medium round scoop to scoop the batter onto the prepared baking sheets, spacing the cookies about ½ inch apart. If the coconut mixture crumbles a little as you place the scoops on the baking sheet, you can use wet fingers to shape them into mounds. Bake the macaroons for 15 to 18 minutes, or until they begin to lightly brown. Slide the parchment paper and macaroons onto a wire rack and let the macaroons cool completely before peeling them off the paper. They can be stored in an airtight container for up to 5 days.

EGGS

All roads lead back to the egg.

When we first set out on our quest to bolster a cooking style based on ingredients, eggs were our first waypoint. We featured them as the subject of our very first Short Stack Edition because they held all of the pieces of the puzzle. Eggs are a column in the temple of technique, central to so many great cooking lessons, such as soufflés and omelets. But they also feel like the farthest thing from pedagogical in the kitchen—a staple that has neither affectations or airs. Eggs are often one of the first ingredients we encounter when learning to cook, usually in the form of a simple scramble (or maybe by cracking eggs into a batter alongside a parent or grandparent).

More than anything, though, thinking about egg-driven recipes is a deliriously fun exercise in imagination. There is always more to discover, whether it's a new way to dress up deviled eggs or an improved method to making a creamier carbonara.

So we're revisiting eggs here with new recipes that push us further as cooks, and push eggs further as ingredients. From egg yolks that have been salt-cured into a shavable condiment to whole eggs braised in coffee grounds and onion skins, this chapter features recipes that are at the heart of what excites us about cooking.

Country Soufflé

MAKES 4 TO 6 SERVINGS

French cookbooks and years of whipping egg whites would suggest that there's nothing "country" about the soufflé. But in the mind of Libbie Summers (Vol. 12: Brown Sugar), this dish has all the flavors of the country breakfasts she grew up on: pork from her grandmother's farm, eggs, butter and a dash of mustard. The only difference is the treatment of the eggs, which, when separated, whipped and reunited, become an extraordinarily light and visually arresting dish.

Our hope is that by serving soufflés for breakfast, the technique for making them will lose some of its haughtiness, and soufflés can be embraced with relaxation. At least, that's what we'll be telling ourselves as we pace back and forth in front of the oven waiting for ours to rise (old habits die hard).

3	tablespoons unsalted butter, divided
½	cup plus 3 tablespoons (65 g) finely grated Parmesan cheese, divided
¼	pound (55 g) pancetta, diced (about ¾ cup/170 g)
½	cup (40 g) all-purpose flour
1⅔	cups (405 ml) whole milk
1	tablespoon whole-grain mustard
	Flaky sea salt and freshly ground black pepper
4	large eggs, separated
¼	teaspoon cream of tartar

Place a rack in the center of the oven and preheat the oven to 375°F (190°C). Coat the inside of a 1½-quart (1.4-L) soufflé dish with 1 tablespoon of the butter and dust with 3 tablespoons of the Parmesan cheese. Set aside.

Arrange the pancetta in a large cold skillet and set over medium heat. Cook, stirring often, until browned and crispy, 5 minutes. Using a slotted spoon, transfer the cooked pancetta to a paper towel–lined plate to drain. Return the skillet (with the rendered pancetta fat) to the stove and reduce the heat to medium-low.

Add the remaining 2 tablespoons of butter to the pan and stir into the pancetta fat. Whisk in the flour and cook until the roux is bubbling and lightly browned, about 2 minutes. Whisking constantly, add the milk in a steady stream. Bring the mixture to a boil and cook for 2 minutes longer, whisking constantly.

Remove the pan from the heat and whisk in the mustard and the remaining ½ cup of Parmesan; season with 1 teaspoon of salt and ½ teaspoon of pepper. Whisk in the egg yolks one at a time, then whisk in the pancetta. Transfer to a large mixing bowl and set aside.

In the bowl of a stand mixer fitted with a whisk attachment, add the egg whites and a pinch of salt. Beat at medium speed until foamy. Turn off the mixer and add the cream of tartar. Increase the mixer speed to high and continue to beat the egg whites until stiff peaks form and the whites are smooth and shiny, 1 to 2 minutes.

Whisk about 1 cup (240 ml) of the egg whites into the yolk mixture, then gently fold in the remaining whites and stir until thoroughly combined. Pour into the prepared soufflé dish (the mixture will fill the dish) and bake until golden brown and puffed, about 40 minutes. Remove from the oven and serve immediately.

Egg Crêpe Stir-Fry Wraps

MAKES 4 SERVINGS

One of the fundamental benchmarks of becoming a great home cook is the moment when you break up with authenticity. There's a place for making recipes according to tradition, but doing so as a rule is a hindrance at home. It straightjackets creative impulses and makes it particularly joyless to cook based on what you have on hand. This recipe is a great example of letting creativity drive you when scouring the contents of your fridge. It floats between a classic French omelet and a Vietnamese rice crêpe (*banh xeo*). Using eggs as the base of the crêpe instead of flour makes a batter that cooks quickly and doesn't need to be flipped. The stir-fry can and should be interpreted as a suggestion. Don't have a carrot? Use cubed sweet potato, or throw in a few mushrooms or swap cabbage for any hearty green.

4	large eggs
3	tablespoons low-fat milk
4	tablespoons (about 10 g) snipped chives, cilantro and/or parsley, divided
	Kosher salt and freshly ground black pepper
4	garlic cloves, very finely chopped
2	teaspoons finely chopped fresh ginger
½	teaspoon red pepper flakes
½	teaspoon Chinese five-spice powder
2	teaspoons soy sauce
2	tablespoons seasoned rice wine or dry sherry
2	tablespoons canola oil
½	red bell pepper, cored, seeded and cut into strips
1	celery stalk, thinly sliced on the bias
1	medium carrot, cut into matchsticks
¼	small cabbage, cored and cut crosswise into ⅛-inch shreds
¼	cup (35 g) chopped unsalted peanuts

In a bowl, whisk together the eggs, milk, 3 tablespoons of the herbs and ½ teaspoon each of salt and pepper. Heat an 8-inch nonstick skillet over medium-high heat and coat with nonstick spray. Add ¼ cup (60 ml) of the whisked eggs to the center of the skillet and tilt the skillet so the egg spreads out and thinly coats the bottom and edges of the skillet. Return the skillet to the heat and cook the crêpe until the edges turn golden brown and lacy and start to pull away from the sides of the skillet, about 60 to 90 seconds. Using a rubber spatula, work around the edge of the crêpe to loosen from the skillet. Do not flip the crêpe, but once the side facing up has set and is no longer loose, wet, or runny, slip the crêpe out of the pan onto a baking sheet and keep warm in a 200°F oven until ready to use. Repeat with remaining egg mixture (you have enough batter to make 4 crêpes).

In a small bowl, combine the garlic, ginger, red pepper flakes and five-spice powder. In a separate small bowl, combine the soy sauce and wine or sherry. Set aside.

Heat the oil in the same nonstick skillet until shimmering. Add the garlic, ginger, pepper flakes and five-spice powder. Stir-fry for a few seconds, just until fragrant, then add the bell pepper, celery and carrot. Stir-fry for 1 to 2 minutes until the bell pepper begins to wilt, then add the cabbage. Continue to cook until the cabbage begins to wilt, 1 to 2 minutes longer. Add the reserved wine and soy sauce mixture. Cover and cook over high heat for 1 minute until just wilted. Uncover and stir-fry for another 30 seconds, until the cabbage is crisp-tender. Stir in the remaining 1 tablespoon of herbs and remove from the heat.

To serve, place an egg crêpe on a plate. Scatter a scant cup of the vegetable mixture over one half of the crêpe. Sprinkle with about 1 tablespoon of peanuts and fold the other half of the egg crêpe over. Repeat with the remaining crêpes. Serve immediately.

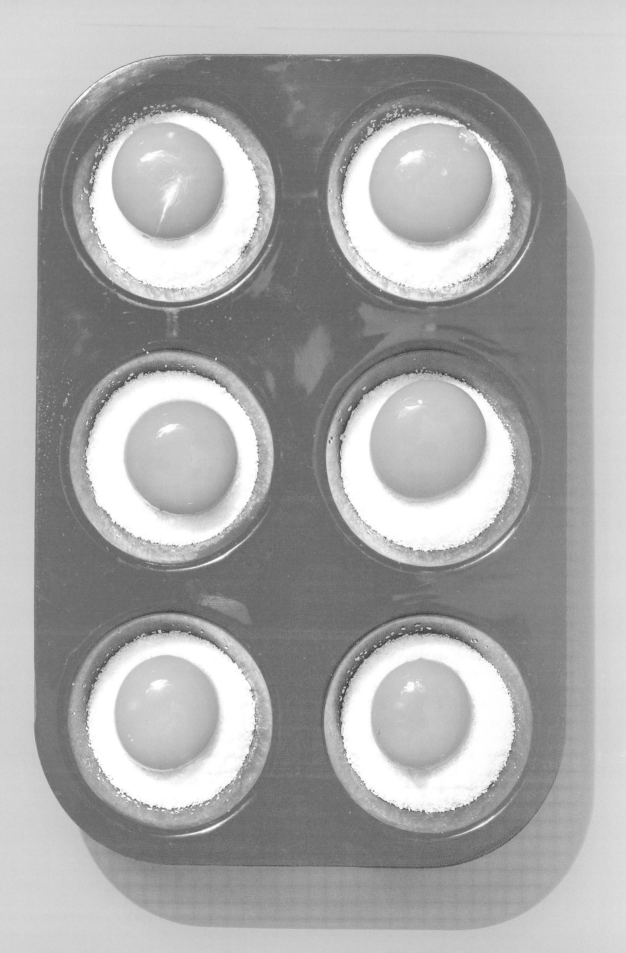

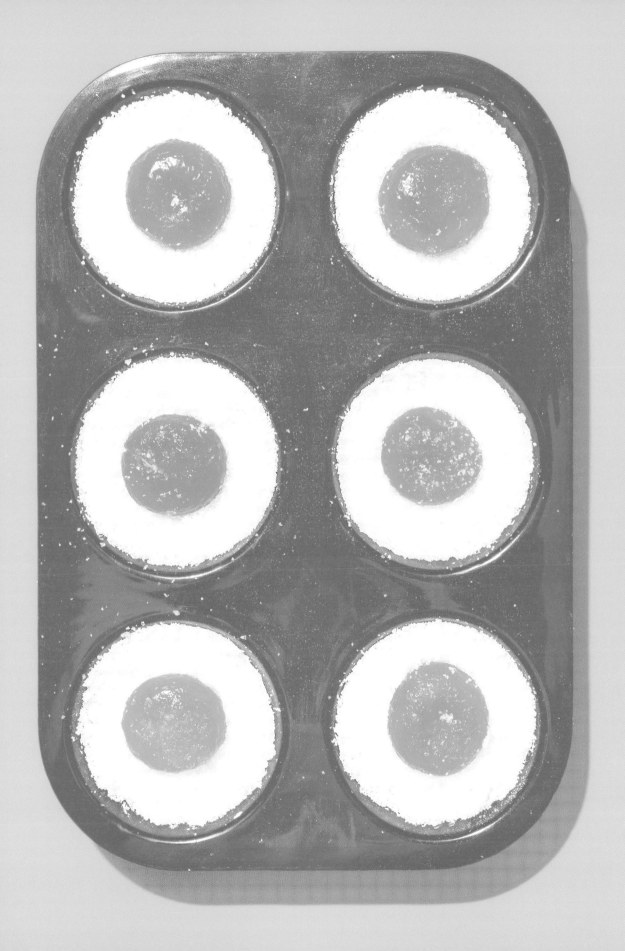

Cured Egg Yolks

MAKES 6 YOLKS

Curing food at home can be intimidating. We associate the technique with large hunks of meat or fish, mysterious neon-colored salts we're not supposed to eat, botulism nightmares and weeks (or months) of patience. Salt-cured egg yolks are a simple way to quickly introduce yourself to the practice, and they're very hard to mess up. The bulk of actual work in curing is done by salt; the sugar is mostly there to prevent the yolks from tasting too salty. We use more sugar than salt in our cure, but you can play around with the amounts if you want a saltier egg.

Treat these little golden gems like a poor man's *bottarga* and shave or grate them over anything that tastes better with eggs: salads, pasta, vegetables, toast, etc. They're especially good grated over battered and fried stuff. The little yellow flecks will melt in your mouth like cheese, leaving behind a rich, concentrated eggy flavor.

We use a muffin tin to cure yolks to keep everything snug (and to save a little on salt and sugar), but you can also cure yolks in a food-safe plastic container or in a small rimmed baking sheet.

1½   cups (300 g) sugar

¾   cup (185 g) kosher salt

6   egg yolks (use the best organic, pastured eggs you can find)

In a mixing bowl, whisk together the sugar and salt. Pour about 2 tablespoons of this mixture into each of 6 cups of a muffin tin and shake the tin to form an even layer. Carefully place an egg yolk inside each cup, then spoon more of the sugar-salt mixture over each yolk until completely covered (fill the cups all the way to the top). Cover the tin with plastic wrap and refrigerate for 1 week.

Retrieve the yolks from the tin and brush off any remaining sugar-salt mixture with a paper towel. Cover the tin with a piece of cheesecloth, then place the yolks on top of the cloth and over the muffin holes (this will help with air circulation). Cover the tops of the yolks with another piece of cheesecloth and refrigerate until the yolks are dry and firm, at least 1 week longer and up to 2 weeks.

Store the cured yolks by wrapping each in plastic wrap and placing the wrapped yolks in a resealable plastic bag. Refrigerate for up to 2 months or freeze for up to 6 months.

To use, grate the yolks with a fine grater. If there's a tough skin on the outside (depending on how long you air-dried the yolks), peel it with a paring knife before grating.

Nacho Tortilla

MAKES 6 SERVINGS

We first fell in love with Spanish tortilla, the savory cake of egg and potato, at Saltie, a slim sandwich shop in Brooklyn's Williamsburg neighborhood. The secret to Saltie's custardy version, we discovered, is that the potato is poached in olive oil before the eggs are folded in, which produces an extra flavorful base. Then we tried our hand at making Ferran Adriá's famous tortilla, wherein crispy potato chips take the place of raw potato.

　　The chip shortcut led us to another idea: What if we put the tortilla back in a tortilla by using corn chips as the base? Answer: great things. The chips soak up the eggs, creating a masa-like texture with enough heft to support a squad of nacho toppings: cheese, tomatoes, jalapeños, sour cream and cilantro. It's a knockout brunch dish (especially because it comes together so quickly), and leftover slices make great late-night snacks.

1	large tomato, cored and diced
	Kosher salt
10	large eggs, divided
2	cups (170 g) crushed tortilla chips
1	cup (115 g) shredded Cheddar or Montery Jack cheese
1	jalapeño chile, thinly sliced crosswise into rings, seeds and core punched out
1	teaspoon Tabasco hot sauce
½	teaspoon salt
1	tablespoon canola oil
½	red onion, thinly sliced
	Sour cream, for serving
	Chopped cilantro, for serving
	Sliced scallions, for serving

Place the diced tomato in a colander, sprinkle with a pinch of salt and let drain. Beat 4 of the eggs in a medium bowl and add the tortilla chips. Stir to combine and let sit until the tortillas have soaked up the liquid and softened into a paste, about 10 minutes. In a separate bowl, beat the remaining 6 eggs and add to the tortilla mixture along with the cheese, jalapeño, Tabasco and salt. Stir until well combined.

Preheat the broiler. In a medium cast-iron skillet, heat the oil over medium heat. When it shimmers, add the onion and cook, stirring, for about 1 minute. Cover the onion and cook for 4 minutes, until the slices are shrunken and softened. Uncover and spread the onion out in an even layer in the bottom of the pan. Add the egg mixture and spread evenly in the skillet. Cook for about 4 minutes, occasionally running a rubber spatula around the perimeter of the tortilla and pushing the edges gently in toward the center. Transfer the skillet to the oven and cook for 3 more minutes.

Remove the tortilla from the oven and let it rest for 5 minutes. Flip the tortilla out onto a flat surface, cut into slices and serve with the sour cream, cilantro and scallions.

Huevos Haminados

MAKES 4 SERVINGS

Enough onion skins (the loose, papery layers) to cover the eggs (from about 8 onions)

8 large eggs

3 tablespoons olive oil

1 teaspoon kosher salt

2 tablespoons coffee grounds

Greek olives, fresh feta, melon, more olive oil and flaky salt for serving

This method of braising eggs in their shells with onion skins and coffee grounds is a holdover from a Sephardic Jewish recipe in observant households and a favorite technique of Victoria Granof (Vol. 17: Chickpeas). By putting this dish in the oven on Friday night before the beginning of the Sabbath, observant cooks had a meal that was ready to eat on Saturday morning without breaking the rule about not cooking on holy days.

We're taken with the gorgeous burnished-amber shells that emerge from the oven. They make a stunnng centerpiece of a lunch platter with olives, feta cheese and fresh fruit. One more added bonus: We finally have a reason to save our onion skins; you can store them in a resealable bag in the freezer until you have enough to use.

Preheat the oven to 200°F (90°C).

In a heavy saucepan or Dutch oven large enough to fit the eggs snugly in one layer, place half of the onion skins in the bottom of the pan in one layer, followed by the eggs, oil, salt, coffee grounds and the rest of the onion skins. Add 1½ cups (360 ml) of water (the water doesn't need to completely cover the eggs and onion skins), cover tightly and transfer to the oven for at least 4 hours and up to overnight. (The eggs are cooked through after 4 hours, but they'll continue to darken in color if cooked longer.) Rinse and peel the eggs and serve warm with Greek olives, chunks of feta and fresh melon.

South-Indian Egg Roast

MAKES 4 SERVINGS

Eggs are just as much a protein as chicken or steak, but Americans rarely think to treat them that way in our kitchens. This recipe remedies that by stewing the eggs in a robust sauce flavored with the holy trinity of Southern Indian cooking: hot peppers, mustard seeds and curry leaves.

To let the sauce season the eggs to the core, score them gently with a knife as you would with meat before roasting.

8	eggs
2	tablespoons coconut oil, divided (if you can't find coconut oil, vegetable oil is fine)
1	small onion, chopped
3	garlic cloves, crushed
1	3-inch piece fresh ginger, peeled and minced
1	serrano chile, halved and seeded
2	cups (330 g) canned crushed tomatoes
2	teaspoons coarsely ground coriander seeds
1½	teaspoons garam masala
1½	teaspoons kosher salt
½	teaspoon freshly ground black pepper
10	curry leaves
⅓	cup (75 ml) unsweetened coconut milk
	Plain Greek yogurt, for serving
	Cilantro leaves, for serving

Place the eggs in a saucepan, cover with water and bring to a boil. As soon as the water is boiling, turn off the heat, cover and let sit for 6 minutes. Drain the eggs, run them under cold water and peel them. With a sharp knife, score the eggs four times from top to bottom (as if you were marking it into quarters).

In a skillet, warm 1 tablespoon of the coconut oil over medium-high heat. Add the onion, garlic, ginger and chile and cook until fragrant and beginning to brown, about 5 minutes. Add the tomatoes, coriander, garam masala, salt and pepper, bring to a simmer and cook for 10 to 15 minutes.

Meanwhile, melt the remaining 1 tablespoon of coconut oil in a small skillet over medium heat. Add the curry leaves and cook just until fragrant, about 1 minute. Add the leaves and oil to the tomato sauce. Add the reserved eggs and simmer for 3 to 4 minutes, turning the eggs in the sauce. Stir in the coconut milk and cook just until warmed all the way through. Divide the eggs among four bowls and top with the sauce. Serve alongside yogurt and cilantro.

Spaghetti Carbonara

MAKES 4 SERVINGS

For years, making pasta carbonara was a bit of a struggle for us. There were more than a few occasions when the eggs curdled or when the sauce wouldn't thicken up just right. Then we went to Italy. You know when people talk about cooking like an Italian grandmother? Well, this recipe is cribbed directly from a Tuscan *nonna*, and it creates the creamiest, most reliable carbonara we've ever made.

There are two tricks that help transform the egg into a creamy sauce without curdling it. First, the order in which you combine the ingredients matters tremendously. Coating the pasta in the bacon and bacon grease before adding it to the eggs brings the temperature down a bit, which in turn naturally tempers the eggs. Second, by leaving some of the pasta water in the pot at a simmer, you have a double boiler ready. Adding this burst of gentle heat while you stir your noodles and egg sauce together solves the previous issues we've had with carbonara; it thickens, but this also ensures that the pasta is hot when it gets to the table.

8   thick-cut bacon slices, diced

6   eggs

1   cup (100 g) finely grated Parmigiano-Reggiano cheese, plus more for serving

       Salt and freshly ground black pepper

1   pound (455 g) dried spaghetti

Bring a large pot of salted water to a boil.

Place the bacon in a large skillet and place over medium-low heat. Cook, stirring occasionally, until the fat has rendered and the bacon is crisp, 15 to 20 minutes. Reduce the heat to the lowest possible setting.

In a large heatproof bowl, beat the eggs well. Add the cheese and 1 teaspoon of black pepper. Set the bowl near the stove.

Add the spaghetti to the boiling water and cook until almost al dente (the pasta will finish cooking in the sauce). When the spaghetti is ready, do not drain; instead, use tongs to transfer the spaghetti to the skillet with the bacon. Stir to coat and cook for 1 minute. Pour out all but 2 inches (5 cm) of pasta water from the pot and return to medium-high heat.

Transfer the contents of the skillet to the bowl with the eggs, stirring constantly. Continue stirring quickly for about 2 minutes; the sauce should start to coat the noodles. Place the bowl over the pot with the simmering water to form a double boiler. Cook, stirring constantly, for 2 to 3 minutes, until the sauce has thickened and turned glossy and clings to the noodles. Season to taste with salt and pepper and serve immediately with extra cheese.

Poppy Seed Pavlovas with Lemon Curd

MAKES 4 TO 6 SERVINGS

FOR THE CURD:

3   large eggs

3   egg yolks (reserve the whites for meringues)

½   cup (100 g) sugar

     Zest and juice of 3 lemons

½   teaspoon kosher salt

½   cup (1 stick/115 g) unsalted butter, cut into small cubes

FOR THE MERINGUE:

3   egg whites (from the curd recipe)

1   cup (200 g) sugar

1   teaspoon poppy seeds

We can't help but love a dish that's as clever as it is delicious. This Pavlova is an homage to the egg in every possible way: visually, philosophically and practically. The curd shows off the rich custardy properties of egg yolk, while the meringue is a textbook demonstration of egg whites in action. The egg, dissected into white and yolks during cooking, comes back together on the plate and shares a remarkable resemblance to a fried egg. (Even the poppy seeds are in on the performance, posing as cracked pepper.)

Tromp l'oeil notwithstanding, this is a perfect brunch dessert, especially because it's best when the components are made the night before. The curd improves when given time to set up in the fridge, and the Pavlovas need to dry out in the oven overnight for that ideal crunchy-on-the-outside, soft-on-the-inside texture.

Make the curd: Fill a medium saucepot with 1 inch of water and bring to a gentle simmer over medium-low heat. Place a metal bowl over the pot to create a double boiler and add the eggs, egg yolks, sugar, lemon zest and juice and salt to the bowl. Whisk constantly for 10 to 12 minutes, or until the mixture is almost pudding-like. Remove from the heat, let cool for 5 minutes, then add the butter slowly, piece by piece, whisking constantly to incorporate between additions. Cover the curd with plastic wrap pressed onto the surface so a skin doesn't form. Chill overnight.

Make the meringue: Preheat the oven to 325°F (165°C). In a stand mixer fitted with a whisk attachment, beat the egg whites at low speed until foamy, then beat at high speed and gradually add the sugar. Whip until stiff peaks form, about 5 minutes.

Line a baking sheet with aluminum foil. Spoon the meringue out into a dozen 3-inch circles, so they look like fried egg whites, using the back of the spoon to make a little indentation in the center of each one. Place the meringues in the oven on the bottom rack, then promptly turn the oven off. Let the meringues sit in the oven overnight.

Peel the meringues off the foil. Put a spoonful of lemon curd in the center of each meringue and sprinkle with poppy seeds. Divide the Pavlovas among 4 to 6 plates or arrange on a platter and serve.

Mess It Up

Transform any leftover Pavlovas into a free-form Eton Mess by crumbling them up and serving them with strawberries, whipped cream and an additional spoonful of curd.

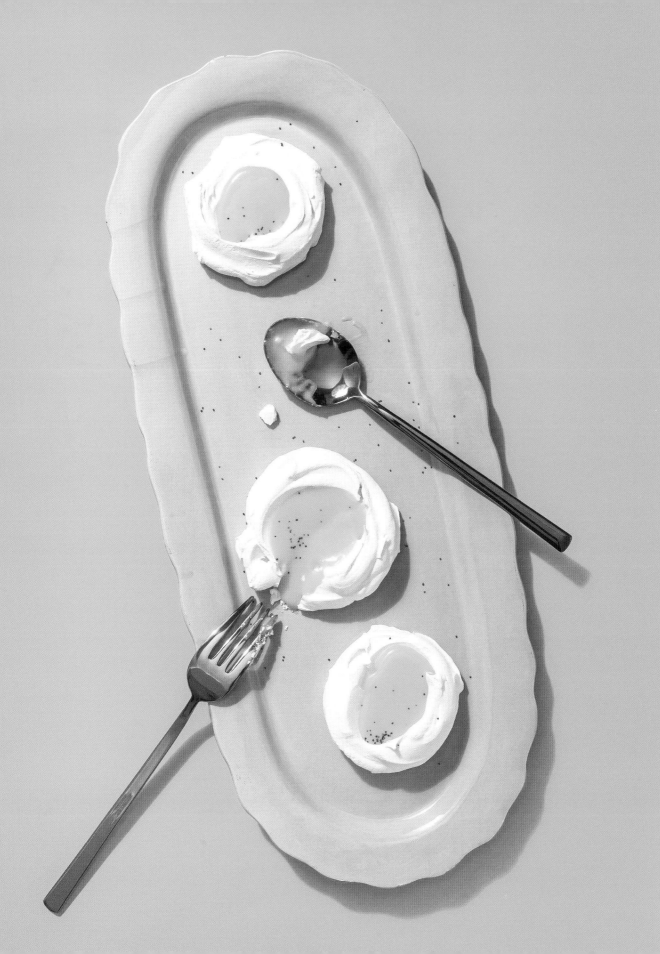

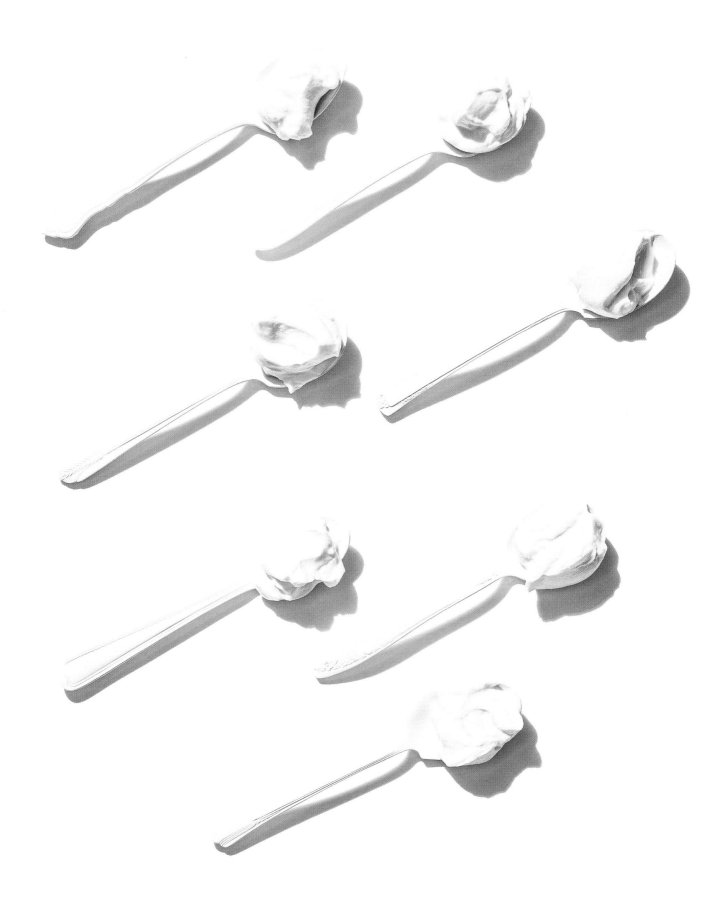

GREEK YOGURT

Few ingredients can follow you around all day without becoming annoying. But Greek yogurt is a welcome, unobtrusive guest at every meal, from breakfast through dinner and into dessert. It can steal the show with its unmistakable tanginess, but it is equally happy to be a supporting player.

This chapter offers a full day's worth of yogurt-based recipes, but first let's agree on what we're cooking with, because it's important and rarely discussed. "Greek yogurt" is what Americans usually call strained yogurt, which is nothing more than its name implies. Although you can strain your own or find freshly strained yogurt at some Greek markets, most of us buy the commercial stuff in plastic tubs. But since there's no regulation on the term "Greek yogurt" in the United States, the contents inside can vary a lot.

The only way to know what you're getting is to read the label. The main (or only) ingredients should be milk and live cultures. The yogurt should be simply strained and not thickened with additives (such as cornstarch) or pumped with richness-enhancing milk proteins or whey concentrates. Some commercial brands contain lots of added sugar, which really sucks, but luckily the most ubiquitous brand in America, Fage, passes the sniff test. With anything else, check out the ingredient list first, then give it a taste: Its texture should be rich and satiny, and it should have a distinct tartness—like yogurt-flavored yogurt.

Beet Raita

MAKES 3 CUPS (720 ML)

2   medium beets, root ends trimmed

1   tablespoon plus 2 teaspoons grapeseed oil, divided

     Kosher salt

¼   cup (25 g) cumin seeds

2   medium shallots, halved and thinly sliced

1½   cups (360 ml) Greek yogurt

     Juice of ½ a lime

½   teaspoon *chaat masala* (available at Indian markets or spice shops)

¼   cup (10 g) finely chopped cilantro leaves

You'll usually find a bowl of raita next to a fiery Indian or Pakistani dish, where it serves as an edible fire extinguisher for spicy foods. But where most raitas are made with cucumber, Raquel Pelzel (Vol. 22: Eggplant) discovered that roasted beets—hastily swapped in during a no-cucumber emergency one evening—makes the best version she (and we) have ever tasted.

Speaking of the Subcontinent: This recipe calls for *chaat masala*, which is a wondrous, salty-tangy-hot spice blend that adds extra layers of saltiness, tanginess and heat to anything it touches thanks to the inclusion of pungent *asafetida* (a dried root that tastes like onion on steroids) and *amchoor* (salty mango powder). You'll find it at Indian markets or online.

Preheat the oven to 375°F (190°C). Place each beet on a large square of foil, coat each with 1 teaspoon of oil and a pinch of salt, wrap tightly and roast until a paring knife easily slips into the center of the beet, 1 hour to 1 hour 15 minutes. Remove the beets from the oven and open the foil; once the beets are cool enough to handle, peel and chop them into bite-size pieces. (If stained hands are a concern, wear a pair of gloves when you're handling the beets.)

While the beets roast, place the cumin in a medium skillet and toast over medium heat, shaking the pan often, until wisps of smoke rise from the seeds and they're golden and fragrant, 2 to 3 minutes. Transfer the cumin to a spice grinder (or mortar and pestle) and pulverize until fine. Measure out 1 teaspoon of toasted cumin and store the rest in an airtight container for up to 6 months. (Toasting spices activates their essential oils, so ground toasted spices don't keep their freshness as long as ground untoasted spices—but it shouldn't be challenging to use up this spice. It's that good.)

In the saucepan used for the cumin, heat the remaining 1 tablespoon of oil over medium-high heat. Add the shallots and cook, stirring often, until they start to brown, 3 to 4 minutes. Reduce the heat to medium low, add ½ teaspoon of salt and continue cooking, stirring often, until the shallots are browned and frizzled, 4 to 5 minutes longer. Transfer half of the shallots to a medium bowl. Add the yogurt, lime juice, *chaat masala*, cilantro, the reserved 1 teaspoon of cumin and 1 teaspoon of salt. Taste and add more salt, if needed. Add the beets and use a spoon to stir them twice—more if you want pink raita. Sprinkle the remaining shallots over the top and serve.

Yogurt Soup with Rice & Mint

MAKES 4 SERVINGS

Hang around with yogurt long enough and you'll get to know its best friends: olive oil, garlic and mint. This foursome of ingredients features prominently in cuisines all around the Mediterranean, including in *ashe mast*, this traditional Persian yogurt soup. Well, almost traditional: The classic version is made with dried mint instead of fresh, but we can't recall the last time we had dried mint in our spice drawer. If you have some, add 1 tablespoon to the brown butter and omit the fresh—or double up!

This is the rare soup that you shouldn't bring to a simmer—the yogurt will curdle. Just heat it enough to warm through.

2   tablespoons olive oil

4   garlic cloves, smashed

4   cups (960 ml) homemade chicken stock or low-sodium broth

2   cups (320 g) cooked long-grain rice

½   cup (120 ml) Greek yogurt

4   tablespoons (½ stick/115 g) unsalted butter

¼   cup (13 g) loosely packed mint leaves, chopped

    Kosher salt

1½ teaspoons Aleppo pepper or red pepper flakes

2   tablespoons toasted pine nuts (optional)

In a large heavy-bottomed saucepan, heat the oil over low heat. Add the garlic and cook, stirring occasionally, until softened, about 3 minutes. Whisk in the stock, rice and yogurt and gently heat through, whisking occasionally, about 8 minutes; if the soup simmers, the yogurt will curdle. Cover and keep warm.

Meanwhile, place a skillet over medium heat and melt the butter; cook until the butter is light amber and smells nutty, 1 to 2 minutes. Turn off the heat and add the chopped mint, tossing it in the butter; it will sizzle and crisp up a bit.

Season the soup with salt, ladle it into bowls and drizzle with the mint brown butter. Sprinkle with the Aleppo pepper and pine nuts, if using, and serve.

Yogurt-Braised Pork Shanks with Fennel & Sage

MAKES 2 SERVINGS

Throughout history, royals and the powerful elite (Cleopatra and Elizabeth I among them) have taken to bathing in milk to aid their complexions. Leave it to the Italians to treat their pork with the same reverence that queens treat their skin. *Maiale al latte*, pork braised in milk, is a special-occasion dish in which loins are slowly cooked in a mixture of milk and cream until the dairy curdles and caramelizes into a sweet sauce.

Pulling the strings behind this whole operation is the lactic acid in the milk, which acts as a tenderizer for the pork. Here's where we saw a golden opportunity: Yogurt has a higher concentration of lactic acid than milk, and folding it into the braising liquid yields tender, richly flavored pork. We're also partial to the slightly acidic kick that the yogurt imparts to an over-the-top rich dish.

---

2   bone-in pork shanks (1½ pounds/570 g each)

     Salt and freshly ground black pepper

4   tablespoons (60 ml) olive oil, divided

1   fennel bulb, stems removed, bulb halved lengthwise and cored

¼   cup plus 2 tablespoons (¾ stick/85 g) unsalted butter, divided

16   sage leaves, divided

3   garlic cloves, finely chopped

4   cups (960 ml) Greek yogurt

4   cups (960 ml) cream

     Strips of zest from 2 lemons

Season the pork shanks generously with salt and pepper. In a large Dutch oven, heat 2 tablespoons of the oil over medium heat. Add the pork shanks and sear until browned on all sides, about 10 minutes. Transfer the shanks to a plate. Add the remaining oil to the pot and when it's hot, add the fennel, cut-side down. Sear until caramelized. Add the ¼ cup (55 g) of butter, 10 of the sage leaves and the garlic and cook until fragrant, about 2 minutes. Return the pork shanks to the pan.

In a large bowl, whisk the yogurt and cream together. Pour the mixture over the pork and stir in the lemon peel, 2 teaspoons of salt and 1 teaspoon of pepper. Bring the mixture to a boil, then lower the heat to a gentle simmer. Cover and cook until the pork is very tender and pulls easily from the bone, about 2 hours, turning the shanks over and scraping the bottom of the pan every 30 minutes.

While the pork is braising, heat the remaining 2 tablespoons of butter in a skillet over medium heat. When the butter has stopped foaming, add the remaining 6 sage leaves and fry until crispy, about 5 minutes, then transfer to a paper towel–lined plate.

To serve, transfer the shanks from the pot to a platter (or individual plates) and top with the fried sage.

Yogurt Fry Bread

MAKES ABOUT 16

4 cups (500 g) all-purpose flour, plus more for dusting

1 tablespoon plus 1 teaspoon baking powder

1½ teaspoons fine sea salt

1 cup (240 ml) full-fat Greek yogurt, at room temperature

1 cup (240 ml) whole milk, warm

1 tablespoon unsalted butter, melted

Corn, vegetable or canola oil, for frying

Confectioners' sugar, honey or jam (optional)

Fry bread has roots in both Indian and Native American cooking traditions. This one comes from the latter via Libbie Summers (Vol. 12: Brown Sugar). "My mother's side of our family is Osage, and this is a take on that recipe," she says. "It wasn't until I was much older that I realized this fried heaven that always seemed to be hanging around my mother's kitchen was in fact part of her heritage and not just an obsession with donuts." The crispy, fluffy triangles can be served either unadorned as a savory bread or sprinkled with powdered sugar to make something very close to a beignet. Libbie calls these "the down jacket of breads; the yogurt makes it light, puffy, warm and cozy on the inside."

Line a baking sheet with a couple of layers of paper towels and set aside.

In a large mixing bowl, whisk together the flour, baking powder and salt. In a large measuring cup, whisk together the yogurt, milk and melted butter. Make a well in the center of the dry ingredients and slowly whisk in the liquid. Mix and knead with your hands just until the dough comes together and starts to pull away from the side of the bowl. Let rest for 10 minutes (the dough will relax and puff up slightly).

Add enough oil to a deep cast-iron skillet or large saucepan to come halfway up the sides. Heat the oil to 360°F (180°C) on a deep-fry thermometer.

While the oil is heating, turn the dough out onto a well-floured work surface and pat it into a 24-inch square about ½ inch thick. Using a knife, cut the dough in half horizontally and then again vertically to make 4 squares. Cut each of the 4 squares into 4 triangles. You'll end up with 16 triangles. Punch your thumb through the middle of each triangle to make a 1½-inch hole.

Working in batches of 2 to 4 (depending on the size of your skillet), fry the dough until golden brown on both sides, flipping halfway through, about 5 minutes. Using a slotted spoon, transfer the fry breads to the paper towels. Return the oil to 360°F (180°C) between batches and repeat until all the dough is fried.

Serve immediately as a savory bread, or sprinkle with powdered sugar, drizzle with honey or spread with jam and eat as a dessert. The fry bread can also be fried ahead of time; it'll retain its crispness for a few hours. Rewarm in an oven, if desired, before serving.

Full-Fat, 2%, or Fat-Free?

Greek yogurt comes in various fat contents. We've found that full-fat yogurt has the best texture and flavor (it should, as it's the most concentrated version), but you can swap in 2% or fat-free yogurt if necessary. But when our recipes call for the full-fat stuff, it's for good reason: Anything skinnier might not give you the best result.

Brûléed Grapefruit with Vanilla Cream Yogurt

MAKES 4 SERVINGS

1 cup (240 ml) Greek yogurt

¼ cup (30 g) confectioners' sugar

1 teaspoon pure vanilla extract

4 grapefruits, about 1 pound (455 g) each

¼ cup (50 g) granulated sugar

Creator Virginia Willis (Vol. 5: Grits) calls this a "cheater's dessert," or the kind of sweet you can throw together when you forget to prepare a last course. With some powdered sugar, vanilla extract and a whisk, Greek yogurt is transformed into a fluffy, spoonable substance that falls somewhere between whipped cream and gelato. No grapefruit? Virginia often serves her vanilla cream with icebox cookies or store-bought shortbread.

In a bowl, whisk the yogurt with the confectioners' sugar and vanilla until fluffy. Refrigerate until ready to use.

Preheat the broiler to high and position an oven rack about 6 inches from the heat source. Slice off the tops and bottoms off the grapefruits with a sharp knife so they'll stand upright. Place a grapefruit upright on a cutting board. Working from top to bottom, slice off the peel, pith and outer membranes from the grapefruit to expose the sections. Slice the grapefruit horizontally into ½-inch-thick slices. Repeat with the remaining grapefruits and arrange the slices in a single layer in a shallow baking dish (use multiple pans or batches, if necessary) and sprinkle evenly with the granulated sugar.

Place the dish under the broiler and cook until the sugar has melted and caramelized, about 3 minutes. (You can also use a blowtorch to brûlée the sugar.) Divide the yogurt cream among bowls, top with the grapefruit slices and serve immediately.

Yogurt-Granola Muffins

MAKES 12 MUFFINS

Muffins and granola both already toe the line between breakfast and dessert, so it only makes sense to put them together. These muffins have a moist, fluffy crumb thanks to the yogurt, and the recipe can be tweaked very easily. In addition to using different granolas, you can swap out the whole-wheat flour for spelt or rye flour, the olive oil for coconut oil or the cinnamon for ground ginger or cardamom. The batter can also be baked into a loaf at 350°F (175°C) for about 1 hour.

Butter, for greasing the pan

1	cup (125 g) all-purpose flour
¾	cup (125 g) whole-wheat flour
2	teaspoons baking powder
½	teaspoon baking soda
1	teaspoon ground cinnamon
¼	teaspoon kosher salt
¾	cup (165 g) packed light brown sugar
2	large eggs
1½	cups (360 ml) full-fat Greek yogurt
½	cup (120 ml) mildly flavored extra-virgin olive oil
1	cup (100 g) prepared granola, plus more for sprinkling

Grease a 12-cup muffin tin or line the cups with paper liners. Preheat the oven to 375°F (190°C).

In a medium bowl, whisk the flours with the baking powder, baking soda, cinnamon and salt. In a large bowl, whisk the sugar with the eggs, yogurt and oil. Mix the dry ingredients into the wet ingredients, then stir in 1 cup of the granola. Let the batter stand for 15 minutes.

Spoon the batter into the muffin cups so each is just full. Sprinkle the tops with additional granola, pressing it into the batter slightly.

Bake the muffins for 15 to 18 minutes, until a tester inserted into the center of the muffins comes out clean. Let the muffins stand in the tin for 3 minutes, then pop them out and transfer to a wire rack to cool. The muffins are best the day they're made but can be kept in a resealable plastic bag for up to 2 days. Gently warm to refresh, and serve with more yogurt.

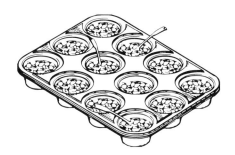

Yogurt-Honey Panna Cotta

MAKES 4 SERVINGS

We discovered that if you stir Greek yogurt into the base of a panna cotta, you don't need to use as much gelatin. This was good news, because most gelatin-based panna cottas are either too firm or too loose and wobbly. Here, yogurt adds not only body and a silky creaminess, but also a lovely tang that's missing in a traditional version of the dessert.

1   cup (240 ml) heavy cream, cold

1   teaspoon unflavored powdered gelatin

⅓   cup (75 ml) wildflower honey, plus more for serving

1   cup (240 ml) full-fat Greek yogurt

1   teaspoon pure vanilla extract

     Pinch of salt

     Fresh berries or other sliced or chopped fruit

In a medium saucepan, add the cream and sprinkle the surface evenly with the gelatin; let the gelatin bloom for 5 minutes.

Place the saucepan over medium-low heat and bring the cream and gelatin to a simmer, whisking to completely dissolve the gelatin, about 3 minutes. Add the honey and continue whisking until dissolved, 2 minutes longer. Don't let the liquid come to a boil; it needs to be heated only enough so that no gelatin granules remain. Remove the pan from the heat and whisk in the yogurt, vanilla and salt.

Pass the yogurt mixture through a fine-mesh sieve—or give the mixture a good buzz with an immersion blender—to ensure that it's smooth and free of lumps. Pour into four 4-ounce (120-ml) ramekins, custard cups, parfait glasses or teacups and refrigerate until set, about 4 hours.

Garnish the panna cottas with berries, drizzle with honey and serve.

Frozen Greek Yogurt

MAKES 6 TO 8 SERVINGS

This is definitely the tangiest frozen yogurt we've ever tasted, but we like lots of "yo" in our fro-yo (otherwise we'll just have ice cream). Because Greek yogurt is so thick, you have to add some liquid back in or you'll end up with an unscoopable brick when it freezes. This means you get to play around with what you add to it. Buttermilk adds the extra tang here, but you can mellow the flavor with an equal amount of whole milk or, for something more surprising, a semi-sweet and very aromatic white wine, such as Riesling or Gewurztraminer.

1   cup (240 ml) cold buttermilk, shaken well

1   tablespoon fresh lemon juice, plus more to taste

½   teaspoon pure vanilla extract

¾   cup (150 g) sugar

¼   teaspoon fine sea salt

2   cups (480 ml) full-fat Greek yogurt, cold

In a large bowl, whisk the buttermilk, lemon juice, vanilla, sugar and salt together until the sugar is dissolved. Add the yogurt and whisk until smooth. Taste and add more lemon juice, if desired.

Transfer to an ice cream maker and process according to the manufacturer's instructions. Serve immediately, or freeze for at least 2 hours for a firmer consistency.

Labne & Roasted Grapes

4   cups (960 ml) full-fat Greek yogurt

½   teaspoon kosher salt, divided

2   pounds (910 g) seedless red grapes, washed

2   tablespoons extra-virgin olive oil, plus more for serving

    Freshly ground black pepper

5   rosemary sprigs

    Ground sumac (available at Middle Eastern markets and spice stores)

    Toasted flatbread, for serving

Yogurt is one of those ingredients typically used to elevate other ingredients, whether it's mixed into a batter, soup, marinade, sauce or dip. But labne is Greek yogurt's chance to jump up and down and wave its arms. As if Greek yogurt weren't dense enough already, straining it more gives you this extra-tangy soft cheese that can be eaten on its own or used as a thick spread or dip. Here, we pair it with roasted grapes, creating a stunning cheese course or savory dessert. Sumac provides a visual trick: This dried and ground berry looks like spicy chile flakes but tastes like lemon. Like salt, it enhances the flavor of anything it touches—almost anything that benefits from a squeeze of lemon juice can be sprinkled with sumac instead—and you should use this recipe as an excuse to stock up and start sprinkling.

To make the labne: Line a fine-mesh strainer with a few layers of cheesecloth. Set the strainer over a deep bowl, making sure the strainer is set a few inches above the bottom of the bowl to leave room for the strained liquid.

In a medium bowl, stir together the yogurt and ¼ teaspoon of salt. Transfer to the lined strainer, fold the corners of the cheesecloth over the yogurt and refrigerate for at least 8 hours and up to 24 hours.

Preheat the oven to 425°F (220°C). Separate the grapes into small clusters (leave the fruit on the stem). Toss with the oil and season with the remaining ¼ teaspoon of salt and pepper. Arrange the rosemary sprigs on a small rimmed baking sheet and top with the grape clusters.

Roast, turning the grapes halfway through cooking, until most of them have burst and their juices bubble and thicken, about 15 minutes. Remove the baking sheet from the oven and set aside to cool to room temperature; discard the rosemary.

Remove the labne from the cheesecloth and transfer it to a bowl; discard the cheesecloth. Drizzle with oil, sprinkle with sumac and top with the roasted grapes. Serve with flatbread.

Saving Labne for Later

Anytime we make labne, we strain a double batch and roll half of it into small balls, then stack them in a sterilized jar and cover them with olive oil. Sometimes we add chopped or dried herbs, lemon zest and/or sliced chiles, which will flavor the cheese as it marinates. If you can find some good za'atar, coat the balls in it and let them sit in the oil for a couple days before eating. Oil-packed labne can be refrigerated for up to 2 months.

HONEY

Second only to fat, sugar is the most polarizing and controversial ingredient category in cooking. It's impossible to keep all the opposing opinions about quantities, choices, politics and health straight. In our minds, honey is the serene yoga teacher sitting quietly in a room of shouting suits. It's the sweetener we can all get along with.

But choosing honey for health benefits or trends doesn't give it enough credit for how it excels in the kitchen. Honey's liquid state adds moisture along with its sweetness, making it ideal for baking. As a glaze for roasted meats and vegetables, it encourages a perfectly caramelized surface. Its syrupy consistency adds value to cocktails and salad dressings. The recipes you'll find in this chapter show off all of these attributes.

Then there's the fact that honey is the Meryl Streep of ingredients, its flavor shape-shifting to reflect location and biological diversity. There are more than 300 varietals of honey in the United States, and each is a prism of its origins—the sweetest form of terroir.

Cooking with honey offers an adventure. Seek out different varietals and prepare yourself to pivot your plans accordingly, depending on the taste. Honey is a prime example of an ingredient that should be valued for nuance rather than consistency, and doing so will lead you to new and exciting discoveries.

Beer- & Honey-Battered Fish with Honey-Sriracha Sauce

MAKES 4 SERVINGS

1¼ cups (160 g) all-purpose flour, divided

¾ teaspoon kosher salt, plus more for seasoning

¼ teaspoon freshly ground black pepper

½ teaspoon smoked paprika (either sweet or spicy)

¼ cup (60 ml) milk

¼ cup plus 2 tablespoons (90 ml) honey, divided

¾ cup (180 ml) beer (preferably a lighter style such as a lager)

1 large egg

1 tablespoon butter, melted

2 tablespoons Sriracha or other chile sauce

Canola oil, for frying

2 pounds (910 g) fish fillets, such as catfish or flounder

We're devout followers of the gospel that salty fried things taste better in the presence of something sweet (see: chocolate-covered potato chips). In this version of beer-battered fish, honey delivers on that command in two ways: First, in the batter, in which it renders a richer golden brown color, and second, in sauce form, mixed with tangy hot Sriracha. It's crucial to watch the temperature of your frying oil carefully to ensure a crispy crust; otherwise, when you drizzle your fish with the sauce, it'll turn into a soggy mess.

In a large bowl, combine ¾ cup (95 g) of the flour, the salt, black pepper and paprika. In a small bowl, whisk together the milk and 2 tablespoons of honey until the honey is well dispersed. Add the beer, egg and butter and whisk. Slowly whisk the milk mixture into the flour mixture, whisking until there are, ideally, no lumps. Set aside for at least an hour.

Meanwhile, make the sauce: In a small bowl, stir the remaining ¼ cup (60 ml) honey with the Sriracha.

After the batter has rested, add the remaining ½ cup (65 g) of flour to a large bowl. Line a large plate with paper towels. Set the bowl of flour and the bowl of batter next to each other near the stove. Fill a wok or large pot with 2 inches of oil. Heat the oil over medium-high heat until it reaches 360°F (180°C) on a deep-fry thermometer.

Dry the fish well and salt lightly. Then, working in batches, coat the fish in flour, shaking off any excess. Add the floured fish to the bowl of batter, shaking off excess batter. Fry the fish until it's deep golden brown, flipping halfway through, about 3 to 4 minutes for each piece. Remove and set on a paper towel–lined plate. Repeat with the remaining fish.

Serve the dish with the honey-Sriracha sauce drizzled on top or on the side as a dipping sauce.

Measuring Honey

To avoid ending up with a sticky mess when you measure honey, spray a measuring spoon or cup with nonstick cooking spray (or coat it in a neutral-flavored cooking oil) before measuring.

Pork Tenderloin with Honey-Peach Barbecue Sauce

MAKES 4 SERVINGS

We've all had that moment: It's the last stretch of winter, and maybe it's been snowing for two weeks straight. The memory of fresh ripe tomatoes, peaches and corn has all but faded, and you've braised everything in your kitchen, including the eggs (see the South Indian Egg Roast on page 140). All you want is something to remind you that the sun will return, eventually.

Here you go. Essentially a barbecue hack for the homebound or grill-less, it imbues pork tenderloin with a smoky-sweet shellac of peaches, bacon and vinegar. Honey provides the earthy, sweet backbone, both sticky and binding. If you close your eyes while eating this dish, you can almost feel the sun on your face. Almost.

4	slices smoked bacon
½	cup (70 g) finely chopped shallot
1	1-inch piece fresh ginger, peeled and grated (2 teaspoons)
¼	teaspoon kosher salt
¼	teaspoon freshly ground black pepper
¼	teaspoon red pepper flakes
1	cup (240 ml) peach preserves
⅓	cup (75 ml) multifloral honey
½	cup (120 ml) plus 1 tablespoon apple cider vinegar, divided
1	tablespoon tomato paste
2	tablespoons extra-virgin olive oil
2	pork tenderloins (about 1 pound/455 g each), trimmed of silver skin

In a large ovenproof skillet over medium-high heat, cook the bacon, turning occasionally, until crisp, about 6 to 8 minutes. Transfer the bacon to a paper towel–lined plate; pour off 2 tablespoons of rendered bacon fat and reserve. Save the skillet to brown the pork later (there's no need to clean it out).

Heat the reserved rendered bacon fat in a medium saucepan. Add the shallot, ginger, salt, black pepper and red pepper flakes and cook over medium heat, stirring occasionally, until the shallot is translucent and tender, about 3 to 5 minutes. Add the peach preserves, honey and ½ cup (120 ml) of vinegar, then lower the heat and simmer, stirring occasionally, until lightly thickened to a porridgy consistency, 12 to 15 minutes. Remove the pan from the heat, then whisk in the tomato paste and the remaining 1 tablespoon of vinegar.

Preheat the oven to 375°F (190°C) and place a rack in the center position.

In the reserved skillet, heat the oil over medium-high heat. Season the pork on all sides with salt and pepper, then add it to the skillet and brown on all sides, about 8 minutes total.

Add about a third of the sauce to the skillet and use a spoon to coat the pork liberally, then transfer the skillet to the oven and cook for 10 minutes. Remove the pork from the oven, coat it again with another third of the sauce and return to the oven to finish cooking, about 10 minutes longer, until an instant-read thermometer inserted into the center registers 140°F (60°C). Transfer the pork to a cutting board and let rest for about 10 minutes. Finely chop the reserved bacon, then slice the tenderloins into ¾-inch-thick medallions and drizzle with the remaining sauce and the chopped bacon.

Help the Bees

Since 2006, the cause and effect of colony collapse disorder (a sudden and large-scale disappearance of adult bees) has been a hotly debated topic. What isn't disputed is this: Honeybees are the world's most celebrated pollinators, and close to a third of our food supply is linked to pollination (including blueberries, raspberries, cucumber, cabbage, citrus, carrots and peanuts). Researchers are studying CCD in order to understand and counteract it, but there's plenty you can do on a smaller scale. Plant bee-friendly flowers, support local beekeepers, eliminate the use of pesticides in your garden and buy pesticide-free produce.

Earl Grey Ice Cream with Honey Caramel Swirl

MAKES 1 QUART (960 ML)

As kids, we took our tea extra sweet with honey, heavy on the milk. And that's exactly the flavor that comes to the fore with this elegant ice cream created by Susan Spungen (Vol. 3: Strawberries). This is a recipe that thrives on good ingredients, especially the tea; forego the six-month-old stale tea bags in favor of high-quality loose-leaf tea. We're big fans of Bellocq's No. 35 and Extra Regal Earl Grey from the Rare Tea Cellar in Chicago.

2 cups (480 ml) whole milk

¾ cup plus 2 tablespoons (175 g) sugar

¼ cup (50 g) loose Earl Grey tea (or 4 tea bags)

6 large egg yolks

2 cups (480 ml) heavy cream, cold

1 teaspoon pure vanilla extract

Pinch of salt

¼ cup (60 ml) Honey Caramel (recipe at right)

In a small saucepan, combine the milk, sugar and tea. Heat until the milk is just about to start boiling, then cover and remove from the heat. Let the tea steep for 10 to 15 minutes. In a medium bowl, beat the egg yolks until well combined.

Strain the milk mixture, then return the milk to the pan and reheat it until it's steaming. Whisk half of the hot milk mixture into the eggs, a little at a time, then whisk the egg mixture back into the milk mixture in the pan. Cook, stirring constantly, over medium heat until the mixture thickens enough to coat the back of a wooden spoon. The time will vary depending on many factors, such as the size and style of your pan and the heat of your stove. It could take as little as 5 minutes or as many as 20. Once the custard coats the back of the wooden spoon, reduce the heat to low and cook for an additional 5 minutes.

Remove the custard from the heat and stir in the cold cream to stop the cooking. Stir in the vanilla and salt. Strain the ice cream base into a bowl or container and let it cool to room temperature, then refrigerate until thoroughly chilled. It's best to do this the night before you want to churn the ice cream (by the way, put your ice cream canister in the freezer now, too). If you're in a hurry, you can chill the mixture over an ice bath.

Churn the ice cream according to the manufacturer's directions, then layer the ice cream into a chilled loaf pan, alternating each layer with thick drizzles of honey caramel. Swirl a knife through the loaf pan a few times and freeze until firm, at least 4 hours.

Honey Caramel

MAKES ¼ CUP (180 ML)

¾ cup (180 ml) orange blossom honey

¼ cup (60 ml) heavy cream

2 tablespoons butter, cold

1 teaspoon pure vanilla extract

¼ teaspoon flaky sea salt

Combine the honey and cream in a small deep saucepan. Set over medium heat and stir until the honey has melted and the mixture is smooth. Bring to a boil, stirring occasionally. Cook until the temperature reaches 238°F on a candy thermometer (114°C) (soft-ball stage). Immediately and carefully stir in the butter. Transfer the mixture to a glass jar or heatproof measuring cup and let cool completely. Add the vanilla and salt and stir to combine thoroughly. Chill until needed. When you're ready to use the caramel, warm it gently to a liquid consistency by placing it in a heatproof bowl and heating in a microwave, uncovered, for 30 seconds, or by putting the container in a bowl of hot water and stirring occasionally.

Burnt Honey-Harissa Chicken Wings

MAKES 4 SERVINGS

1 cup (240 ml) honey

⅓ cup (75 ml) Asian fish sauce

2 tablespoons *harissa*

1 pound (455 g) chicken wings

Salt and freshly ground black pepper

3 tablespoons unsalted butter, divided

2 limes

For most children, sweetness is synonymous with dessert, the reward that waits beyond a plate of forced-down vegetables. But our palates mature, and suddenly we want our dessert with a sprinkle of salt or a side of bitter *amaro*. Likewise, we start to take delight in the way that a little sugar can make the flavor of a short rib pop. The line between sweet and savory dissolves in the name of balance, and honey is a crucial diplomat in making this peace. Of all the sweeteners in a cook's arsenal, it has the depth necessary to pair with pretty much anything you can put on a plate.

The first time we (intentionally) tasted burned honey was a revelation. Exposed to heat, the natural sugars caramelize into something that begs to be a glaze for proteins or hearty vegetables. Mix burnt honey with whiskey and use it to glaze a pork chop (as Rebekah Peppler did in Vol. 8: Honey), stir it into aioli for a dip to accompany crispy fried vegetables, add it to a cocktail for a decidedly sophisticated twist or use it to glaze roasted carrots.

For chicken wings, we mixed burnt honey with fish sauce to evoke *nuoc mau*, or fish sauce caramel, a Vietnamese condiment that everyone from David Chang to Andrew Zimmern has replicated. And *harissa* adds the trademark heat that every chicken wing should offer; feel free to swap it out for your favorite chile-based condiment, or omit it altogether if heat isn't your thing.

Place the honey in a medium saucepan and cook over medium-high heat. When the honey begins to bubble, lower the heat to medium-low and simmer until the honey has darkened to a deep amber color, about 7 minutes. Remove from the heat and stir in the fish sauce and *harissa*.

Season the chicken wings with salt and pepper. In a large skillet, melt 1 tablespoon of butter over medium-high heat. Add the chicken wings in a single layer and cook until browned, about 2 minutes on each side. Add the burnt honey sauce and the remaining 2 tablespoons of butter and reduce the heat to medium. Cook, occasionally turning the wings over to coat them with the sauce, until the wings are cooked through, about 15 minutes. Transfer the wings to a plate and squeeze the juice of both limes over them. Let them sit for 2 to 3 minutes, then serve.

Honey Laundering

Store-bought honey is one of the most frequent victims of labeling fraud. According to the World Health Organization, the FDA and other food safety organizations, honey that's been filtered so much that it's devoid of pollen—which can be used to identify its source—shouldn't be labeled *honey*. However, about 75 percent of the honey on American shelves doesn't contain a trace of pollen, which, although legal by USDA standards, is impossible to trace back to its origin. Even worse, there have been cases of commercial "honey," much of it imported from China, that isn't honey at all, but a blend of cane sugar, food coloring and artificial flavors. To make sure you're getting the real thing, read labels carefully (there shouldn't be any ingredients listed other than *honey*) and buy honey from small, local producers whenever possible.

Honey-Glazed Grilled Eggplant with Burrata

MAKES 4 SERVINGS

2   pounds (910 g) chinese eggplant, halved lengthwise

     Kosher salt

2   tablespoons canola oil

2   tablespoons butter

¼   cup (60 ml) honey

1   sprig rosemary

1   ball fresh burrata (or another creamy cheese, such as chèvre), about 8 ounces

The first time we ate fried eggplant drizzled in honey was in Asheville, North Carolina, the unlikely location of chef Katie Button's imaginative restaurants.

Her version of *berenjenas con miel*, a classic tapa, is still among the best preparations of eggplant we've ever had. Battered and gently fried, the eggplant is crunchy on the outside and soft on the inside, with a sweet glaze of honey and a hint of rosemary—the garden's answer to a doughnut. This dish is a lighter take: The eggplant is grilled rather than fried, then finished with creamy burrata. It's delicious right off the grill, but we also enjoy it at room temperature.

Place the eggplant halves in a colander in the sink or over a bowl and sprinkle with 2 teaspoons of salt. Stir to coat and let sit for 30 minutes. Prepare a medium-high charcoal or gas grill.

Pat the eggplant halves dry with a paper towel, then brush oil on both sides. In a small saucepan over medium heat, combine the butter, honey and rosemary. Cook, stirring, until the butter melts and stops foaming. Remove from the heat and discard the rosemary sprig.

Grill the eggplant until browned on both sides, about 5 minutes a side, brushing throughout with the honey-butter mixture.

Transfer the eggplant to a platter and drizzle with 1 teaspoon of the remaining honey-butter mixture. Tear the burrata into pieces and scatter over the eggplant. Serve immediately.

Storing and Reviving Honey

Honey is about 80 percent sugar and 20 percent water. Store honey in a cool, dark place. It keeps indefinitely—millennia-old samples found in King Tut's tomb were still edible, despite spending more than 2,000 years beneath the desert sand—though it may crystallize over time. If your honey does crystallize, heat it briefly by placing the jar in a pan of warm water.

Honey-Cardamom Coffee Cake

MAKES 12 SERVINGS

This richly flavored cake came to us from Raquel Pelzel (Vol. 22: Eggplant). And it came with a story: "During Rosh Hashanah, the Jewish New Year, you dip apples into honey, you braise carrots with honey and, of course, you make a honey cake, all to welcome the sweet year to come. If dropped from the right altitude and with precision, my mom's honey cake could kill a small animal. Heavy, with sad little flour-creased raisins shamefully suspended within, it was the kind of loaf that required an inch of cream cheese to help you choke it down. One year, she told me she was sending a loaf to me in Brooklyn from Chicago. I was walking back to my house and saw the FedEx guy ahead of me, ringing my bell. I paused mid-block. Rather than do the right thing and run to retrieve the honey cake, I stood statue-still and did nothing. The FedEx guy returned to his truck and drove away—with my cake. Oddly, FedEx never tried to redeliver the honey cake (or not so odd if you've dealt with package deliveries in Brooklyn), so I made my own. The funny thing is that after a few weeks, my mom's cake was returned to her. Of course she ate it—with lots of cream cheese—and said it was the best honey cake she had ever made, naturally."

¼ cup (60 ml) brandy

¾ cup (110 g) golden raisins

½ cup (1 stick/115 g) plus 1 tablespoon unsalted butter, at room temperature

1½ cups (190 g) white whole-wheat flour

½ cup (45 g) rolled oats

½ cup (50 g) almond meal (or ground almonds)

1 tablespoon whole green cardamom pods

2 teaspoons baking powder

1 teaspoon ground ginger

½ teaspoon ground allspice

½ teaspoon baking soda

½ teaspoon kosher salt

¼ teaspoon freshly ground black pepper

½ cup (120 ml) strong-brewed coffee, warm

½ cup (120 ml) honey

1 2-inch piece fresh ginger, peeled and grated

1 teaspoon pure vanilla extract

¾ cup (150 g) packed light brown sugar

2 large eggs, at room temperature

¼ cup (30 g) confectioners' sugar

Preheat the oven to 350°F (175°C). Pour the brandy into a heat-safe bowl and microwave until hot, 15 to 30 seconds. Stir in the raisins, cover the bowl with plastic wrap and set aside.

Lightly coat an 8½- to 9-inch loaf pan plus two 6-ounce (180-ml) ramekins with about 2 teaspoons of the butter. Line the loaf pan with a long strip of parchment paper lengthwise, making sure at least a couple of inches of parchment hangs over the edges of the loaf pan (don't worry about the ramekins— the cake will pop out with just the butter coating). Use another 1 teaspoon of butter to grease the parchment.

In a food processor, combine the flour, oats, almond meal, cardamom pods, baking powder, ground ginger, allspice, baking soda, salt and pepper and process until the oats and cardamom are finely ground,

about 30 seconds. Transfer the mixture to a medium bowl. In a separate medium bowl, whisk together the coffee, honey, fresh ginger and vanilla.

Add the remaining ½ cup (1 stick/115 g) of butter and the brown sugar to the bowl of a stand mixer (or a large bowl if using a hand-held mixer) fitted with the paddle attachment. Cream the butter and sugar at medium speed until combined. Raise the speed to medium-high and cream until the butter is light and airy, about 2 minutes. Add the eggs, one at a time, beating well and scraping down the bottom and side of the bowl between the eggs.

Reduce the speed to low and add a third of the flour mixture. Increase the speed to medium-low and, when only a few dry spots remain, add half of the honey mixture, then stop the mixer to scrape down the bottom and side of the bowl. On low speed, add half of the remaining flour mixture, then increase the speed to medium-low and add the remaining honey mixture. Reduce the speed again to add the remaining flour mixture, then jack the speed up to medium-high and beat for 15 seconds. Remove the bowl from the stand. Drain the raisins and fold them into the batter (reserve the leftover brandy; you'll use it later in the glaze). Be sure to scrape the bottom and side of the bowl to make certain all the ingredients are worked into the batter.

Use a rubber spatula to scrape the batter into the prepared loaf pan and the ramekins and even out the tops. Bake until the center of the cake springs back to light pressure and a wooden cake tester or toothpick inserted into the center comes out clean or with a crumb or two attached (not wet batter, just a couple of nice crumbs), 50 minutes to 1 hour (25 to 30 minutes for the ramekins).

Remove the cake from the oven. Cool it completely, then run a paring knife around the edges of the cake to loosen it from the pan and lift it out from the loaf pan (or invert it from the ramekin). Whisk the confectioners' sugar into the reserved brandy and spoon it over the cake. Slice and serve. The cake can be wrapped in plastic and stored at room temperature for up to 2 days.

Buckwheat Dark & Stormy

MAKES 1 DRINK

Buckwheat honey is a completely different creature from the light, multifloral honeys that act as the ingredient's standard bearer. Rich and a bit bitter, buckwheat honey is malty and thick—the Ryan Adams to clover honey's Taylor Swift.

This Dark & Stormy plays to buckwheat honey's strengths, using its notes of molasses and malt to fortify the molasses flavor in the rum. (It's that molasses-ginger punch that gives this drink its edge.) It's also an insurance policy: If you don't have molasses rum, this is the recipe that'll hack your regular aged rum to the necessary spice level.

FOR THE SIMPLE SYRUP:

1   cup (240 ml) buckwheat honey

FOR THE DARK & STORMY:

2   ounces (60 ml) dark rum (preferably a molasses-based rum, such as Gosling's)

½   ounce fresh lime juice

     Ginger beer

     Lime wheels, for garnish

     Candied ginger, for garnish

Make the buckwheat simple syrup: In a small saucepan, combine the honey and ½ cup (120 ml) water. Heat over medium-low heat until the honey melts and is fully combined with the water. Transfer to a covered container, cool and store in the refrigerator.

Make the cocktail: In cocktail shaker, combine ½ ounce of the buckwheat simple syrup, the rum and lime juice. Fill with ice, cover and shake vigorously. Pour into an ice-filled Collins glass and top with ginger beer. On a toothpick, skewer a lime wheel over a piece of candied ginger; garnish the drink and serve.

Peach Pie with Honey-Sherry Syrup

MAKES ONE 9-INCH PIE

Most peach pies are simply too cloying for our taste. At peak ripeness, the fuzzy stone fruit is plenty sweet enough, yet most recipes ignore this, calling for cup after cup of additional sugar. It turns out that honey is a far better enhancement to this classic fruit pie. It helps the peaches caramelize while baking, just as white sugar would, but is mellow enough to avoid a teeth-chattering end result. (This lesson is something to bear in mind in any kitchen situation where you're worried about balancing sugar.)

Another reason to love this pie: The magical top crust is easier to manage than a full-blown lattice, but still allows steam to escape easily, which keeps the crust flaky.

FOR THE CRUST:

2½ cups (315 g) all-purpose flour

½ teaspoon fine sea salt

1 cup plus 2 tablespoons (2¼ sticks/ 255 g) cold unsalted butter, cut into ½-inch pieces

5 to 8 tablespoons (75 to 120 ml) ice water, as needed

FOR THE FILLING:

3 pounds (1.4 kg/8 or 9) peaches— halved, pitted and cut into 1-inch wedges

¼ cup (35 g) tapioca starch

1 vanilla bean, split and scraped

Freshly grated zest of 1 lemon

¼ teaspoon kosher salt

½ cup (110 g) packed light brown sugar

6 tablespoons (90 ml) mild honey (such as acacia or orange blossom)

¼ cup (60 ml) dry sherry

2 tablespoons unsalted butter

2 tablespoons heavy whipping cream

Turbinado sugar

FOR THE SHERRY WHIPPED CREAM:

1 cup (240 ml) heavy cream, cold

2 tablespoons dry sherry

Make the crust: In a large bowl, combine the flour and salt. Use your fingers to cut the butter into the flour until chickpea-size pieces form. (You can also do this in a food processor.) Add the ice water a little at a time, just until the dough begins to hold together. Gather the dough into two balls, wrap each in plastic wrap and refrigerate for at least 1 hour or up to 3 days.

Make the filling: In a large heatproof bowl, combine the peaches, tapioca starch, vanilla bean seeds, lemon zest and salt. In a small saucepan, combine the sugar, honey and sherry and bring to a boil over medium heat. Cook, without stirring, using a pastry brush to brush the side of the pan with water to prevent recrystallization, until the caramel is dark amber and thickened, about 5 minutes. Stir the butter into the caramel until it's melted, then pour the mixture over the peaches. Remove from the heat and set aside to cool while you roll out the crust.

Assemble the pie: Preheat the oven to 400°F (205°C). On a lightly floured surface, roll one of the dough balls into a 12-inch disk. Fit the dough into a 9-inch pie plate. Trim the overhang to ½ inch and refrigerate the bottom crust while you roll out the second one. Roll out the second ball into a 12-inch disk. Use a knife or pizza cutter to cut the dough into ½-inch-wide strips.

Remove the pie plate from the refrigerator and pour the peach filling into the crust. Top with the strips of dough, leaving a little space between each strip. Trim the edges of the strips to a ½-inch overhang and fold the top strips and bottom edges under, pressing them together to seal. Refrigerate the pie for at least 30 minutes and up to 1 hour.

Brush the crust lightly with the cream, then sprinkle with turbinado sugar and place on a rimmed baking sheet. Bake the pie until it's golden and crisp, the peaches are tender and the juices bubble thickly through the top crust, 45 minutes to 1 hour. Transfer the pie to a rack and cool until lukewarm, about 2 hours.

While the pie is cooling, make the sherry whipped cream: In a medium bowl, beat the cream to medium-soft peaks. Fold in the sherry and serve alongside the pie. The pie can be wrapped in plastic and stored overnight at room temperature.

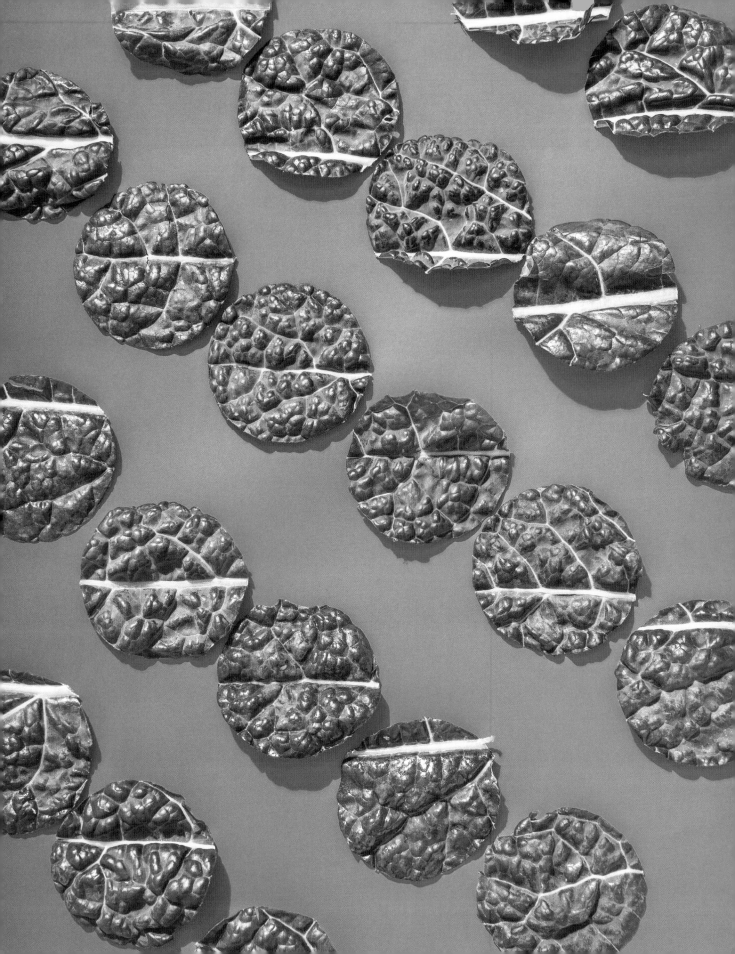

KALE

The precursor to the modern foodie was, in many ways, the health nut. The foodie fixates on his or her diet from a perspective of pleasure and flavor, while the health nut channels the same fixation, only from a perspective of health and wellness. And thanks to ingredients such as kale, these two fanatics are beginning to merge into one hyperenergetic breed of eater.

With high marks in both sets of values, kale is exceptionally well suited to be the poster child of today's health-conscious food lover. On the health side, kale is one of the most nutrient-dense vegetables we know: 1 cup of kale offers more than double your daily vitamin A target and six times your daily vitamin K. It's also loaded with antioxidants and has been linked to lowering cholesterol.

On the cook's side of the equation, kale's hearty flavor and leaf structure lends itself to a huge range of recipes. A relative of cabbage, kale holds up well without wilting (thus the salad trope), but it can also be cooked into a tender, mild state. We're most fond of Lacinato kale (aka Tuscan or black kale), which has dark, flattish leaves and thinner stems, but curly kale has an amazing shape for capturing liquid in pasta or soup.

Kale's rise to prominence has incited the inevitable haters, but we're on the side of the more balanced approach to the food that it represents, one where our diets are governed in equal measure by the "good" and "good for you."

Kale Salad with Turmeric Cauliflower, Spiced Cashews & Pumpkin Seeds

FOR THE CAULIFLOWER:

- 2 tablespoons grapeseed oil or coconut oil
- 2 teaspoons ground turmeric
- 1½ teaspoons ground coriander
- 4 cups (540g) bite-size cauliflower florets (less than 1 inch large), from about 2 large heads
- 1½ teaspoons kosher salt
- Juice of 1 lime

FOR THE SPICED CASHEWS:

- 1 tablespoon grapeseed oil or coconut oil
- 1½ teaspoons garam masala
- ¼ teaspoon cayenne pepper or Piment d'Espelette (optional)
- 1 cup (120 g) raw cashews
- 5 thyme sprigs
- 1 tablespoon sugar
- 1 teaspoon kosher salt
- ½ cup (65 g) pumpkin seeds (pepitas)

FOR THE KALE SALAD:

- 1 small red onion, thinly sliced
- 1 teaspoon kosher salt, divided
- 2 bunches Lacinato kale, tough stems removed, leaves stacked and sliced crosswise into thin ribbons
- 2 tablespoons lemon juice
- 2 tablespoons lime juice
- ½ teaspoon freshly ground black pepper
- 5 tablespoons (75 ml) grapeseed oil

The definition of salad is a mutable, transitory thing. But one thing we know for sure is that it goes way beyond lettuce. In fact, for anything denser than cucumbers and tomatoes, lettuce is a weak ride. When roots and starchy heads of cauliflower enter into the salad discussion, hearty greens step up. Kale is a natural for these types of salad—so much so that its ubiquity has prompted pushback and accusations of shark-jumping. Well, we haven't grown cynical on the kale salad, particularly a version like this one. Warm Indian spices seep into every bite, and all those bites have a satisfying crunch that will resonate even if you prepare the salad hours beforehand.

Make the cauliflower: Heat the oil in a large skillet over medium heat for 2 minutes. Add the turmeric and coriander and cook for 20 seconds, then add the cauliflower and salt and stir to combine. Cook the cauliflower, stirring often, until it is tender and golden brown in spots, 5 to 6 minutes. Transfer the cauliflower to a medium bowl and toss with the lime juice.

Make the spiced cashews: Return the skillet to medium heat and add the oil, garam masala and cayenne (if using). Once the spices start to sizzle, 1 to 2 minutes, add the cashews, thyme, sugar and salt. Cook, stirring often, until the cashews are golden brown, about 2 minutes. Stir in the pumpkin seeds and cook, stirring constantly, until they start to pop, 1 to 2 minutes longer. Transfer the nuts and seeds to a plate. Strip the fried leaves from the thyme sprigs and set aside.

Make the kale salad: Add the red onion to a fine-mesh sieve and toss with ½ teaspoon of salt. Set aside while you prepare the kale.

Add the kale to a large serving bowl. In a small bowl, whisk together the lemon and lime juices, the remaining ½ teaspoon of salt, the pepper and the grapeseed oil. Pour the mixture over the kale and massage the greens with your hands for 3 to 4 minutes, until they start to soften and wilt.

Rinse the onion slices under cold water, then use a paper towel to blot them dry. Add the onion to the salad along with the cauliflower and toss to combine. Sprinkle the fried thyme leaves over the salad. Sprinkle with the cashew–pumpkin seed mixture and serve.

Garlicky Kale, Clam & Chorizo Pasta

MAKES 4 SERVINGS

As much as we love pasta, in this recipe it's just a vehicle that delivers the insanely great combination of chorizo, clams, garlic and kale. The first three ingredients are a trifecta in Portuguese cooking; here, they're given a new vantage point by the leafy green tourist. We love the bitter, almost-brown-butter-esque flavor that the kale imparts, but the texture is what gives it job security. The craggy surfaces of Lacinato capture the juices and flavors in every bite and stand up to high heat. If you can't find Portuguese *chouriço*, Spanish chorizo is more or less interchangeable, so use what you can find.

Kosher salt

3   tablespoons extra-virgin olive oil

4   ounces (115 g) dried Portuguese or Spanish chorizo, halved lengthwise and cut into thin half-moons

6   medium garlic cloves, finely chopped

¼   cup (25 g) fine dried bread crumbs

1½ teaspoons sweet paprika

1   cup (240 ml) dry white wine

24 littleneck or Manila clams, scrubbed

1   cup (240 ml) clam juice

2   small bunches kale, preferably Lacinato, stems discarded and leaves chopped

12 ounces (340 g) dried linguine

Red pepper flakes

Bring a large pot of salted water to a boil. Heat the oil in a Dutch oven or wide, shallow pot over medium heat. Add the chorizo and garlic and cook, stirring occasionally, until the chorizo starts to release its oil and the garlic is light golden, about 3 minutes. Add the bread crumbs and cook, stirring, until golden, about 2 minutes. Stir in the paprika. Add the wine, increase the heat to medium-high and bring to a boil.

Add the clams, cover and cook, stirring occasionally, until the clams have opened, about 8 minutes. Use tongs to fish out the clams and transfer to a bowl, leaving the sauce in the pot (discard any clams that don't open). Cover the clams with foil to keep warm.

Add the clam juice and kale to the sauce. Bring the liquid to a boil, then reduce the heat to maintain a gentle simmer and cook until the kale is wilted and tender, about 3 minutes.

Meanwhile, cook the linguine in the boiling water until just barely al dente. Reserve 1 cup (240 ml) of the pasta cooking water, then drain the pasta. Add the linguine and ½ cup (120 ml) of the cooking water to the pot with the kale and simmer until the pasta is al dente, about 2 minutes. Season to taste with salt. Add a little more of the cooking liquid to loosen if desired. Divide the pasta and sauce among four shallow bowls. Top with the clams, sprinkle with pepper flakes and serve.

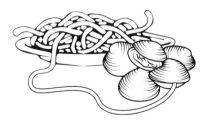

Before It Was Famous

Before kale's rise to stardom in mainstream culture, its biggest fan was Pizza Hut. Yes, you read that correctly. Prior to 2013, the fast food pizza company was the largest consumer of kale, which it used to decorate its salad bars. Another strange moment from kale's road to stardom: It was a staple food in the United Kingdom during World War II because it was easy to grow, even in cold weather.

Kale Potlikker

MAKES 4 TO 6 SERVINGS

Few recipes are named after their remnants (which is why you'll never see a recipe for "Pile of Pizza Crusts" or "Lobster Shells" in a cookbook), but this one deserves to be.

Smoky, tangy and loaded with umami, potlikker is the byproduct of traditional Southern-style braised greens. The elixir left behind is one of the most important liquids in American food history (Google "The Potlikker and Cornpone Debate of 1931"). But it also gives you a pot of tender braised kale, which stands in for the usual collard, mustard or turnip greens. Any kind of kale will work here, and you can adjust the cooking time from 1 to 3 hours, based on how much flavor you want to draw out of the greens and into the broth (our sweet spot is about 1 hour 30 minutes, wherein both broth and kale will be plenty tasty).

We save every drop of leftover potlikker and use it in soups and gravies, for cooking beans and dumplings and (more often than not) sipping down as a nourishing, nutrient-rich soup. No ham hock? Double the amount of bacon (and use hickory- or double-smoked if possible).

About the spelling: Some sources, including the dictionary, refer to this liquid as "pot liquor." But we defer to former Georgia Lieutenant Governor Zell Miller, who wrote a letter to the *New York Times* in 1982 in reaction to their spelling of the word in an article: "Only a culinarily-illiterate damnyankee (one word) who can't tell the difference between beans and greens would call the liquid left in the pot after cooking greens "pot liquor" (two words) instead of "potlikker" (one word) as yours did. And don't cite Webster as a defense because he didn't know any better either."

---

2   bunches kale (1½ to 2 pounds/680 to 910g total)

4   slices thick-cut bacon (preferably hickory-smoked), cut into ½-inch (12-mm) pieces

2   garlic cloves, finely chopped

1   small smoked ham hock, rinsed

12   ounces (180 ml) pilsner beer

½   cup (120 ml) cider vinegar

2   tablespoons dark brown sugar

   Pinch of red pepper flakes

1   teaspoon kosher salt

1   teaspoon freshly ground black pepper

   Hot sauce, for serving (optional)

Pull the kale leaves from the thick stems (pinch the thickest part of the stem and zip your fingers down the spine, as you would to strip thyme leaves from a sprig). Wash and drain the leaves (no need to dry them thoroughly), then coarsely chop.

In a Dutch oven or large saucepan, cook the bacon over medium-low heat until some of the fat has rendered and the bacon begins to brown slightly, 8 to 10 minutes. Add the garlic and cook until fragrant, about 2 minutes.

Add the ham hock, beer, vinegar, 6 cups (1.4 L) water, the sugar, red pepper flakes, salt and pepper and bring to a boil. Add the kale and pack it down until it's submerged in the liquid. Reduce the heat and cover the pot, leaving a crack for steam to escape. Simmer the kale, stirring occasionally, until very tender, about 1 to 2 hours. The kale will be tender enough to eat after about an hour, but the potlikker is best when it's given the extra time to develop. You can cook it longer than 2 hours if you like. The greens will have given up a lot of flavor by this point, but the broth will get better and better.

Turn off the heat and remove the ham hock from the pot. When the hock is cool enough to handle, remove the skin and pull the meat from the bone. Coarsely chop the meat and return it to the pot.

Season the greens to taste with more salt, pepper and vinegar, if needed. Serve with hot sauce, if desired. The kale can be refrigerated for up to 1 day.

Kale Pakoras

8 ounces (225 g) kale (about 1 bunch), stemmed and finely shredded

¾ cup (70 g) chickpea flour (besan)

2 teaspoons garam masala or curry powder

1 teaspoon black onion seeds or nigella seeds, optional

1 teaspoon red pepper flakes, optional

1 teaspoon mustard seeds

1 teaspoon salt

1 small onion (6 ounces), thinly sliced

Neutral oil (such as safflower) for deep-frying (about 6 cups)

Cilantro and mint leaves, for serving

Tamarind chutney, for serving

Raita or Greek yogurt, for serving

Deep-frying can cause anxiety for some cooks, but the Klonopin of kitchen tools to calm your nerves is a good deep-fry thermometer. This inexpensive piece of equipment will end the Goldilocks guessing game, ensuring reliably golden and crunchy results. For these Indian vegetable fritters, the kale crisps up beautifully within the light chickpea batter, turning into brittle shards that offer maximum crunch.

Bring a large pot of water to a boil. Add the kale and give it a stir; when the kale is a deep, rich green color, use a slotted spoon to remove it and place it in a strainer. Drain the kale well (if you have a salad spinner, this is the time to use it; alternatively, drain it in a colander, shaking it around to remove as much water as possible).

In a bowl, whisk together the chickpea flour, garam masala, black onion seeds (if using), red pepper flakes (if using), mustard seeds and salt.

Add the kale and onion to the bowl and toss to combine. Add just enough water to bind the ingredients, about 4 tablespoons (60 ml). Let the mixture stand for about 15 minutes.

Preheat the oven to 250°F (120°C). Heat the oil in a Dutch oven or large saucepan until it reaches 350°F (175°C) on a deep-fry thermometer. Working in batches, carefully drop ¼-cup (60-ml) spoonfuls of the kale mixture into the oil. You can use a spider or slotted spoon to help you lower the fritters into the oil safely. Fry the fritters, flipping once, until they turn golden brown on both sides, about 2 minutes. Be sure to allow the oil to come back up to 350°F (175°C) between batches, and avoid crowding the pan. (If you have a splatter screen, use it to avoid any mess.)

Use a slotted spoon to transfer the pakoras to a paper towel–lined baking sheet. Place the baking sheet in the oven to keep the pakoras warm while you fry the rest.

Serve the pakoras hot with cilantro, mint, tamarind chutney and raita.

Kale & Maitake Mushroom Soup

MAKES 4 SERVINGS

3   tablespoons vegetable oil

4   garlic cloves, thinly sliced

2   tablespoons finely grated ginger, divided

1   large bunch kale, preferably Lacinato, ribs and leaves separated

½   pound (225 g) maitake mushrooms, ends trimmed, torn into small pieces (you can also use quartered creminis)

1   tablespoon soy sauce

1   tablespoon mirin

¼   cup (40 g) dried wakame seaweed

    Fine sea salt

8   ounces (225 g) dried soba, udon or ramen noodles, cooked al dente (optional)

2   scallions, thinly sliced on the bias

1   Persian (or half a hothouse) cucumber, thinly sliced

2   teaspoons toasted sesame and/ or chile oil

It's never fun to be under the weather, but there's something particularly unjust about a cold in the summer. None of the usual palliatives, such as hot tea and heavy blankets, seem appropriate when the air conditioner is blasting and the sun is shining. This soup was created during one such summer illness. It's loaded with vitamins and cold-busting agents, thanks to kale and ginger, with a broth that feels as appropriate for summer as a hot soup can get. That said, you can also slurp it cold.

Heat the oil in a large pot over medium heat. Add the garlic and 1 tablespoon of ginger. Cook, stirring occasionally, until the garlic and ginger are super fragrant and starting to brown on the bottom, about 5 minutes.

Meanwhile, slice the kale ribs about ¼ inch thick. Tear the leaves into bite-size pieces and set aside.

Add the kale stems and mushrooms to the pot, stirring to coat. Cook, stirring frequently, until the mushrooms have browned and released most of their water, 8 to 10 minutes.

Add the soy sauce, mirin and kale leaves. Cook just a minute or two, enough to slightly wilt the kale. Add 4 cups (960 ml) of water along with the seaweed and remaining 1 tablespoon of ginger. Bring the soup to a simmer and cook, uncovered, until the flavors have melded and the liquid has reduced by a third, 25 to 35 minutes. Season to taste with salt as needed.

You can most definitely eat this soup alone, but it's also great over noodles—just divide the noodles among four bowls and ladle the soup over them. Either way, sprinkle with scallions, cucumber and sesame and/or chile oil before serving.

Kalekraut

MAKES ABOUT 1 QUART (960 ML)

There's a gassy edge to traditional sauerkraut that can be off-putting. Using kale in the place of cabbage diminishes that flavor while still packing in funk. It also offers a little bit of bitterness (in contrast to cabbage's sweet, mild flavor), which goes a long way in rich, meaty dishes such as choucroute garni. You can welcome this kraut anywhere that traditional kraut has a home (as a topping on hot dogs or stuffed into a Reuben), or consider braising it with apples in a little bit of beer. It would also make an excellent side to the Cider-Braised Bacon on page 46.

1	bunch kale
3	scallions, cut into 1-inch pieces
1	dried hot chile, such as chile de àrbol
3	tablespoons fine sea salt

Thinly slice the kale stems and cut the leaves into bite-size pieces. Place the kale, scallions and chile in a 1½- to 2-quart (1.4- to 2-L) crock or ceramic container and press the ingredients down.

In a saucepan, bring 4 cups (960 ml) of water and the salt to a simmer, stirring until the salt is dissolved. Let the brine cool completely, then pour it over the kale mixture. Fill a 1-gallon (3.8-L) resealable plastic bag halfway with water, then seal well. Place the bag on top of the vegetables to weight them down and submerge them with the brine. Let the kraut ferment at room temperature for 1 to 2 weeks. At the end of 1 week, check the kale: Scrape off and discard any mold that may have formed on any exposed kale. Taste the kraut for sourness. If you prefer a more sour kraut, then let it ferment for another few days at room temperature. When the flavor is to your liking, drain the kraut, discarding most of the liquid, then refrigerate, covered, until ready to use. The kraut will keep in a sealed container in the refrigerator for up to 6 months (or even longer).

Charred Kale Spanakopita

MAKES 24

Spinach is the standard filling when it comes to the savory, flaky-crusted pies that run rampant in Greek and Middle Eastern cooking. But kale, in our opinion, is better suited for the job. The hearty, dense leaves don't get waterlogged like spinach, so they create a tighter, more concentrated filling. (And the filling goes beyond triangle-shaped spanakopita; try it as the base of an artichoke dip or whipped with eggs to form a deep green, vegetal pie.)

Charring the kale gives it a caramelized, stronger flavor without affecting the structure. The pleasantly bitter edge, barely distinguishable, sets the end product apart.

FOR THE FILLING:

	Canola oil
2	bunches kale, preferably Lacinato, tough stem ends removed
½	pound (225 g) high-quality feta cheese, drained well, divided
2	tablespoons sour cream
6	scallions, coarsely chopped
3	garlic cloves, finely chopped
½	cup (25 g) chopped parsley
½	cup (120 ml) extra-virgin olive oil
1	tablespoon fresh lemon juice
1	teaspoon toasted sesame oil

FOR THE PASTRIES:

½	pound (225 g) frozen phyllo sheets, thawed
½	cup (1 stick/115 g) unsalted butter, melted
	Honey, for garnish
	Sesame seeds, for garnish

Make the filling: Heat a large cast-iron skillet over high heat and add about 1 teaspoon of canola oil. When the skillet is very hot, add a layer of kale leaves (cook the kale in batches so that you don't overcrowd the pan). Sear the kale until the leaves begin to brown and crisp up, about 90 seconds. Flip and sear the other side for an additional 30 seconds. Transfer the kale to a baking sheet and repeat with the remaining kale, adding another teaspoon or so of oil to the pan between each batch. When the kale leaves are cool enough to handle, roughly chop them into bite-size pieces.

In a food processor, combine half of the feta with the sour cream, scallions, garlic, parsley and charred kale and process until finely chopped. With the motor running, add the olive oil; the mixture should form a pesto-like consistency. Transfer the mixture to a mixing bowl. Crumble the remaining feta with your hands and fold it into the kale. Stir in the lemon juice and sesame oil.

Assemble the pastries: Preheat the oven to 375°F (190°C). On a clean work surface, lay one phyllo sheet out lengthwise (keep the other sheets covered with a damp towel while you work so they don't dry out). Use a pastry brush to lightly brush the sheet with melted butter. Lay a second phyllo sheet directly on top of the first and gently press down so the sheets affix (the melted butter is your glue that will hold the pastry together for rest of this process).

Cut the sheets lengthwise into thirds so you have 3 long strips, each roughly 3 inches wide. Spread a heaping teaspoon of filling into a triangle shape in the bottom left corner, leaving a small (¼-inch) margin. Brush the surface of the strip with additional butter, then fold the strip up as if you were folding a flag, bringing the bottom left corner to meet the right edge, then folding the bottom right point up and over, continuing to fold until a triangle forms. (Take care not to press down too hard as you fold or the filling will spill out.) Brush the exterior of the triangle with melted butter and place it on a greased baking sheet. Repeat with the remaining phyllo and filling.

Bake the triangles for 20 to 25 minutes, until they're golden brown. While they're still hot, brush them with honey and sprinkle with sesame seeds. Serve warm.

Putting Your Kale Filling to Use

KALE-ARTICHOKE DIP: Make the filling according to the recipe. Drain and chop one 6-ounce (170-g) jar of artichoke hearts. Add the artichoke and 8 ounces (225 g) of softened cream cheese to the filling. Season with additional salt and pepper to taste. Transfer the filling to a buttered 1-quart (960-ml) soufflé dish. Sprinkle with ½ cup (55 g) of shredded mozzarella and bake in the oven at 375°F (190°C) for 20 minutes. Serve with pita chips.

KALE PIE: Make the filling according to the recipe. Stir in 1 cup (240 ml) of heavy cream and 4 eggs. In a blind-baked deep-dish pie shell, arrange a layer of roasted tomato halves (drained, diced roasted red peppers would work here as well). Pour the kale filling into the shell, and sprinkle the surface with 1 cup (110 g) of shredded cheese (we prefer a mix of Parmesan and mozzarella). Bake in the oven at 375°F (190°C) for 45 to 50 minutes, until the center is set. Let the pie cool for 10 to 15 minutes before cutting and serving.

Kale Salsa Verde

MAKES ABOUT 3 CUPS (720 ML)

1   jalapeño chile, stem and seeds removed, very finely chopped

½   medium shallot, very finely chopped

2   tablespoons lime zest

2   tablespoons fresh lime juice

2   tablespoons fresh lemon juice

Kosher salt and freshly ground black pepper

1   bunch curly or Tuscan kale, ribs removed, leaves very finely chopped (about 2 cups/130 g)

½   cup (20 g) very finely chopped cilantro or parsley

1   cup (240 ml) olive oil

1   teaspoon Worcestershire sauce

Kale's sturdy physical structure is one of its best qualities; its unwillingness to wilt or bend without major interference is what makes it great for frying (see the Pakoras on page 178), charring (see the Spanakopita on page 182) and sautéing (see the Pasta on page 176). But sometimes it's the flavor we're after, not that bossy texture. When you need to beat kale's toughness into submission, as is the case for this brassy condiment, it's time for a massage.

Massaging kale sounds like a joke, but working raw kale with your hands truly does break down the hearty green's cell walls, tenderizing it until it plays well with others. Do it here and you'll be rewarded with a condiment that you can drizzle over chicken, fish or grains.

Combine the jalapeño, shallot, lime zest and juice and lemon juice in a medium bowl. Season with salt and pepper and let sit about 5 minutes. Add the kale, cilantro and oil. Using your hands, massage the mixture for a couple of minutes to tenderize the kale. Stir in the Worcestershire and season again with salt and pepper, adding more lime or lemon juice if you feel it needs it. Spoon the salsa over everything, and refrigerate for up to 3 days.

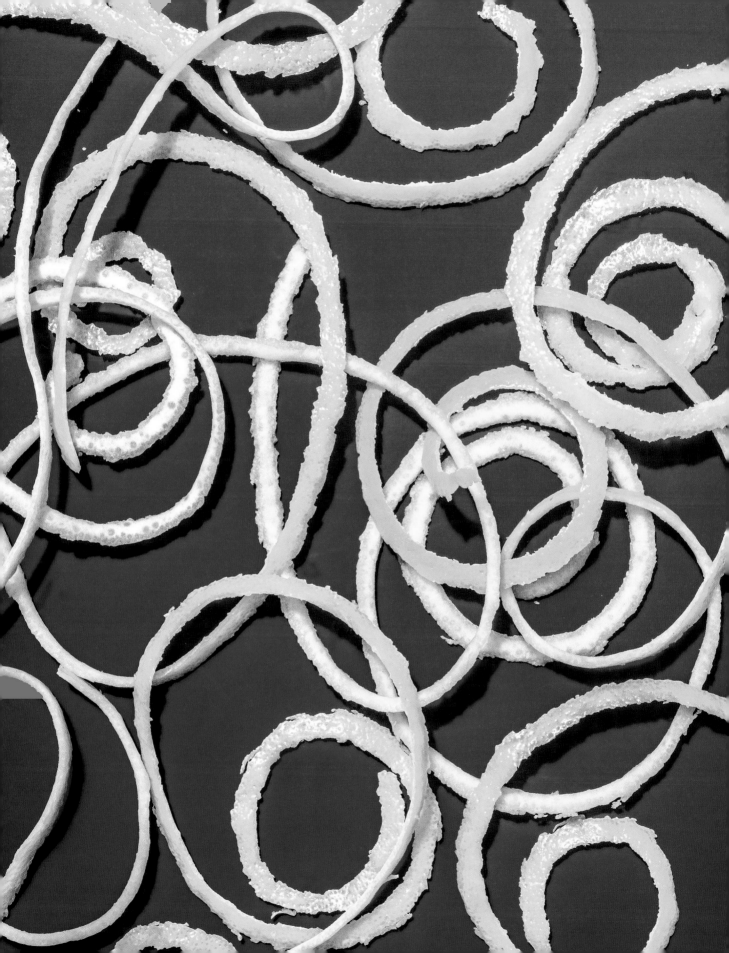

LEMONS

Professional cooks like to play a game wherein they ask each other which few ingredients they can't live (or at least cook) without. It's not a very fun game, because the answers are usually the same: salt, pepper, olive oil and lemon.

When you think about it, it's remarkable that lemons are so universally indispensable to cooks. Most of us don't eat them out of hand (at least more than once), and there are countless other ways to add acidity to our food. But no, it's always the lemon left standing on the podium. Why?

Like salt and pepper, lemon is a flavor enhancer. Depending how you use it, it delivers complexity, acidity, bitterness and/or brightness to other foods. But lemons can be much more than a flavor enhancer or ubiquitous garnish. Through the recipes in this chapter, we've learned how to apply the nose-to-tail cooking philosophy to the sunny fruit, finding as much virtue in the maligned pith as we do in the juice and zest. We began using whole lemons in our cooking, learned the transformative effects of roasting and grilling the fruit and started thinking of the lemon first, not last, when creating new recipes.

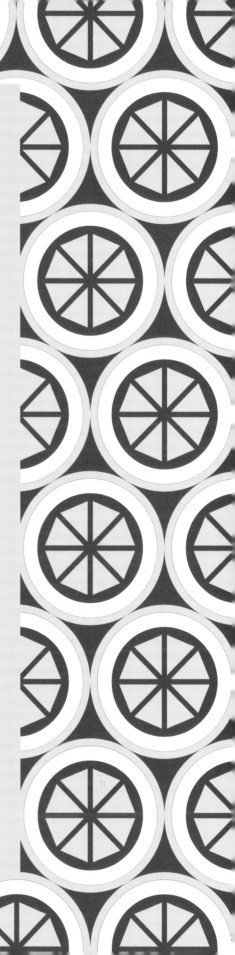

Candied Lemon Salad

MAKES 4 SERVINGS

2 Meyer lemons

1 teaspoon pink peppercorns

2 tablespoons sugar

1 tablespoon fresh Meyer lemon juice (from about ½ lemon)

1 teaspoon honey

3 to 4 tablespoons extra-virgin olive oil

Coarse salt and freshly ground black pepper

1 tablespoon chopped chives, plus more for garnish

2 heads little gem or 1 head butter lettuce, torn into pieces

We have Francis Nicholas Meyer to thank for his namesake lemons, which he brought to the United States from China in the early 20th century. They're thought to be a cross between a conventional lemon and a Mandarin orange, and the flavor of a Meyer lemon matches its parentage: sweeter and more herbaceous than a lemon, with a thin skin and less puckery acidity. If you're lucky enough to find fresh Meyer lemons (and may we emphasize *fresh*; many of the Meyers we encounter on the East Coast are old and mushy), don't hesitate to swap them in for regular lemons. If you have a surfeit of them, pack them in salt to make the best version of preserved lemons.

Cut the Meyer lemons crosswise as thinly as possible, knocking away any seeds with the tip of your knife.

Preheat the broiler (use low heat if that's an option). Line a large rimmed baking sheet with foil and arrange the lemon slices in a single layer.

Using a mortar and pestle (or the side of a chef's knife and a cutting board), crush the pink peppercorns. Place them in a small bowl, add the sugar and combine.

Sprinkle the peppercorn mixture over the citrus slices and place the baking sheet under the broiler, watching closely to make sure the citrus doesn't burn. Broil for 2 minutes, then rotate the pan and broil until the citrus slices are lightly browned and the sugar is bubbling (you can also use a blowtorch for this task, because your mom gave you one of those, right?). Remove the baking sheet from the oven and, using a spatula, immediately transfer the citrus to a wire rack; let the citrus slices cool until they are chewy and slightly crunchy.

In a large bowl, whisk together the Meyer lemon juice and honey. Slowly add the oil, whisking until the dressing is emulsified; season to taste with salt and pepper and stir in the chopped chives. Place the lettuce in a serving bowl and toss with dressing to taste. Season with salt and pepper, arrange the candied citrus slices (in whole wheels or broken into pieces) over the salad, garnish with more chopped chives and serve.

Slow-Roasted Lemon Slices

MAKES 10 SLICES PER LEMON

If food is fashion, then roasted lemons have been the neon yellow of the past few seasons, adding a bright accent to every imaginable ensemble. This version is the brainchild of Martha Holmberg (Vol. 9: Plums), who wanted to re-create the flavor and texture of the lemon slices she often roasts beneath whole chickens. After a few attempts that produced brittle, bitter disks of lemon, she isolated the three common problems with roasted lemon: The rind is too bitter; the rind is too tough; the juices burn. To avoid these fates, she first cures the lemons with salt and sugar, then roasts them at a fairly low temperature, which mitigates the bitterness and softens the zest and pith, making the finished slices delightfully chewy rather than leathery or overly crunchy.

Pay close attention to the lemons as they cook; you should remove them from the oven just as they're lightly caramelized and "chewy-tender." Once you get the technique down, you can play around with different seasonings: In addition to rosemary, try other herbs, such as thyme and oregano, a dusting of ground fennel seeds, za'atar, smoked paprika—any ingredient that plays well with lemon and complements the rest of your meal. And while they're highly snackable on their own, the roasted lemons can be chopped and mixed into dressings, dips and relishes, or used as an eye-catching garnish for pretty much anything.

PER LEMON (WE RECOMMEND MAKING 1 OR 2 AT A TIME):

½ teaspoon sugar

1 teaspoon kosher salt

Extra-virgin olive oil

10 1-inch rosemary sprigs (1 per slice)

Rinse and dry the lemon and cut it into 10 slices between ⅛ and ¹⁄₁₆ inch thick. Discard the ends.

Mix the sugar and salt together. Spread the lemon slices on a work surface and sprinkle with half of the sugar-salt mixture; flip the slices and sprinkle them with the rest of the sugar-salt mixture. Stack the slices together and put them in a small bowl or container. Cover tightly with plastic and refrigerate for at least 4 hours, preferably overnight, to cure.

When you're ready to roast, heat the oven to 275°F (135°C) and line a baking sheet with parchment paper. Pour about ¼ cup (60 ml) of oil into a bowl or on a plate. Dip each lemon slice in the oil, coating both sides, and arrange it on the baking sheet. Top each slice with a rosemary sprig.

Roast the lemon slices for about 20 minutes, then flip each slice and continue roasting until the slices are deeply golden with a few touches of light brown and they're chewy-tender, another 20 minutes. Don't over-roast the slices, or they'll end up being too stiff after they cool (unless you want really crispy lemons, which are pretty good, too).

Transfer the slices to an airtight container and keep covered until you're ready to serve. If you refrigerate the slices, be sure to bring them to room temperature before serving.

Lemony Cornmeal Pound Cake

MAKES 8 SERVINGS

This is the kind of cake that takes an hour to prep, an hour to make and another hour to wash all the dishes and utensils you just used. But sometimes this is exactly the kind the cake we want to make: labor-intensive, immersive, afternoon-consuming. And so worth it.

Two little things that can make a considerable difference: Use fine-ground cornmeal (our favorite brand is Anson Mills); a coarser grind will result in a more cornbread-like cake (which is fine, but probably not what you want). And, as with all pound cakes, a light metal loaf pan works better than a dark or non-stick pan, which will produce a darker, thicker crust.

FOR THE CAKE:

1 cup (125 g) all-purpose flour

½ cup (90 g) fine-ground cornmeal

¼ teaspoon baking soda

¼ teaspoon fine sea salt

½ cup (1 stick/115 g) butter, at room temperature

1½ cups (300 g) granulated sugar

3 large eggs, at room temperature

2 tablespoons fresh lemon juice

2 teaspoons finely grated lemon zest

½ cup (120 ml) sour cream

FOR THE SYRUP:

3 tablespoons fresh lemon juice

3 tablespoons granulated sugar

FOR THE GLAZE AND TOPPING:

1 cup (100 g) sifted confectioners' sugar

1 tablespoon fresh lemon juice

1 tablespoon lightly packed finely grated lemon zest

1 tablespoon granulated sugar

Make the cake: Preheat the oven to 325°F (165°C). Grease and flour a 9-by-5-inch (23-by-12-cm) pan. In a medium bowl, whisk together the flour, cornmeal, baking soda and salt. In a large bowl, beat the butter with a handheld mixer at medium speed until fluffy. With the mixer running, gradually add the sugar. Beat at high speed for 5 minutes, or until light and fluffy. Beat in the eggs, 1 at a time, beating after each addition only until the yellow disappears into the batter. Beat in the lemon juice and zest. Add the flour mixture and stir with a rubber spatula just until the batter is smooth. Add the sour cream and stir with a rubber spatula just until smooth.

Scrape the batter into the prepared pan. Bake for 50 to 60 minutes, or until a tester inserted into the center of the cake comes out clean. Place the pan on a wire rack and let the cake cool for 15 minutes.

Meanwhile, make the syrup: In a small saucepan, stir together the lemon juice and sugar. Cook over medium heat, stirring, until the sugar dissolves. Continue cooking until the mixture thickens slightly, about 3 minutes.

Turn the cake out on the rack and place it top-side up. Brush the top and sides of the warm cake with lemon syrup. Let the cake cool to room temperature.

Make the glaze and topping: In a small bowl, stir together the confectioners' sugar and lemon juice until smooth. Spoon evenly over the top of the cake, letting it drip down the sides.

In a separate small bowl, stir together the lemon zest and granulated sugar until the mixture looks shiny and crumbly; sprinkle over the top of the cake. Slice the cake and serve it warm or at room temperature.

Store the cake at room temperature in an airtight container or wrapped in nonstick foil for up to 2 days.

Grilled Lamb Chops with Lemon-Walnut Relish

MAKES 4 SERVINGS

½ cup (50 g) walnut halves

1 lemon

½ cup (25 g) chopped dill

¼ cup (13 g) chopped parsley

⅛ teaspoon ground cumin

½ cup (120 ml) extra-virgin olive oil, plus more for brushing

Salt and freshly ground black pepper

4 8-ounce (225-g) lamb chump chops or eight 4-ounce (115-g) lamb loin chops

Never heard of a "chump chop"? Until recently, neither had we, but once we got our hands on this incredibly tender cut, taken from the rump between the leg and top loin, it became our favorite lamb for grilling. It's a popular cut in the United Kingdom but might require a special request from your butcher here in the U.S., or you can use the more common lamb loin chops. If you're not a lamb lover, this relish is equally good with beef or pork. Mixing pieces of lemon flesh into relishes and other chunky condiments is a fun way to add surprising little pops of lemon juice to a dish.

Preheat the oven to 350°F (175°C). Spread the walnuts on a baking sheet and bake for about 4 minutes, or until lightly toasted. Let the walnuts cool slightly, then coarsely chop them.

Using a sharp knife, remove the rind and bitter white pith from the lemon. Cut between the membranes to release the sections onto a cutting board, then coarsely chop the flesh, removing the seeds as you go.

In a bowl, mix the walnuts with the chopped lemon, dill, parsley, cumin and oil. Season with salt and pepper.

Prepare a medium-hot grill or heat a grill pan over high heat. Rub the lamb chops all over with oil and season generously with salt and pepper. Grill the chops over medium-high heat, turning once, 3 to 5 minutes a side for medium-rare meat (an instant-read thermometer inserted into the thickest part of the meat should read 125°F/50°C.)

Transfer the chops to a platter and let them rest for a few minutes. Spoon the relish on top or serve alongside.

Lemony Ricotta Pancakes

MAKES ABOUT 12 PANCAKES

1 cup (245 g) ricotta cheese

2 cups (330 g) hulled sliced strawberries (from about 4 cups/ 580 g strawberries)

3 tablespoons sugar, divided

Finely grated zest and juice of 1 lemon, plus more for garnish

1¼ cups (155 g) all-purpose flour

1 teaspoon baking powder

Pinch of fine sea salt

3 large eggs, separated

¾ cup (180 ml) whole milk

¾ teaspoon pure vanilla extract

Unsalted butter or canola oil, for the pan

These puffy pancakes are a fixture on the brunch menu at Porsena, the Manhattan restaurant run by Sara Jenkins (Vol. 14: Prosciutto di Parma). Where normal pancake batter would get weighed down by ricotta cheese, here, beating the egg yolks and whites separately—as you would in a soufflé—makes the batter puff and rise as it cooks, yielding a very fluffy pancake with an extra-crisp exterior. Lemon—juiced into the batter and zested throughout—lightens these fluffy pancakes even further.

Line a fine-mesh strainer with cheesecloth and set it over a small bowl. Add the ricotta and let it drain for 15 minutes; set aside.

In a small bowl, toss the strawberries with 1 tablespoon of sugar and the lemon juice. Set aside.

In a medium bowl, whisk together the flour, 1 tablespoon of sugar, the baking powder and salt.

In a separate medium bowl, combine the ricotta, egg yolks, milk, lemon zest and vanilla and whisk until thoroughly mixed. Whisk in the flour mixture until a smooth batter forms.

Using a stand mixer fitted with a whisk attachment or bowl and handheld mixer, beat the egg whites and the remaining 1 tablespoon of sugar at low speed until frothy, about 30 seconds. Increase the speed to medium-high and beat the egg whites and sugar until stiff and glossy. Fold the beaten egg whites into the batter.

Heat a cast-iron griddle or large heavy skillet over medium heat. Add a spoonful of butter and heat until the foaming subsides. Working in batches, drop ⅓ cup (75 ml) of pancake batter onto the hot griddle and cook over medium heat until the tops of the pancakes are bubbling and slightly dry and their bottoms are golden brown, about 2 minutes. Flip the pancakes over and cook through until browned on the other side, 1 to 2 minutes. Transfer the pancakes to a platter and repeat with the remaining batter.

Spoon the strawberries and their juices over the top of the pancakes, zest some lemon over the top and serve.

Oleo Saccharum

MAKES ABOUT ⅓ CUP

"Oleo saccharum," or "oil sugar," has been a critical ingredient in punch—the boozy, festive kind—since the 19th century. When citrus peels and sugar make extended contact, the sugar pulls the essential oils from the peels, dissolving into a syrup with an intense aroma and flavor you can't get from juice alone.

This heady sweetener can be made with other types of citrus—we like to make a mixed-citrus oleo saccharum and use it to sweeten Old Fashioneds and Sazeracs—but the best cocktail for putting lemons on a pedestal is the French 75, which we scale up here into a large-format punch. You're probably used to French 75s served neat in Champagne flutes, but the original version was served over cracked ice—and that's how we prefer them, too.

4   large lemons

¾   cup (150 g) superfine sugar (see Note)

Wash the lemons with warm water and pat dry. Using a sharp vegetable peeler, peel the lemons from tip to tip, leaving as much white pith attached to the lemon as possible. (Reserve the denuded lemons for juicing.) Place the lemon peels in a jar or bowl and add the sugar. Using a cocktail muddler or large wooden spoon, smash the sugar and peels together for about 1 minute to release the fruit's oils, then let the mixture sit until all (or most) of the sugar has dissolved, at least 4 hours and up to 12 hours. The leftover peels should look like shriveled remnants of themselves; this is a sign that they've surrendered all of their oil.

Pour the contents of the jar or bowl into a fine-mesh strainer and strain into a resealable container. (If your lemons weren't particularly oily, there might be some undissolved sugar left over. Add a splash of fresh lemon juice and stir until the sugar dissolves; repeat if necessary.) Cover and refrigerate until ready to use; the oleo saccharum will keep for up to 1 week.

NOTE: We suggest using superfine sugar here, as it'll dissolve more easily. But you can make your own by whizzing granulated sugar in a blender or food processor until fine. Very important: Don't use confectioners' sugar, as it contains cornstarch.

French 75 Punch

MAKES 8 TO 10 SERVINGS

⅓   cup (75 ml) Oleo Saccharum (left)

¾   cup (180 ml) fresh lemon juice

1½   cups (360 ml) cold gin (from the freezer)

1   bottle (750 ml) cold brut Champagne

2   lemons, sliced into thin wheels, for garnish

     Cracked ice, for serving

In a punch bowl, whisk together the Oleo Saccharum, lemon juice and gin. Pour the Champagne over the top. Garnish with the lemon wheels and ladle into cups filled with cracked ice.

More Uses for Sugar Oil

In addition to cocktails and punches, oleo saccharum can service many non-alcoholic applications. Use it to sweeten iced tea, add a few drops to vinaigrettes, drizzle over sweets and desserts or combine with fresh lemon juice and water to make the best lemonade you'll ever taste.

Grilled Clams with Grilled Lemon Butter & Tarragon

MAKES 4 SERVINGS

This is one of the laziest ways to cook clams: Just set them directly on the grill grates and don't take them off until they pop open. If you have a charcoal grill, they'll take on lots of great smoky flavor. It's also an excuse to grill some lemons, because lemons are about 100 times better in their charred state.

Be sure to arrange the clams on the grill so that the hinge sides are facing away from you. That way, after they open, you can easily grab them with tongs and retain as much of the delicious briny juice as possible.

2   garlic cloves

Extra-virgin olive oil, for brushing

1   lemon, cut into 4 wedges, plus half a lemon

4   tablespoons (½ stick/55 g) unsalted butter, melted

2   dozen littleneck clams, scrubbed

2   tablespoons roughly chopped tarragon or parsley

Crusty bread, for serving

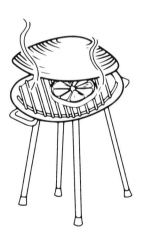

Prepare a medium-hot grill. (A pretty hot grill is important here; you should be able to hold your hand a few inches above the grill grate for only a few seconds. If you're using a gas grill, you'll probably need to crank it to high.)

Place the garlic cloves on skewers and brush with oil. Brush the lemon wedges and the cut side of the halved lemon with oil. Grill the garlic and lemon wedges, turning once, until grill marks form, 2 to 4 minutes a side. Grill the lemon half, cut-side down, for about 3 minutes.

Slide the cloves off the skewer onto a cutting board and finely chop, then transfer to a large bowl. Add the butter to the garlic. Squeeze the lemon half (catching any seeds in your hand) into the butter and mix to combine.

Arrange the clams on the grill, placing them as flat as possible so the juices don't leak out when they open. Cover the grill and cook until the clams open, 4 to 8 minutes. As they open, remove the clams from the grill and add them to the butter; discard any clams that don't open.

Toss the grilled clams with the butter, garnish with tarragon and serve with the grilled lemon wedges and plenty of crusty bread.

Main Event

To quickly turn this dish into a main course, add some linguine or creamy gigante beans to the bowl with the cooked clams and toss.

Lemonade Stand Gummy Candy

MAKES ABOUT 8 DOZEN PIECES

1 tablespoon plus 1½ teaspoons finely grated lemon zest (about 2 to 3 lemons)

½ cup (120 ml) fresh lemon juice (about 2 to 3 lemons)

3 envelopes Knox unflavored gelatin or 2 tablespoons plus 1 teaspoon powdered gelatin

3 cups (600 g) sugar, divided

¼ teaspoon kosher salt

3 drops yellow food coloring (optional)

Research has shown that the scent of lemons increases alertness and lowers anxiety, which is probably why we add it to so many products both edible and otherwise. These chewy confections, a hybrid of French *gelée* (or *pâte de fruit*) and American gummy candy, can be cut into any shape you like—break out your little cookie cutters and make some happy candy.

Line an 8-by-8-inch (20-by-20-cm) square baking pan with aluminum foil and spray with a nonstick cooking spray. Set aside.

In a shallow bowl, stir together the lemon zest and juice and ¼ cup (60 ml) of water and sprinkle the gelatin evenly over the surface of the juice. Stir well, making sure all of the gelatin is thoroughly mixed, and let stand for 10 minutes.

In a medium saucepan fitted with a candy thermometer, combine 2 cups (400 g) of sugar, ½ cup (120 ml) of water and the salt and bring to a boil over medium heat without stirring, about 5 minutes. Continue cooking until the syrup reaches the softball stage (240°F/116°C), about 5 minutes longer. The mixture will be foamy and have a syrupy consistency. Remove from the heat and whisk the lemon-gelatin-juice mixture into the syrup until smooth. Stir in the yellow food coloring if using. Pour the syrup into the prepared baking pan, cover and let set overnight at room temperature.

Line a rimmed baking sheet with parchment paper.

Generously coat the top of the set gummy mixture with ¼ cup (50 g) of sugar. Lift the foil around the edges of the pan to loosen the gummy, place a clean cutting board over the top of the pan and invert it onto the cutting board; peel away the foil and coat all sides of the gummy with the remaining ¾ cup (150 g) of sugar—it won't all stick, but the excess will be enough to coat the gummies as they're cut into pieces. Grease a chef's knife with nonstick cooking spray and cut the candy into ½-by-1-inch pieces. Gently roll each piece in sugar until well coated and set on the baking sheet to dry for 2 days, rolling in sugar again after the first day if necessary. The longer the gummy candy sets, the crunchier the outside will get. Store the candy in a covered container at room temperature for up to two weeks.

THE SHORT STACK COOKBOOK

MAYONNAISE

We grew up thinking unkind thoughts about mayonnaise. It was the bane of our brown bag lunch, affixing the contents of our turkey sandwich together into an unappetizingly smooshy puck.

What a difference a few years and a recipe can make. Of all the ingredients (and yes, mayonnaise is as much an ingredient as a stand-alone recipe) to benefit from the return to DIY, mayonnaise comes out on top. Breaking out the whisk (or, better yet, a food processor) is no longer an outrageous task, and the process of preparing mayonnaise from scratch has had a profound effect on how we think about it. The process of emulsifying oil into yolks and watching it turn into the most lovely emulsion right before our eyes forever changed our viewpoint on mayonnaise. It's not only a condiment; it's a sauce—the most important sauce in our arsenal.

Just think, for a moment, about mayo's attributes: It provides richness like dairy, but without the sweetness of cream or the tang of yogurt or cheese. It's the best conveyor of flavors we can think of. Like a vinaigrette, it can enrobe vegetables in a kind of swaddling that accentuates their flavors, but it doesn't lead with acid. And because it's made with eggs, it can even function as a leavener in baking by creating structure and acting as a source of fat. As the recipes in this chapter prove, there's nothing—from shrimp to chocolate—that mayonnaise doesn't like.

Homemade Mayonnaise

MAKES 2 CUPS (480 ML)

1   large egg

2   egg yolks

½   teaspoon Dijon mustard

1   teaspoon fresh lemon juice

1¾ (420 ml) cups canola oil

    Fine sea salt

The first time we made mayonnaise from scratch—with a whisk and a bowl set on a damp kitchen towel—was the first time we saw how vital and brilliant it really is. This recipe produces thick, creamy foolproof mayonnaise in 2 minutes and allows us to doctor it as the occasion requires.

We started adding a whole egg to our mayo (instead of the usual yolks only) at the urging of one of our favorite chefs, Ashley Christensen of Poole's Diner in Raleigh, North Carolina. She's something of a mayonnaise savant and swears by the addition of the egg white in creating a lighter, creamier texture. As with any recipe that uses raw eggs, purchase the best that you can find.

In a food processor, combine the egg, egg yolks, mustard and lemon juice. Turn on the machine and let it run for about 1 minute, then slowly add the oil in a steady stream. The mixture will thicken and emulsify. When all of the oil has been incorporated, transfer the mayonnaise to a bowl. Season with salt to taste. Store in an airtight container and refrigerate for up to 1 week.

Spicy Mayonnaise

MAKES 1 CUP (240 ML)

1   tablespoon *ssamjang* or *gochujang* (available at Asian markets, spice shops, or online)

1   cup (240 ml) mayonnaise, homemade (recipe above) or store-bought

This mayo variation was born out of a hangover. The combination came together to amp up a greasy, headache-busting breakfast sandwich, and we've never looked back. It's great when made with *gochujang*, a Korean fermented red pepper paste, but we like it even better with *ssamjang*, a *gochujang* variation with soybean paste, sesame seeds and garlic mixed in.

In a small bowl, combine the *ssamjang* and about ¼ cup (60 ml) of mayonnaise. Stir with a fork until the *ssamjang* is well incorporated. If your *ssamjang* is old, you may need to smash pieces of it up against the side of the bowl to break it down. Add the remaining mayonnaise and stir until mixed. Refrigerate for about a week if the mayonnaise is store-bought or about 3 days if the mayonnaise is homemade.

Mayo 2.0

Armed with the base recipe above, your condiment opportunities increase exponentially. Stir in mashed garlic for classic aioli; add capers, scallions and pickles for a homemade spin on tartar sauce; and whip in roasted tomatoes for a remoulade.

Mayonnaise Biscuits

MAKES 15

These are the simplest scratch biscuits you will ever make. No butter to cut into flour, no kneading or resting or layering. Just dump, stir and bake.

For those who are struggling to think of mayonnaise as more than a condiment, trust us when we say that the mayo has a very mild effect on flavor here. This isn't a biscuit masquerading as tuna salad or a turkey sandwich. Instead, mayonnaise gets a behind-the-scenes production credit with these biscuits: It does the heavy lifting (literally, as it helps the biscuits rise) as well as filling in for the butter in supplying fat. Since these are quick breads, they're best when eaten straight out of the oven; they'll harden the longer they sit.

2½ cups (315 g) all-purpose flour

1 tablespoon baking powder

1 teaspoon sugar

1 teaspoon fine sea salt

1 cup (240 ml) 2% milk

3 tablespoons mayonnaise, homemade (see page 204) or store-bought

Soft unsalted butter or Cultured Butter (see page 82), for serving

Salted Apple Jam (page 38) or other jam, for serving

Preheat the oven to 375°F (190°C). Line a rimmed baking sheet with a silicone baking mat or parchment paper and set aside.

In a large bowl, combine the flour, baking powder, sugar and salt. In a measuring cup, whisk the milk with the mayonnaise until combined. Make a well in the center of the dry ingredients and pour in the milk-mayonnaise mixture. Use a fork to combine the wet and dry ingredients until a soft dough forms. Do not overmix the dough or it will be tough.

Scoop 15 rounds of dough onto the prepared baking sheet (each round should be about 2 tablespoons). Bake until golden brown, 20 to 23 minutes. Transfer the biscuits to a wire rack to cool slightly. Serve warm with butter and jam.

Curry-Grilled Shrimp

MAKES 4 SERVINGS

We're familiar with using mayonnaise as a condiment for seafood (tartar sauce for the win!), but until we tried this recipe from Susie Heller (Vol. 18: Chocolate), we hadn't used it as a straight-up marinade. Now that we've been turned on to the technique, there'll be plenty of mayo-swabbed shellfish in our future. Not only does mayo do a better job of keeping herbs and spices (curry, in this case) affixed to the protein, but it also acts a protective shield that allows caramelization without burning.

1 pound (455 g) large (16 to 20 count) shrimp, shelled and deveined

½ cup (120 ml) mayonnaise, homemade (see page 204) or store-bought

1 teaspoon curry powder

½ teaspoon honey, plus some for drizzling, optional

Lime wedges

Flaky sea salt, for serving

Prepare a medium-high charcoal or gas grill.

Dry the shrimp well. In a bowl, whisk together the mayonnaise, curry powder and honey. Just before you're ready to grill, fold the shrimp into the mayonnaise mixture until they are well coated.

Using tongs, lift the shrimp out of the mayonnaise and place them on the grill. Let the shrimp cook for 30 seconds to 1 minute to allow the coating to set, then flip the shrimp over and repeat on the other side. Continue cooking, flipping occasionally, until the shrimp are cooked through, about 4 minutes total.

Transfer the shrimp to a platter. Squeeze some lime juice over the top and drizzle with a small amount of honey. Sprinkle with salt and serve.

Elote Orecchiette

MAKES 4 SERVINGS

This unorthodox recipe is our defense that classic French technique is still relevant in today's kitchen, specifically an understanding and appreciation for the mother sauces. Without that framing, heating up mayonnaise to make sauce for pasta might sound, well, gross. But when we think about mayonnaise as an offspring of hollandaise (just swap oil for clarified butter), and beyond that, a classic Carême-worthy *allemande*, the ground opens up and something like orecchiette with roasted corn and mayonnaise, which marries Mexican street food and Escoffier, sounds like the greatest invention of all time.

The key to making this dish is to treat it almost as if you would carbonara (see page 141) or custard. You have to temper the mayonnaise (especially if it's homemade)—by stirring the warm pasta in slowly—to keep it from breaking.

1	teaspoon red pepper flakes
2	ears corn, shucked (or about 1½ cups/205 g frozen corn, thawed)
1	cup (240 ml) mayonnaise, homemade (see page 204) or store-bought
1	cup (100 g) finely grated Parmigiano-Reggiano or Pecorino-Romano cheese
	Freshly ground black pepper
1	pound dried orecchiette pasta
½	cup (20 g) chopped basil and parsley
	Hot sauce, for serving

In a large skillet, toast the red pepper flakes over medium heat until fragrant, about 1 minute. Transfer the flakes to a bowl and set aside.

Cut the kernels from the corncobs. Heat the skillet over medium-high heat and add the kernels. Toast the corn, stirring occasionally, until browned in spots, about 5 minutes. Transfer to a bowl.

Bring a large pot of salted water to a boil.

In a food processor, combine the mayonnaise with half of the corn and puree until smooth. Transfer the mixture to a large bowl and fold in half of the Parmesan cheese and the toasted red pepper flakes. Season generously with black pepper.

Cook the orecchiette until al dente. Drain, reserving about 1 cup (240 ml) of the pasta water.

Stirring constantly, slowly add the pasta to the mayonnaise mixture. If needed, add a splash or two of the reserved pasta water to make a creamy sauce. Fold in the remaining corn and the herbs. Sprinkle with the remaining cheese and serve with hot sauce.

Japanese Potato Salad

MAKES 4 SERVINGS

2   pounds (910 g) medium Yukon Gold potatoes

½   medium English cucumber

½   sweet onion

½   cup (120 ml) plus 2 teaspoons rice wine vinegar, divided

1   teaspoon sugar

1   tablespoon salt, plus more for seasoning

¾   cup (180 ml) mayonnaise, homemade (page 204) or store-bought

2   teaspoons dark soy sauce

1   teaspoon freshly grated ginger

½   teaspoon wasabi paste

2   hard-boiled eggs, roughly chopped

     Freshly ground black pepper

It might surprise you to learn that mayonnaise-bound potato salad is claimed by Japan as much as it is by the U.S. There are some distinctions that separate the Japanese version, however. Firstly, potatoes share the spotlight with hard-boiled eggs and vegetables like onions, carrots and cucumber. But the biggest difference is in the mayonnaise. Japanese mayonnaise uses sweet rice wine vinegar for its acidic base and is slightly less thick in consistency. (Oh, and it often contains MSG, for what it's worth.)

To approximate a version, we brined cucumbers and onions directly in rice wine vinegar and doctored basic American-style mayo with the punchy flavors of ginger, wasabi and soy sauce (which would be stellar on its own as a dipping sauce for tempura, or edamame). The result: a Japanese-style potato salad with texture and bite. It's sure to be the star of your next potluck, whether here or abroad.

Bring a large pot of salted water to a boil. Add the potatoes and simmer until fork tender, 35 to 40 minutes. Drain the potatoes and, when cool enough to handle, remove the peels.

Slice the cucumber and the onion as thinly as possible into a medium bowl (use a mandoline if you have one) and toss to combine. In a saucepan, combine ½ cup (120 ml) vinegar, 1 cup (240 ml) water, the sugar and salt. Bring to a simmer over medium heat, stirring until the sugar and salt have dissolved. Pour the brine over the cucumber-onion mixture and let stand for at least 15 minutes and up to 1 hour. Drain well and pat the vegetables dry with a paper towel.

In a small bowl, whisk together the mayonnaise, soy sauce, the remaining 2 teaspoons vinegar, ginger and wasabi.

In a large bowl, smash the warm potatoes with the back of a fork so that they break down but don't entirely lose their shape. Add the pickled cucumber-onion mixture, the chopped eggs and the mayonnaise and stir until combined. Season to taste with salt and pepper. The potato salad can be refrigerated for up to 3 days.

Chicken Sandwiches with White Barbecue Sauce

MAKES 4 SERVINGS

Like butter, mayonnaise is a fabulous mood board on which to pin other flavors. Mix in garlic and you have classic aioli; a bit of chopped tomato and pickle makes it remoulade (the sauce, not the salad). White barbecue sauce, known to the lucky few as "Alabama white sauce," is a lesser-known member of the mayo-based canon, but not for lack of flavor or fervor of its devotees. There's enough cider vinegar and mustard to steer this almost into vinaigrette territory and enhance the flavor of vegetables or give pasta salad a lift. But where it really shines is next to grilled or smoked meat, classically chicken. These sandwiches are a messy, fork-and-knife affair, so do like the barbecue joints of Alabama do and bring a whole roll of paper towels to the table.

FOR THE SAUCE:

1½ cups (360 ml) mayonnaise, homemade (see page 204) or store-bought

¼ cup (60 ml) apple cider vinegar

1 tablespoon Creole or spicy brown mustard

1 tablespoon prepared horseradish

2 garlic cloves, finely chopped

1 teaspoon freshly ground black pepper

1 tablespoon sugar

1 teaspoon kosher salt

¼ teaspoon paprika

¼ teaspoon ground cayenne pepper

FOR THE SANDWICHES:

1 smoked or grilled whole chicken

2 tablespoons unsalted butter

4 white hamburger buns, split

Dill pickle slices, for serving

Make the sauce: Whisk together all of the ingredients in a medium bowl. Cover and refrigerate until chilled, preferably overnight. Stir well before serving. The sauce can be refrigerated for up to 1 week.

Make the sandwiches: Pull the chicken meat off the bones and pull or cut the meat into medium pieces. You should have about 3 cups (585 g) of meat.

In a large heavy skillet, melt the butter over medium-high heat. Arrange the buns, cut-side down, in the skillet and twist them around to make sure they're coated in butter. Cook the buns until the bottoms are golden brown, about 1 to 2 minutes.

Divide the buns among serving plates. Place a couple of pickle slices on each half. Pile the chicken on top. Drizzle with sauce, about 3 to 4 tablespoons a sandwich. Top the chicken with the bun tops and serve at once.

Celery Root Remoulade

MAKES 3 CUPS (720 ML)

The vegetable-and-mayonnaise salad is well-covered territory. It has spawned more twists and turns than a telenovela, as chefs and cookbook authors have sought to say something new about it. But the truth is, the best version of the genre is almost monastically straightforward: celery root remoulade.

This bistro staple of France binds julienned celery root with mayo that's been sharpened to a point with good Dijon. Our tweaks to the classic version have a small range of motion: We like to grate the celery root on the large side of a box grater rather than julienne it, and we add celery stalks and leaves to enhance that sharp, salty flavor. The addition of preserved lemon is about as unorthodox as we're willing to go.

1   tablespoon Dijon mustard

½   teaspoon red wine vinegar

½   cup (120 ml) mayonnaise, homemade (see page 204) or store-bought

2   tablespoons sour cream

1   tablespoon chopped preserved lemon peel (or 1 tablespoon lemon zest)

     Salt and freshly ground black pepper

1   celery root bulb (about 1 pound), peeled, tops removed

     Juice of 1 lemon

3   celery stalks (with leaves intact), finely chopped

½   cup (25 g) chopped parsley

2   tablespoons chopped tarragon

2   tablespoons extra-virgin olive oil

In a small bowl, whisk together the mustard, vinegar, mayonnaise, sour cream and preserved lemon peel. Season to taste with salt and pepper.

Grate the celery root using the large holes of a box grater and place in a large bowl. Toss the celery root with the lemon juice. Add the celery, parsley and tarragon. Add the mayonnaise mixture to the celery root mixture and stir to combine. Stir in the oil, season with additional salt and pepper to taste and serve. The remoulade is best eaten the day it's made, but it'll keep in the refrigerator for up to 2 days.

Chocolate Chicory Cake

MAKES ONE 8-INCH CAKE

During the Great Depression, when ingredients like fresh eggs, granulated sugar and coffee were hard to come by, cooks got creative to make ersatz versions of their favorite dishes. Store-bought mayonnaise suddenly had newfound value in baking as a substitute for eggs.

Although we no longer need to use mayonnaise as a placeholder, this cake is an instance in which the understudy outperforms the lead. Not only does mayonnaise add the richness and leavening, but the oil in its makeup also acts as the fat that brings the batter together.

Chicory is another nod to the days of rationing; it was used as a substitute for coffee, except in New Orleans where, in many kitchens, it's still preferred over coffee.

FOR THE CAKE:

Butter or nonstick cooking spray, for greasing the pan

¼ cup (60 g) granulated, roasted chicory (available in spice shops or online)

1 cup (240 ml) boiling water

¾ cup (165 g) packed dark brown sugar

1 cup (240 ml) store-bought mayonnaise

1¾ cups (220 g) all-purpose flour

⅓ cup (30 g) cocoa powder

½ teaspoon baking soda

½ teaspoon baking powder

1 teaspoon pure vanilla extract

FOR THE ICING:

12 ounces (340 g) bittersweet chocolate, chopped

4 tablespoons (½ stick/55 g) salted butter, chopped

1 cup (240 ml) heavy cream

Make the cake: Grease three 8-inch round cake pans, and line the bottoms with parchment paper. Preheat the oven to 350°F (175°C).

Place the chicory in a heatproof bowl. Pour the boiling water over the chicory and let it steep for 10 minutes. Strain the brewed chicory through a fine-mesh sieve and measure 1 cup (240 ml) into a large measuring cup. Discard the solids. Whisk the brown sugar and mayonnaise into the brewed chicory until no sugar lumps remain (if it looks curdled, that's fine) and set aside.

In a large bowl, whisk together the flour, cocoa, baking soda and baking powder. Add the chicory liquid and vanilla to the dry ingredients and whisk until smooth. Divide the batter among the three prepared pans and smooth their tops. Bake for 20 minutes or until the tops spring back when lightly pressed. Let the cakes cool in their pans for 15 minutes, then invert onto cooling racks; remove the pans, carefully peel away the parchment paper and let the cakes cool completely, about 1 hour.

Meanwhile, make the icing: Place the chocolate and butter in a small mixing bowl.

In a small saucepan, heat the cream over high heat until it's just about to boil. Remove the cream from the heat and immediately pour it over the chocolate and butter. Let the mixture sit for about 5 minutes, or until the chocolate is melted, then stir to combine. Don't stir too vigorously or the icing will lose its shine. It should be thick, but still loose enough to pour.

When the cakes are cooled, turn them right-side up on the cooling rack and place the rack over a rimmed baking sheet. Starting with one layer, pour a generous ½ cup (120 ml) of the icing over the center of the layer. Use an offset spatula to smooth the icing over the top and down the sides (the rimmed baking sheet will catch your drips). Repeat with the second layer and another ½ cup (120 ml) of icing.

Top with the third layer and spread some of the remaining icing over the top (you can coat the sides of the cake as well if you like). The icing will become firm as it cools. Use a large spatula to transfer the cake to a serving plate.

The cake can be covered and stored at room temperature for up to 3 days.

RICE

It's a weighty thing to consider the importance of rice, one of the oldest and most essential crops on the planet. The grain provides more than one fifth of the calories consumed by humans worldwide, a statistic that makes our heads pop.

In the beginning, our reasoning for including rice in this ingredient yearbook was more philosophical, but as we began to dig into the recipes, our hearts started to flutter, and the arranged marriage became true love.

There were several pivotal moments in the courtship. We came to rely on rice for its starch content, adding the creaminess to horchata and the necessary crunch to fried chicken batter. We also got weak in the knees over its ability to relax into a creamy, spoonable pudding (the Soubise on page 220 and the Sweet Risotto on page 216). But the discovery that sealed the deal was when rice presented itself as a physics project, trapped between two states, with a crispy shell protecting a soft interior. It's this balance that makes the Crispy Rice Cakes on page 221 work so well, and it's the result that rules our Persian Rice technique on page 218.

But more than anything, rice is a staple in the truest definition of the word—not in the way that people toss it around when talking about how to shop for your pantry. Within each grain is enough to keep the human body sustained, and unlocking the contents of those tiny universes is a truly magical thing.

Sweet Cardamom Risotto with Ginger-Stewed Plums

MAKES 4 SERVINGS

FOR THE RISOTTO:

2   ¼-inch-thick coins fresh ginger, smashed with the flat side of a knife, divided

3   cups (720 ml) unsweetened almond milk

2   tablespoons salted butter

½   cup (95 g) Arborio rice

⅓   cup (65 g) sugar

Scraped seeds from ½ vanilla bean

Seeds from 3 green cardamom pods, crushed (or ¾ teaspoon powdered cardamom)

1   cup (240 ml) whole milk, divided

½   cup (120 ml) heavy cream

FOR THE PLUMS:

2   tablespoons salted butter

3   ¼-inch-thick coins fresh ginger, smashed with the flat side of a knife

3   purple or red plums—halved, pitted and cut into eighths

¼   cup (50 g) sugar

Welcome to the nexus of the dessert universe. This risotto meets at the intersection of two sweets: the rich milky flavor has emotional ties to *gulab jamun*, an Indian dessert of caramelized milk solids, while the chewy, thick bite of Arborio rice will seem familiar to anyone who's spooned up rice pudding.

While you can force a risotto, sweet or savory, out of any rice, Arborio is the standard bearer with good reason. The short-grained Italian rice has a higher starch content than other grains, which contributes greatly to risotto's porridge-like texture. If there's no Arborio in sight, any short-grain rice can work.

Make the risotto: In a small saucepan, warm 1 piece of ginger and the almond milk over medium heat until scalding. Remove the pan from the heat and let sit for 10 minutes. Remove the ginger and discard; keep the almond milk warm.

In a large shallow skillet, melt the butter. Add the rice and cook, stirring, until opaque, about 3 minutes. Add the sugar, the remaining piece of ginger, vanilla and cardamom, along with ½ cup (120 ml) of whole milk. Cook over medium heat, stirring constantly, until the rice absorbs the milk. Add the warm almond milk, ½ cup (120 ml) at a time, stirring constantly after each addition and waiting until most of the milk has been absorbed before adding more. Remove the risotto from the heat, add the last ½ cup (120 ml) of whole milk, stir and set aside, covered, until cooled to room temperature. Discard the ginger. The risotto will thicken as it cools.

Meanwhile, make the plum compote: In a shallow skillet over medium-high heat, melt the butter until foamy. Stir in the ginger, then the plums. Stir in the sugar.

Cook and stir the mixture until the plums are softened and the sugar is melted and forms a thick syrup, about 10 to 15 minutes. Remove and discard the ginger.

In a chilled bowl, whip the cream to soft peaks, then fold gently into the risotto. Serve with the compote on the side.

Jeweled Persian Rice

MAKES 8 SERVINGS

There are certain dishes that bring out a cook's goal-oriented edge. Perfectly risen soufflés, unblemished omelets, a tarte Tatin that releases from the pan without a fight—each offers a sense of accomplishment and confidence that takes the act of cooking from mundane to magical.

For us, the white whale of these trophy recipes is Persian rice, complete with a crispy, golden crust known as *tadig*. Generally made for celebrations, this pilaf-style dish is studded with candied fruit and nuts and scented with baking spices. It's a kinetic dish that hurtles through the textural spectrum of rice with every bite and sums up the grain's vast potential. A rice chapter without it would be remiss, so here's our best attempt at sticking the landing.

FOR THE SPICE MIXTURE:

½	cup (65 g) shelled pistachios
1	tablespoon light brown sugar
	Pinch of saffron threads
1	teaspoon ground cardamom
1	teaspoon ground cinnamon
½	teaspoon ground cumin
½	teaspoon sea salt

FOR THE RICE:

2	cups (360 g) basmati rice
⅓	cup (45 g) shelled pistachios, roughly chopped
⅓	cup (35 g) slivered almonds
1	generous pinch saffron threads
1½	cups (360 ml) boiling water, divided
⅓	cup (50 g) dried sour cherries
⅓	cup (40 g) dried barberries or goji berries
½	cup (100 g) granulated sugar
	Peels of 2 oranges, julienned
2	medium carrots, julienned
⅓	cup (65 g) diced dried apricots
¼	cup plus 1 tablespoon (75 ml) canola oil, divided
1	medium onion, thinly sliced
	Sea salt
2	tablespoons unsalted butter, melted

Make the spice mixture: In a food processor, combine the pistachios, sugar, saffron, cardamom, cinnamon, cumin and salt. Pulse 10 to 15 times, until the nuts are coarsely ground. Set the mixture aside.

Make the rice: Place the rice in a fine-mesh sieve and rinse under cold water for 1 minute. Set aside. Preheat the broiler. Place the pistachios and almonds on a baking sheet and toast under the broiler until they're just beginning to brown, 3 minutes. Let the nuts cool, then set aside.

Place the saffron in a small bowl and pour ⅓ cup (75 ml) of boiling water over the threads. Set aside. Place the sour cherries and barberries in a medium bowl and cover with the remaining boiling water. Let the fruit steep for 10 minutes, then drain and set the fruit aside.

In a medium saucepan, combine the sugar and 1 cup (240 ml) of water and bring to a simmer, stirring until the sugar dissolves completely. Add 1 tablespoon of the reserved saffron liquid, along with the orange peels and carrots. Cover and simmer until the carrots are tender, 8 to 10 minutes. Drain the mixture and discard the syrup. Place the carrot-orange mixture in a large bowl and add the sour cherry mixture and the apricots.

In a large skillet, heat 1 tablespoon of the oil over medium-high heat. Add the onion and cook, stirring frequently, until the onion has softened, about 8 minutes. Add the reserved spice mixture and stir to coat. Add the carrot-fruit mixture and 1 tablespoon of the saffron liquid. Season with salt and stir to combine. Remove the skillet from the heat and set aside.

Bring a large heavily salted pot of water to a boil. Add the rice and let it return to a boil; cook for 3 minutes, until the grains have elongated but still have some bite. Drain the rice and set aside.

In a large enamel-coated Dutch oven, heat the remaining ¼ cup (60 ml) of oil and 1 tablespoon of the saffron liquid over medium heat. When the liquid starts to sizzle, add a layer of rice to the pan. Forming a pyramid shape, layer half of the fruit mixture on the rice, followed by half of the nuts, then half of the remaining rice, then the remaining fruit mixture and nuts. Finish with the rest of the rice. Carefully insert the handle of a wooden spoon directly down the center of the pyramid (as if you were drilling a hole) until it reaches the bottom of the pan. Pour the remaining saffron liquid and the butter around the perimeter of the hole.

Place a clean kitchen towel over the Dutch oven, then cover with a tight-fitting lid. Secure the hanging corners of the towel up around the lid with a rubber band or tape. Cook the rice over medium heat for 7 minutes, then lower the heat to low (as low as your stove goes) and cook until the rice is fluffy and cooked through, 35 to 40 minutes.

To serve, spoon the rice onto a platter. Use a spatula to gently scrape up the layer of crispy rice on the bottom (this is the best part!) and scatter it atop the rice on the platter. Serve.

Spanish Rice Soubise

MAKES 4 SERVINGS

Soubise is generally a term used to describe an onion sauce, sometimes (but not always) thickened by rice. But we go by the definition of our patron saint of cooking, Julia Child, who uses the term to describe a simple side dish of onions and rice, in which the moisture of the onions steams the rice to the point of tenderness. In this version, red onions and a healthy dose of paprika take the geographical influence from France to Spain. Top this dish with a salty Spanish cheese (Manchego would be killer) or bread crumbs, or pair alongside chicken or shrimp.

½   cup (95 g) jasmine rice

2   tablespoons unsalted butter

2   pounds (910 g/4 medium) red onions, halved and thinly sliced

1   teaspoon smoked Spanish paprika

1   cup (240 ml) heavy cream

3   garlic cloves, mashed with kosher salt

1   teaspoon sherry vinegar

Salt and freshly ground black pepper

Bring a medium saucepan of water to a boil. Add the rice and cook for 5 minutes; drain and set aside. Preheat the oven to 325°F (165°C).

In a Dutch oven or large saucepan, melt the butter over medium heat. Add the onions and cook, stirring, until softened, about 7 minutes. Add the rice and paprika and stir to combine. Cover and transfer to the oven; bake until the onions are tender and falling apart and the rice is cooked through, 1 hour.

Stir in the cream, garlic, vinegar, 1 teaspoon of salt and black pepper to taste. Return the pan to the oven and cook for another 15 minutes; there should no longer be liquid in the pan. Serve immediately.

Crispy Rice Cakes with Chinese Sausage

MAKES 4 TO 6 SERVINGS

Most of the time, crunchy rice means undercooked rice. But not in this recipe, which captures the two distinct stages of this powerful grain. The exterior of these seasoned rice cakes are rendered golden and crispy, while the insides stay soft, almost chewy. Using day-old rice offers the best results because the time allows it to dry out, which yields better caramelization in the pan.

The rice cakes are also the ideal canvas for *lap cheong*, a sweetened and highly emulsified sausage that you can pick up at Asian markets. Buried in the seasoned rice, its sweetness isn't overpowering.

FOR THE DIPPING SAUCE:

¼   cup (60 ml) soy sauce

2   tablespoons rice wine vinegar

1   teaspoon toasted sesame seeds

½   teaspoon sugar

¼   teaspoon toasted sesame oil

FOR THE RICE CAKES:

5   medium dried shiitake caps

2   cups (480 ml) boiling water

2½   ounces (70 g) dried Chinese sausage (*lap cheong*) (about 2 links), finely chopped

1   teaspoon Chinese five-spice powder

1½   teaspoons sugar

2   scallions, finely chopped

2   tablespoons chopped cilantro

2½   cups (465 g) cooked short-grain (sushi) rice, cooled and preferably 1 day old

Kosher salt

1   large egg, lightly beaten

About ½ cup (120 ml) vegetable oil

Make the dipping sauce: In a small bowl, combine all ingredients and stir well.

Make the rice cakes: In a heatproof bowl, cover the shiitakes with the boiling water; let stand until completely rehydrated, about 30 minutes. Drain and finely chop the mushrooms.

In a large nonstick skillet over medium heat, cook the sausage until lightly browned and the fat just starts to render, about 4 minutes. Stir in the mushrooms, five-spice powder and sugar and cook, stirring, until the spices are aromatic, about 1 minute more. Transfer the sausage mixture to a large bowl. Stir in the scallions, cilantro, rice and ½ teaspoon salt. Stir in the egg until thoroughly mixed.

Line a baking sheet with parchment paper. Fill a ¼-cup (60-ml) measuring cup with the rice mixture and pack it very tightly. Turn the cup upside down over the baking sheet and tap the cup with the back of a spoon to release the rice cake. Wipe the measuring cup clean and repeat with the remaining rice mixture.

Wipe out the nonstick skillet and add enough oil to coat the bottom with about ⅛ inch (3 mm). Heat the oil over medium heat until it shimmers. Add the rice cakes and cook, undisturbed, until the undersides are golden brown and crispy, about 5 minutes (try not to peek before then because the cakes might break). Flip the cakes with a spatula and cook until golden brown and crisp on the other side, about 5 minutes longer. Transfer to paper towels to drain briefly. Serve immediately with the dipping sauce on the side.

Mujadarra-Stuffed Peppers

MAKES 4 SERVINGS

1   cup (190 g) brown rice, rinsed and drained

1   cup (200 g) green lentils, rinsed and drained

2   tablespoons extra-virgin olive oil

2   medium yellow onions, halved and thinly sliced

1   teaspoon kosher salt

2   teaspoons ground cumin

1   teaspoon freshly ground black pepper

¼   teaspoon ground cinnamon

¼   teaspoon ground nutmeg

4   large bell peppers

¼   cup (13 g) chopped parsley

We hit the cookbook geek's jackpot when we started to dig into the story of *mujadarra*, a rice and lentil stew that is popular all over the Middle East. It led us to discover the *Kitab al Tabik*, a cookbook published in the early part of the 13th century in what is now Iraq. Among descriptions of cooking styles, the book has a recipe for *mujadarra*. Nearly one millennium later, the dish is still a mainstay. That's a version of "classic" that we can hardly comprehend.

Our take uses the *mujadarra* as a stuffing for bell peppers, which adds a sweet, fruity dynamic to the otherwise grounded dish. You'll have a bit of extra *mujadarra* left over; save it for the next day's lunch, or top it with a fried egg for a hearty breakfast. It's also delicious alongside roasted lamb.

Add the rice to a saucepan and cover with 2 cups (480 ml) of water. Bring to a boil, then reduce the heat to very low; cover and gently simmer for 15 minutes (the rice won't be cooked all the way through). Turn off the heat.

Add the lentils to a separate saucepan and cover with 2 cups (480 ml) of water. Bring to a boil, then reduce the heat to a simmer and cook until the lentils are almost cooked through, about 15 minutes.

In a large skillet, heat the oil over medium-high heat. Add the onions and cook undisturbed for about 3 minutes, or until they begin to brown slightly. Stir briefly, then let cook for another 2 minutes. Season with 1 teaspoon of salt. Transfer ¼ cup (60 ml) of the onions to a small bowl and set aside. Place the remaining onions in a large mixing bowl with the rice and the lentils.

In the same pan the onions were cooked in, combine the cumin, black pepper, cinnamon and nutmeg. Toast over medium heat until fragrant, about 1 minute. Deglaze the pan with 1 tablespoon of water, and add the rice and lentil mixture, stirring to combine.

Preheat the oven to 350°F (175°C). Remove the tops from the peppers and scoop out the seeds. Fill each pepper to the top with the rice mixture and place in a 9-by-9-inch baking dish. (Depending on the size of your peppers, you might have extra rice mixture.) Top each pepper with some of the reserved onions and bake, uncovered, for about 30 minutes, or until the peppers are tender. Top with chopped parsley and serve.

Brown Rice Horchata

MAKES 4 SERVINGS

Here's a Harry Potter–worthy magic trick for you: Rice can turn water into delicious, creamy horchata just by soaking in it. That's right: The road to your own horchata is head-scratchingly short. Simply soak rice in water, blend it, strain it and sweeten it. It's no wonder that this beverage has a history dating back centuries.

A nut-milk bag is a cloth bag used for fine-straining the solids from liquids like nut milks and juices. It works great here, but a double layer of cheese-cloth inside a fine-mesh sieve will also do the job.

1½ cups (270 to 285 g) brown rice (long grain or short grain)

¾ teaspoon kosher salt

¾ teaspoon ground cinnamon

3 tablespoons maple syrup or honey

¾ teaspoon pure vanilla extract

  Ice, for serving

In a large bowl, cover the brown rice by 1 inch with cold water. Let the rice soak at room temperature for at least 4 hours or up to overnight.

Drain the rice in a fine-mesh sieve and transfer it to a blender. Cover with 3 cups (720 ml) of cold water. Blend at the highest speed until the rice is finely ground and well mixed. Pass the mixture through a nut-milk bag (or a mesh sieve lined with a double layer of cheesecloth) into a pitcher or large measuring cup. Discard the contents of the bag or sieve.

Whisk the salt, cinnamon, maple syrup and vanilla into the rice milk. Serve the horchata immediately over ice, or refrigerate for up to 2 days, stirring well before serving, as the mixture tends to separate.

Dark Chocolate Bark with Puffed Rice

MAKES 1 POUND (455 G)

Every Halloween, it was the Nestlé Crunch bars that we tore into first. And Rice Krispies treats were always the bake sale item we requested. Since then, we've dabbled in re-creating our favorite childhood foods, from mac and cheese to whoopie pies. But somehow we've never looked under the hood of the puffed rice treats that ruled over our prepubescent cravings.

That ended when we discovered how simple it is to puff rice at home (seriously, it requires the same skillset as making popcorn). We paired the discovery with some high-quality dark chocolate for a faithful take on the classic, but the puffed rice technique has far more of a purpose than helping us satisfy our sweet tooth. Swap it for oats in your favorite granola recipe, or use it as the key ingredient in *bhel poori*, the Indian street snack.

Don't start this recipe without a good thermometer on hand; you'll need it to temper the chocolate.

2 teaspoons vegetable oil

¼ cup (45 g) black wild rice (no blends) or forbidden rice

1 teaspoon kosher salt

1 pound (455 g) 70% to 72% dark chocolate

Heat the oil in a large skillet over medium to medium-high heat until it starts to smoke.

Add the rice and stir, uncovered, until all the grains pop, about 1 minute; when you no longer hear the grains popping, take the pan off the heat (unlike popcorn, the rice kernels won't jump out of the pan as they pop). Transfer the rice to a paper towel–lined baking sheet and season with the salt. Let the popped rice cool completely.

Add 1 inch of water to a medium saucepan and bring to a simmer over medium heat. Finely chop the chocolate. Set aside 4 ounces (115 g) and melt the rest in a stainless steel bowl set over the simmering water until it reaches 115°F (46°C). This happens very quickly, so as the chocolate melts, it's a good idea to remove it from the heat occasionally to measure the temperature while stirring with a spatula. Remove the chocolate from the heat, wipe the bottom of the bowl with a kitchen towel and add the reserved chocolate. Let the chocolate cool to 82°F (28°C), stirring occasionally. Place the bowl of melted chocolate back over the simmering water and warm in 15-second intervals, stirring constantly, until the chocolate reaches 90°F (32°C).

Pour the chocolate onto a silicone or aluminum foil–lined baking sheet and use an offset spatula to spread ¼ inch thick or slightly thinner. Tap the pan several times on your work surface to release any bubbles. Sprinkle the puffed rice over the chocolate. Let the chocolate harden at room temperature for 20 minutes, or refrigerate until firm, about 10 minutes.

Break the bark into pieces and store in an airtight container at room temperature for 1 week, or refrigerate for up to 1 month.

By Any Other Name

Rice is so fundamental in many cultures that it takes on a larger significance in the very language itself.
- In China, the word for rice is the same as the word for food. The greeting "How are you?" is replaced by "have you had your rice today?"
- In Thailand, you announce that a meal is ready by saying "eat rice."
- In Japan, the word for cooked rice is the same as the word for meal.

Super-Crisp Fried Chicken

MAKES 4 SERVINGS

2 tablespoons soy sauce

2 tablespoons apple cider vinegar

2 garlic cloves, finely chopped

1 tablespoon toasted sesame oil

Kosher salt and freshly ground black pepper

2 pounds (910 g) bone-in, skin-on chicken thighs

½ cup (65 g) all-purpose flour

½ cup (60 g) white rice flour

6 cups (1.4 L) vegetable oil, for frying

Change is hard, especially when it comes to fried chicken. We were long-time devotees of the traditional dip-and-dredge method using buttermilk and all-purpose flour, and we had no cause for changing up our game. Then Ian Knauer (Vol. 1: Eggs) turned our world on its head with this recipe, which produces some of the crunchiest fried chicken we've ever attacked. There are two main techniques at play: the wet batter, which helps the starch affix to the meat more uniformly, and two trips into the frying oil. But the secret ingredient that takes this over the edge is the rice flour in the batter, which has a higher level of carbohydrates and less protein than regular flour, which produces the gluten necessary to achieve a thin, crisp crust. If you don't have any rice flour on hand, make your own by pulsing ¾ cup (140 g) of long-grain rice in a spice grinder until very finely ground.

In a bowl, stir together the soy sauce, vinegar, garlic, sesame oil, ¾ teaspoon of salt and ½ teaspoon of pepper. Transfer the marinade to a large bowl, add the chicken and toss it to coat. Refrigerate for at least 30 minutes and up to 2 hours.

In a bowl, whisk the flours together, then whisk in ¾ cup (180 ml) of water and any remaining marinade from the large bowl to combine. You should have a batter with a pancake-like consistency (add more water if necessary). Pour the batter over the chicken and toss to coat completely.

Heat about 2 inches of vegetable oil to 325°F (165°C) in a medium Dutch oven. Add the chicken to the oil and reduce the heat to low, then cook the chicken until it's cooked through, about 15 minutes. (The oil temperature will drop as low as 245°F/120°C.) Transfer the chicken to a paper towel–lined baking sheet and increase the heat until the oil climbs back to 325°F (165°C).

Fry the chicken a second time until the coating is super-crisp and dark golden brown, 2 minutes. Drain on paper towels, then transfer the chicken to a platter and serve.

SOURDOUGH BREAD

This chapter will not teach you how to make sourdough bread at home. A primer on DIY sourdough could fill an entire book, and even then, it's one of those skills best learned in person under the tutelage of a seasoned professional. As with homebrewed beer or homemade mozzarella, it's a fun and educational project to tackle over a weekend, but the end result is rarely better than what you can buy around the corner.

But we sure *can* teach you how to use up a few loaves of sourdough. Before you start cooking, do yourself a favor and buy the best loaf you can find. If you don't have access to a good bakery, sample a few commercial loaves from the supermarket until you find one you like.

Our ideal sourdough loaf has a dark, burnished crust, thick enough that it *thumps* when tapped with a knuckle. Inside, the crumb should be pleasantly chewy with a bit of spring and some noticeable air pockets (evidence of proper fermentation) and a yeasty, gently tangy flavor. A khaki-colored exterior, wet, spongy crumb or unpleasantly sour flavor are all signs of an inferior loaf. Shape-wise, we like the oval-shaped *batards* for sandwiches and round *boules* (or the larger *miche*) for everything else.

Once you've found your sourdough soul mate, you'll find yourself wanting to use up every last crumb. Luckily, the following recipes will help you do just that.

Smoked Mozzarella & Sage in Sourdough Carrozza

MAKES 4 SERVINGS

¼ cup (½ stick/55 g) unsalted butter

16 large or 24 medium sage leaves

¼ cup (60 ml) extra-virgin olive oil

8 slices sourdough bread (about ½ inch thick)

1 pound (455 g) smoked mozzarella, thinly sliced

1 cup (240 ml) whole milk

½ cup (65 g) all-purpose flour

4 large eggs

Kosher salt and freshly ground black pepper

Marinara sauce, for serving, optional

This glorious mash-up of grilled cheese and French toast is a riff on a classic Italian snack that hails from Campania, Italy, the birthplace of mozzarella cheese. It's so easy to make and universally satisfying that it defies a time of day or meal to call its own. Here we use smoked mozzarella both for flavor and its lower moisture content, which prevents the sandwich from turning into the goopy and less-glorious American snack of fried mozzarella sticks. This is a particularly great use for leftover sourdough; the older your bread, the longer you should soak it in milk.

Preheat the oven to 200°F (90°C). Place a wire rack in a rimmed baking sheet and place the baking sheet in the oven.

In a nonstick or cast-iron skillet, melt the butter over medium heat. Add the sage leaves and cook until fragrant, about 2 minutes (don't burn the sage or let the butter brown). Transfer the sage leaves to paper towels and pour the butter into a measuring cup, then stir in the oil.

Assemble a sandwich by placing 2 to 3 sage leaves on top of a piece of bread, then scattering one-fourth of the mozzarella over the top. Place 3 more sage leaves on top of the cheese, then top with another slice of bread. Repeat with the remaining bread, cheese and sage to make 4 sandwiches. If you like, cut off the crusts. Pour the milk into a shallow dish; place the flour in a second shallow dish, and beat the eggs in a third shallow dish. Set all three dishes within close reach of the stove.

Place the skillet over medium heat and add enough of the butter-oil mixture to coat the bottom of the pan. Quickly coat both sides of one sandwich in milk, then dredge both sides in flour, patting off any excess. Coat the sandwich in the egg and allow the excess to drip off.

Gently place the sandwich in the pan and cook one side until well browned, 2 to 3 minutes. Flip the sandwich over, sprinkle the top with salt and cook until browned on the other side, 2 to 3 minutes. Flip the sandwich one more time, sprinkle the top with salt and cook for 30 seconds. (Don't worry if some of the cheese drips out onto the pan—that's a crispy little gift!) Transfer the sandwich to paper towels and blot away any excess oil, then transfer to the prepared baking sheet to keep warm. Wipe out the skillet and repeat with the remaining 3 sandwiches. Serve with marinara sauce, if using.

Bread Crumb Omelet

MAKES 1 SERVING

We firmly believe that this omelet is perfectly suitable for company. Somehow, putting bread crumbs inside the eggs—rather than serving toast on the side—makes it feel fancier. And we have Jessica Battilana (Vol. 10: Corn) to thank for introducing us to this magical combination.

We couldn't decide whether to put this recipe in the egg chapter or here: An omelet is an egg with nothing to hide behind, but bread crumbs operate on the same honest principles. Of course this recipe's success hinges on knowing how to cook a damn omelet—that bicycle of cooking techniques—but it also hinges on crispy bread crumbs that are just the right size. Too small and they dissolve into a weird bread paste when they hit the hot eggs. Too large and they make the omelet difficult to roll and awkward to eat. Pea-size crumbs, fried in olive oil, are the ultimate workhorse ingredient (just don't tell the eggs).

2   large eggs

       Kosher salt and freshly ground black pepper

1   tablespoon butter, divided

2   tablespoons grated Gruyère cheese

¼   cup (25 g) Coarse Bread Crumbs (recipe at right)

2   teaspoons minced chives, optional

In a medium bowl, whisk the eggs until very well combined and season with salt and pepper. The goal here is get a homogenous mixture, but you're not trying to aerate the eggs, so mix them thoroughly but don't beat too vigorously.

Heat an 8-inch nonstick pan over medium-low heat and add half of the butter. Let the butter melt slowly. When a few bubbles appear on the surface, add the eggs. With a heatproof spatula, quickly and vigorously stir the eggs to prevent curds from forming; run the spatula around the edge of the pan from time to time to prevent the edges from overcooking.

When the omelet is set on the bottom but still slightly runny on top, tap the pan firmly on the burner a couple of times (to pop any air bubbles—thanks Julia Child), then turn the heat off but leave the pan on the burner. Sprinkle the cheese evenly over the omelet, then add the bread crumbs in a straight line down the center.

Using your nondominant hand, tilt the pan away from you and use a spatula to lift up the edge of the omelet closest to you. Flip the first couple inches of the edge over and away from you, then add the remaining butter to the pan behind the fold. Continue rolling the omelet away from you, enclosing the bread crumbs inside. The rolled omelet should be about 2 inches thick; you're not aiming for something rolled as tightly as a cigar, but it shouldn't be all loosey-goosey, either. Grab the pan with your dominant hand and turn the omelet out onto a warmed plate. Garnish with chives, if using, and serve immediately.

Coarse Bread Crumbs

MAKES ABOUT ¾ CUP (75 G)

3   thick slices day-old sourdough bread, crusts removed, torn into 1-inch pieces

2   to 3 tablespoons extra-virgin olive oil

       Kosher salt

Preheat the oven to 400°F (205°C). In a medium bowl, toss the bread and oil together, coating the bread evenly with the oil. Arrange the bread in a single layer on a rimmed baking sheet and season with salt. Bake, shaking the pan occasionally, until the bread is deep golden brown. Remove from the oven and let cool. Once the bread is cool, spread it on a work surface and, using a rolling pin, crush the cubes into pea-size crumbs.

Inside-Out Chowder Bowl

MAKES 4 SERVINGS

In the San Francisco Bay Area, chowder bowls are as common as hamburgers. "They are trashy in all the right ways," says local son Scott Hocker (Vol. 6: Sweet Potatoes), who created this version. "The chowder is thick, verging on gummy. The sourdough bowl is, too. The clams are most certainly canned. Ultimately, the one grievous misstep is the sheer volume of the bread-to-soup ratio." Inspired by the chowder at San Francisco's Hog Island Oyster Company, this recipe flips that formula, turning the novelty bread bowl into croutons and repurposing the water used to boil potatoes to thicken the soup without relying on flour to clog the chowder's briny essence.

This is also a hands-on dish, as the clams remain in their shells. The work of alternating between spoon and fingers somehow makes the eating all the more fun.

3	tablespoons unsalted butter, divided
8	ounces (225 g) sourdough (about half a typical loaf), crusts discarded and crumb cut into 1-inch cubes (about 2 cups/180 g)
	Salt
2	large Yukon Gold potatoes, about 1 pound (455 g), cut into ½-inch pieces
36	littleneck clams, scrubbed
¼	pound (55 g) good thick-cut bacon, cut crosswise into ¼-inch slices
2	thyme sprigs
½	celery stalk, thinly sliced crosswise
4	scallions, thinly sliced crosswise, whites and greens separated
½	cup (120 ml) whole milk
½	cup (120 ml) heavy cream
¼	teaspoon freshly ground black pepper

Preheat the oven to 400°F (205°C). Melt 2 tablespoons of butter and toss it with the sourdough cubes and ½ teaspoon of salt in a bowl. Scatter the bread on a rimmed baking sheet and bake until golden brown all over, turning the cubes halfway through, about 10 minutes. Reserve the croutons.

Meanwhile, place the potatoes in a saucepan and cover them with cold water. Bring the water to a boil and salt it well. Cook the potatoes until just tender, about 10 minutes. Drain the potatoes over a measuring cup, saving about 2 cups (480 ml) of the cooking water.

Rinse the clams well and transfer them to a large pot. Add just enough water to cover them. Bring the clams to a boil and shake the pot. After 30 seconds, remove the opened clams. Keep cooking the clams for another minute or two, until most of the other clams have opened. Discard any unopened clams.

Pour the clam broth through a fine-mesh strainer—or pour off the broth slowly, keeping the sandy dregs in the pot. Place the clam broth (there should be about 3 cups/720 ml) in a large bowl, then add enough of the reserved potato water to the clam broth to give you a total of 4 cups (960 ml) of liquid. Reserve the clams while you finish the broth.

Rinse the pot used for cooking the clams. Over medium-low heat, cook the bacon with the remaining 1 tablespoon of butter and the thyme until a good amount of the bacon's fat has rendered, 5 to 8 minutes. Add the celery and white parts of the scallions and cook the vegetables until they're soft and translucent, about 1 minute. Add the potatoes and clam broth liquid. Bring the mixture to a simmer and add the milk and cream. Season with salt and the pepper.

Divide the soup and reserved clams among four bowls. Garnish with croutons and scallion greens and serve.

Caramelized Onion Bread Soup

MAKES 4 TO 6 SERVINGS

3 ⅓-inch-thick slices sourdough, cut into 1-inch pieces (about 3 cups/ 270 g)

¼ cup (½ stick/55 g) unsalted butter

2 large sweet onions, halved and cut into ⅛-inch slices

Salt and freshly ground black pepper

4 to 6 cups (960 ml to 1.4 L) chicken or vegetable stock, preferably homemade

Optional garnishes: Gruyère cheese, sourdough croutons, smoked trout, coarsely grated tart apples, chives

It's remarkable how some dishes, made with just a few ingredients, can taste so much more than the sum of their parts. Caramelized onion soup is perhaps the best example of this, but only if you actually caramelize the onions. So many recipes tell us that it takes only 15 or 20 minutes to complete the task, but we've never been able to do it in less than 40—anything short of that might give you browned onions, but they sure as hell won't be *caramelized*. And the longer you go past the 40-minute mark (we've cooked onions for several hours), the more you're rewarded with the allium's deepest umami and sweetness.

Served on its own, this creamy soup is real *cucina povera*, but you can embellish it with Gruyère (to evoke French onion soup), double-down with sourdough croutons, or top it with an elegant combination of smoked trout, apples and chives.

Preheat the oven to 350°F (175°C). Spread the bread cubes on a baking sheet and toast for about 10 minutes, or until lightly golden.

Meanwhile, in a heavy wide saucepan, melt the butter. Add the onions and a large pinch of salt; cover and cook over medium heat, stirring occasionally, until softened, about 6 minutes. Reduce the heat to medium-low and cook, uncovered, until the onions are deeply golden brown, 40 to 50 minutes (or more!). Stir in a splash of water as necessary to deglaze the pan as the onions cook.

Add the toasted bread and 4 cups (960 ml) of stock to the saucepan and bring to a boil, stirring until browned bits are loosened from the bottom of the pan. Simmer the soup over very low heat just until the bread is very soft, about 5 minutes. Use an immersion blender or transfer the soup to a blender and puree until smooth. (If you're using a blender, be sure to wait until the soup has cooled down a bit.)

Return the soup to the saucepan (if necessary) and cook until it's heated through; add more stock if you want a thinner soup. Season to taste with salt and pepper. Ladle the soup into bowls and garnish as desired.

The soup can be refrigerated for up to 2 days. Reheat gently, adding more stock as necessary to thin it out.

More Caramelized Onion Best Practices

- Use a wide pan to give the onions more surface area.
- Cover the pan for the first 5 to 10 minutes of cooking to help sweat more liquid out of the onions (more liquid equals more caramelization).
- Watch the pan carefully; a dark fond will develop on the bottom of the pan, but the onions shouldn't scorch.
- When they get very dry, deglaze the pan with small amounts of water and scrape the bottom of the pan to release the fond.

Pork Schnitzel

MAKES 4 SERVINGS

Schnitzels are often associated with German cuisine, but most food cultures have their own version of this dish, wherein a thin cut of boneless meat is breaded and fried (versions of it date back to the Roman Empire). Think of this recipe more as a technique that can be applied to a variety of proteins and seasonings (try swapping the caraway and paprika out for other spices), but we love the subtle tang that sourdough bread crumbs add to the finished product.

4   4- to 5-ounce (115- to 140-g) boneless pork loin chops

3   cups (270 g) sourdough bread cubes

1   tablespoon caraway seeds

¾   cup (95 g) all-purpose flour

1   teaspoon smoked paprika

    Kosher salt and finely ground black pepper

3   large eggs, lightly beaten

    Rendered lard or vegetable oil, for frying

    Lemon wedges, for serving

Trim any excess fat from the pork chops. Place 1 pork chop between two sheets of plastic wrap, then pound with the flat side of a meat pounder (or a small saucepan) as uniformly and thinly as possibly (aim for about ¼ inch thickness). Repeat with the remaining 3 pork chops, stacking them on a plate as you go.

Place the bread cubes in a food processor and process until they're finely chopped, about 1 minute. Place the bread crumbs on a large plate and scatter the caraway seeds over the top. In a shallow bowl, stir together the flour, paprika and 1 teaspoon of salt.

Whisk ½ teaspoon of salt and ½ teaspoon of pepper into the eggs and place in a shallow bowl. Dredge the pork chops in the flour mixture, then dip each in the egg mixture to coat and let any excess egg drip back into the bowl. Dredge the egg-dipped pork chops in the bread crumbs, pressing the crumbs into the meat to form an even coating all over.

Heat ½ inch of lard or oil in a medium heavy skillet over medium-high heat. Fry the pork chops, two at a time, turning once, until golden brown and just cooked through, 2 to 3 minutes a side. Transfer the schnitzel to a serving platter. Repeat with the remaining pork chops and serve with lemon wedges.

Bread Dumplings with Lemon-Butter Sauce

MAKES 4 SERVINGS

During any impending weather crisis, newscasters trot out the tired suggestion to go out and stock up on bread and milk, as if these two things are the pillars of the proper prepper diet. But perhaps whoever came up with this shopping list was familiar with *semmelknodel*, a simple Bavarian dumpling made from old bread that's been softened in milk. These smaller versions, coated in lemon-butter instead of classic cream sauce or meat gravy, make a delicious accompaniment to roast chicken or pork chops.

½ pound (225 g) stale sourdough bread, cut into 2-inch cubes

1 tablespoon olive oil

1 leek, white and light green parts only, finely chopped

2 tablespoons all-purpose flour

1 cup (240 ml) whole milk

1 tablespoon Dijon mustard

1 teaspoon minced thyme leaves

1 egg, beaten

Salt and freshly ground black pepper

½ cup (1 stick/115 g) unsalted butter

½ cup (120 ml) fresh lemon juice

Bring a large pot of salted water to a boil. Place the bread in a large heatproof bowl.

In a skillet, heat the oil over medium heat. Add the leek and cook, stirring, until translucent, 7 minutes. Sprinkle the flour over the leek and cook until the flour turns golden brown and smells nutty. Whisk in the milk and cook until the mixture thickens up slightly and the whisk leaves trails in the sauce. Whisk in the mustard, then pour the sauce over the bread and let sit for 10 minutes, stirring occasionally. Add the thyme and egg and use your hands to squeeze the mixture into a dough. Season with about 1 teaspoon of salt and about 1 teaspoon of pepper. Shape the dough into rounds the size of large marbles and set them on a baking sheet.

When the water is boiling, add the dumplings and boil for 8 to 10 minutes. While the dumplings are boiling, melt the butter in a large skillet. Whisk in the lemon juice and season with salt. Using a slotted spoon, transfer the dumplings to the skillet and stir gently to coat them with the butter sauce. Season with additional salt and pepper, if needed, and serve.

Sausage & Mushroom Stuffing/Dressing

MAKES 8 SERVINGS

Stuffing is like pizza (and some of life's other great pleasures): There's an endless supply of perfectly decent encounters, very few "bad" ones, and even fewer that are "most amazing ever."

In our attempt to make the best stuffing you'll ever have, our version pulls a few tricks. We start by making a flavorful soup with double-strength chicken (or turkey) stock and browned vegetables. When it comes time to combine the soup with the bread, we add a little bit at a time to ensure we hit that sweet spot between dry and soggy, then add some brown butter and a mix of sautéed mushrooms to boost the dish's meaty, roasted flavors. If you're serving stuffing with roasted turkey or chicken, use as many leftover scraps and trimmings from the bird as you can gather: Leftover fat can (and should) replace some of the butter; freshly made stock always eclipses canned; and sautéed gizzards—if the gravy hasn't already called dibs—will make your stuffing taste as though it was cooked inside the bird, just like in the old days. (Technically, stuffing is "dressing" if it's not cooked *in cavitatem*, but "dressing" has always sounded so WASP-y to us.)

1	1-pound (455-g) sourdough loaf
4	cups (960 ml) chicken or turkey stock, preferably homemade
1	cup (240 ml) dry vermouth or white wine
8	tablespoons (1 stick/115 g) unsalted butter, divided, plus more for the baking dish
1	pound (455 g) Italian sausage (hot, sweet or a mix), casings removed
1	large yellow onion, diced
1	small fennel bulb, diced
3	celery stalks, diced
1	teaspoon celery seeds, optional
3	garlic cloves, finely chopped
1	tablespoon thyme leaves
1	tablespoon finely chopped sage
¼	cup (13 g) finely chopped parsley
	Kosher salt and freshly ground black pepper
8	ounces (225 g) mixed mushrooms, stems removed, cut into 1-inch pieces (about 4 cups)

Preheat the oven to 300°F (150°C) and grease a 9-by-11-inch baking dish. Using a serrated knife, cut the bottom crust off the loaf and discard or save it and use it to make bread crumbs. Cut the loaf into 1-inch slices, then tear the bread into jagged bite-size pieces (you can also cut the bread into neat, uniform cubes, but we like our stuffing looking rugged). Spread the bread on a rimmed baking sheet and bake until it's dry and lightly toasted, stirring a couple of times, about 30 minutes. (If you're making this a day ahead, you can skip the baking step and let the bread dry out on the counter overnight.) Transfer the bread to the largest mixing bowl you own. Turn the oven up to 375°F (190°C).

Meanwhile, bring the stock and vermouth to a boil in a saucepan and reduce by half, about 10 to 15 minutes. Turn off the heat.

Melt 4 tablespoons (½ stick/55 g) of butter in a large skillet over high heat. Add the sausage and cook, breaking it into small pieces with a metal spatula, until browned and cooked through, 8 to 10 minutes. Using a slotted spoon, transfer the meat to the bowl with the bread. Lower the heat to medium-high and add the onion, fennel, celery, celery seeds, if using, and garlic to the pan; cook, stirring occasionally, until the vegetables are softened, about 7 minutes. Stir in the thyme and sage. Add the reduced stock, bring to a simmer and cook for 5 minutes. Remove the pan from the heat and strain the broth into a measuring cup (you should have 2 to 2½ cups/480 to 600 ml at this point) and pour the vegetables over the bread. Add the parsley and toss well. Season the broth with salt and pepper.

In the same large skillet, melt the remaining 4 tablespoons (½ stick/ 115 g) of butter over medium-high heat. Continue cooking the butter until it just begins to brown and smell nutty, about 2 to 3 minutes, then add the mushrooms. Turn the heat to high and sauté until the mushrooms begin to brown, 3 to 4 minutes; season with salt. Pour the mushrooms over the bread mixture. Add half of the reserved broth and toss well; if the bread soaks up all of the liquid (it should), add a splash more and toss again, adding more broth until the bread stops soaking it up.

Transfer the stuffing to the baking dish, cover with foil and bake for 25 minutes. Remove the foil and continue baking until the top is golden brown and crisp, 25 to 30 minutes longer. Let the stuffing cool for 10 minutes before serving.

Pull-Apart Sourdough Loaf

MAKES 8 SERVINGS

½ cup (1 stick/115 g) unsalted butter

3 garlic cloves, finely chopped

½ teaspoon kosher salt

½ teaspoon freshly ground black pepper

½ teaspoon red pepper flakes

2 tablespoons chopped parsley

1 scallion, thinly sliced

1 1-pound (455-g) round sourdough loaf

8 ounces (225 g) Gruyère cheese (or your favorite melting cheese; anything is awesome here), coarsely grated (about 2 cups/220 g)

True story: One day, a checkerboard-sliced avocado gave us an idea for this spiky party snack. We took a stab at making one, applying our favorite garlic bread recipe to a circular loaf of sourdough, and were *so proud* of the result. But then the Internet told us that millions of other people have already made at least as many versions, which range from savory to very sweet to trashy as heck. And they go by many names, which seem to vary by region: pull-apart loaf, crack bread, tear 'n' share bread, etc. Ours was to be called "porcupine bread," but we surrender to those who came before us.

Preheat the oven to 350°F (175°C). In a saucepan, melt the butter over low heat. Add the garlic and cook over medium-low heat for 5 minutes; the butter should simmer very gently but not brown. Add the salt, pepper, red pepper flakes, parsley and scallion and transfer the mixture to a measuring cup.

Using a serrated knife, slice the bread into 1-inch slices, working from one side to the other and stopping each slice about ½ inch from the bottom of the loaf. Rotate the loaf and repeat to make a crosshatch pattern. Place the loaf on top of a piece of aluminum foil large enough to wrap the entire thing.

Spoon the garlic-herb butter between the columns of bread, then drizzle and brush the remaining over the top of the loaf. (A pair of small spring-loaded tongs will help spread the layers of bread apart, making it easier to get the butter and cheese in there.) Sprinkle and shove the cheese deep between the cracks as well, then sprinkle the remaining cheese over the top.

Wrap the loaf loosely in foil, then place it on a baking sheet and bake for 15 minutes. Remove the foil and continue baking the loaf for 10 minutes longer, or until the cheese is melted and the top is golden brown and crispy. Serve.

TOMATOES

Our favorite summer rite of passage is to amble through a farmers' market without an agenda, only to emerge with overloaded bags of tomatoes and a mental list of 20 or so ways we want to use them. This exact occasion—when you're seduced by an ingredient and form a cooking plan around it—is why we created Short Stack Editions.

A peak-of-the-season tomato is the most concise case we can make for the idea of inspiring ingredients. Its evocative package is the perfect alignment of seasonality, geography, romance, nostalgia and approachability. Yes, perfect-looking tomatoes are available every day of the year in every grocery store, but no other perennial ingredient is so much more superior when it's eaten in season, as though the tomato were nature's reminder that we're actually not supposed to have everything all the time.

The recipes in this chapter are meant to sustain the magic of that first heady bite of a freshly picked Brandywine or the sweet explosion of a Sungold or cherry tomato. A couple dishes will still be great with supermarket tomatoes in mid-January, but only because they capitalize on the transformative properties of roasting the fruit. But the rest of the dishes celebrate the defining principle of this era of American cuisine: that eating ingredients grown nearby and in season is not only the responsible thing to do—for your local food system and the planet—but also the most rewarding.

Orecchiette with Burst Cherry Tomato Sauce

MAKES 6 SERVINGS

Kosher salt and freshly ground black pepper

1 pound (455 g) dried orecchiette pasta

¼ cup (60 ml) extra-virgin olive oil

2 pounds (910 g) mixed bite-size tomatoes, such as cherry, grape, and currant

2 garlic cloves, thinly sliced

1 cup loosely packed basil leaves, chopped (about ½ cup/20 g)

1 cup (115 g) shaved *ricotta salata* cheese (about 4 ounces/115 g)

Sara Jenkins (Vol. 14: Prosciutto di Parma) is, hands down, the best pasta-cooking chef we've ever met, and this speedy recipe of hers is a great way to use up that extra pint of mixed miniature tomatoes you grabbed at the farmers' market. Cooking the tiny orbs until they explode offers the reward of a speedy tomato sauce that works with pretty much any style of pasta, from the ear-shaped orecchiette here to a longer pasta like linguine or spaghetti.

Bring a large pot of salted water to a boil. Add the pasta and cook until al dente. Reserve 1 cup (240 ml) of the pasta water, then drain the pasta and reserve.

Meanwhile, add the oil to a large heavy skillet and set over medium-high heat. When the oil is hot, add half of the tomatoes, sprinkle them with salt and cook, stirring frequently, until the tomatoes start to wrinkle and collapse, 8 to 10 minutes. Reduce the heat to medium and add the rest of the tomatoes and continue cooking and tossing for 2 minutes longer.

Push the tomatoes to one side of the pan and add the garlic to the other side. As the garlic starts to soften, after about 2 minutes, mix it in with the tomatoes, gently pressing on the tomatoes to release some of their juices. If the tomatoes are dry, add some of the reserved pasta water, about ¼ cup (60 ml) at a time, simmering between additions, to make a thick sauce, about 5 minutes. Add about half of the cooked pasta to the sauce and toss until it's coated; remove the pan from the heat and season with salt and pepper.

Transfer the remaining pasta to a warm serving bowl and immediately toss with the tomato-sauced pasta. Stir in the basil and sprinkle with the ricotta salata. Serve immediately.

Tomato Pepperoni

MAKES 1 CUP (200 G)

The gonzo brain of chef Tyler Kord (Vol. 7: Broccoli) dreamed up this faux pepperoni while developing a mostly vegetarian pizzeria concept. Somehow he managed to nail the flavor profile of the funky cured sausage while maintaining its vegetarian (vegan, actually) status. You'll have to taste it for yourself. Make a double or triple batch and freeze the extra, because you'll find yourself wanting to throw these slices on everything from salads and sandwiches to pasta, or just snack on a bowlful—they're that good.

1	tablespoon mustard seeds
1	teaspoon black peppercorns
1	tablespoon fennel seeds
1	teaspoon anise seeds
½	teaspoon red pepper flakes
¼	teaspoon smoked paprika
	Kosher salt
1	garlic clove
2	teaspoons soy sauce
1	teaspoon pure maple syrup
1	pint (290 g) cherry tomatoes

Preheat the oven to 300°F (150°C) and line a baking sheet with parchment paper or a silicone mat. Using a spice grinder or mortar and pestle, grind the mustard seeds, peppercorns, fennel seeds, anise seeds and red pepper flakes until finely ground. Stir in the paprika and ½ teaspoon of salt. This is more than you need for this recipe, so save what you don't use for making more tomato pepperoni or for seasoning fun things like pork chops or roasted cauliflower.

Place the garlic on a cutting board and smash it with the side of a knife, then sprinkle it with salt and mash it into a paste with the knife. In a small bowl, blend the garlic, soy sauce and maple syrup with a fork. Slice the cherry tomatoes crosswise into ⅛-inch rounds that look like pepperoni, if pepperoni were made from fresh tomatoes. In a mixing bowl, gently toss the tomatoes with the soy sauce mixture, then pour off the excess liquid and add 1 tablespoon of the spice blend and toss again.

Arrange the tomato slices in a single layer on the baking sheet and bake for 15 minutes. Reduce the oven temperature to 200°F (90°C) and continue baking for another 50 to 60 minutes, or until the tomatoes are shriveled and lightly caramelized. Remove the tomatoes from the oven and let the slices cool on the baking sheet, then transfer them to a container until ready to use. The tomato pepperoni can be kept frozen for up to 1 month.

Roasted-Tomato Niçoise Salad

MAKES 4 SERVINGS

When you slowly roast them, tomatoes take on a very different flavor and texture than their fresh counterparts, essentially becoming an entirely new ingredient. They can still stand in for fresh tomatoes in most cases and, thanks to their intensely savory flavor and fleshy makeup, are suitable for a lot more ingredient matchmaking as well. We could write an entire book about how to use roasted tomatoes. Maybe we will!

Until then, we're channeling our love with this salad from Martha Holmberg (Vol. 9: Plums), who crafted it after one too many disappointing attempts at making stuffed tomatoes. She eventually had the epiphany that deconstructing the dish would put all the ingredients into the state in which they taste best.

The vital piece of this recipe is roasting tomatoes to the perfect degree of concentration, which takes some patience and judgment, because each batch of tomatoes will behave slightly differently in the way it loses water during cooking. But once you get the hang of it, this technique will live in your top 10.

8	medium tomatoes, cored and halved
	Extra-virgin olive oil
	Kosher salt and freshly ground black pepper
1	tablespoon coarsely chopped rosemary
8	ounces (225 g) green beans, trimmed
1	teaspoon thyme leaves
1	6-ounce (170-g) can oil-packed tuna, drained and broken up into large pieces
3	ounces (85 g) crumbled feta cheese
1	2-ounce (55-g) tin anchovies in oil, drained
1	tablespoon drained capers
4	lemon wedges

Preheat the oven to 375°F (190°C) and line two rimmed baking sheets with parchment paper. Arrange the tomato halves cut-side up on one baking sheet. Drizzle about 3 tablespoons of the oil over the tomatoes, season generously with salt and pepper and sprinkle with the rosemary.

On the other baking sheet, toss the beans with another tablespoon of oil and sprinkle with salt, pepper and the thyme leaves.

Place both baking sheets in the oven and roast. Remove the beans from the oven when they're done—they should be wrinkled and very tender—after about 20 minutes and let cool to room temperature.

Roast the tomatoes until they've shrunk to about half of their original size, about 1½ to 2½ hours; they'll have shriveled somewhat but not completely fallen apart. Remove the tomatoes from the oven and let them cool in the pan. Depending on the moisture content of the tomatoes, lots of juice will accumulate in the pan; you can just spoon the juice back over the tomatoes when they've finished roasting, if you like.

Place 4 tomato halves on each of four plates, overlapping them slightly. Arrange a pile of green beans on each bed of the tomatoes and top the beans with the tuna. Crumble some feta over the tuna, then place a few anchovy fillets on top of each portion in a criss-cross pattern. Scatter the capers over the whole thing, letting some spill onto the plate. Finish the salad with a drizzle of oil and a lemon wedge. Serve slightly warm or at room temperature. If you make any of the components ahead, be sure to bring them to room temperature before assembling and serving the salad.

Green Tomato Shakshuka

MAKES 4 SERVINGS

3 tablespoons extra-virgin olive oil

1 large onion, halved and thinly sliced

2 Cubanelle peppers or other sweet green frying peppers—stemmed, seeded and thinly sliced

Kosher salt and freshly ground black pepper

2 medium garlic cloves, thinly sliced

1 jalapeño chile—stemmed, seeded and thinly sliced lengthwise

1 teaspoon ground coriander

½ teaspoon toasted cumin seeds

1 teaspoon thyme leaves, roughly chopped

4 large green tomatoes (about 2½ pounds/1.2 kg), roughly chopped

4 large eggs

¼ pound (115 g) feta cheese, crumbled, for garnish

Cilantro leaves, for garnish

Gardeners (and CSA subscribers) are often left with an abundance of green tomatoes. They're great fried, obviously, but they also cook down nicely into sauces, soups and chili. Ripe tomatoes have a sweet-savory depth, but green tomatoes offer up a fresh, almost lemony tang, with a texture that adds structure. Shakshuka is a North African dish that's standard breakfast fare in Israel, kind of like a Middle Eastern huevos rancheros. But we're big fans of this dish as eggs-for-dinner, served with a stack of warm pita.

In a large deep skillet, heat the oil over medium-low heat. Add the onion and peppers and a large pinch of salt and cook, stirring frequently, until soft, 15 to 20 minutes. Add the garlic and jalapeño and cook over moderate heat until softened, about 2 minutes. Add the coriander, cumin seeds and thyme and cook until fragrant, about 1 minute. Add the tomatoes, cover the pan and cook over medium-low heat until the tomatoes start to break down, about 10 minutes. Use a spoon to break up the tomatoes and cook, uncovered, until a thick sauce forms, about 10 minutes longer. Season with salt and pepper.

Crack the eggs into the sauce; cover the skillet and cook, basting the tops of the eggs gently with the sauce once or twice, until the egg whites are just set, about 5 minutes.

Garnish the shakshuka with the feta and cilantro and serve in bowls.

Tomato Water

MAKES ABOUT 3 CUPS (720 ML)

When you find yourself with squishy-soft overripe tomatoes that threaten to burst if you look at them too long, please stifle the instinct to throw them out. Instead, use them to make the most tomatoey tomato water you've ever tasted.

Our version of tomato water is as basic as they come, but you can add other ingredients—such as garlic, shallots, lemongrass, chiles and herbs—to the puree to infuse their flavors into the liquid.

3   pounds (1.4 kg) very ripe (or overripe) tomatoes

2   teaspoons kosher salt

Line a large fine-mesh strainer with a double layer of cheesecloth or a clean kitchen towel and place it over a bowl (leave enough room to hold about 3 cups/720 ml of liquid). Rinse the tomatoes, then core and quarter them. Place the tomatoes and salt in a food processor and pulse a few times, until coarsely chopped.

Pour the chopped tomatoes into the prepared strainer and refrigerate for at least 4 hours, or overnight. You should end up with about 3 cups (720 ml) of pale-yellow tomato water.

Discard the solids, cover the liquid and refrigerate it until ready to use. The tomato water will start losing its fresh flavor after a couple of days; discard after 4 days or freeze for up to 1 month.

Tomato-Water Orzo

MAKES 2 SERVINGS

This is a very simple recipe for showcasing tomato water as a cooking medium. Anything you can cook in simmering water—pasta, rice, vegetables, even fish—will taste that much better when tomato water is used instead. It's a luxurious swap, yes, but one that's worth making for a few weeks each year when you have enough surplus tomatoes that tomato water is an inevitability.

2½   cups (600 ml) Tomato Water (recipe at left), divided

1   cup (150 g) orzo

2   tablespoons unsalted butter

½   cup (50 g) finely grated Parmigiano-Reggiano cheese, divided

    Freshly ground black pepper

¼   cup (10 g) shredded basil leaves

1   cup (145 g) cherry tomatoes, thinly sliced

In a saucepan, bring 2 cups (480 ml) of tomato water to a boil. Add the orzo and simmer over medium-high heat until the orzo is al dente (there should be a little bit of liquid left over in the pan). Stir in the butter, then ¼ cup (25 g) of cheese. Crank a good amount of pepper over the top. Divide the orzo between two pasta bowls and pour the remaining ½ cup (120 ml) of tomato water around the orzo. Garnish the pasta with the cherry tomatoes, sprinkle with the remaining cheese and serve.

Uses for Tomato Water

- As a poaching liquid for flaky fish or shellfish
- As a base for ceviche or gazpacho
- As a condiment for oysters
- As a base for Bloody Marys and tomato martinis
- As a base for tomato granita

Baked Salmon with Roasted Tomato Relish

MAKES 6 SERVINGS

Heat is your helper when you're jonesing for tomatoes outside of peak season, as Soa Davies (Vol. 2: Tomatoes) has so wisely demonstrated with this recipe. She gives the contents of a flavorful relish a quick session under the broiler, which charges the batteries with concentrated flavor. As-is, it's delicious on fish, but also try pureeing it to use as a sauce over eggs or roasted potatoes.

FOR THE RELISH:

1   pound (455 g) medium tomatoes (such as beefsteak or plum)

2   jalapeños chiles, halved, seeded and chopped

4   scallions, cut into ½-inch slices

2   garlic cloves, thinly sliced

     Salt and freshly ground black pepper

2   teaspoons sumac

¼   cup (60 ml) extra-virgin olive oil

3   tablespoons apple cider vinegar

3   tablespoons chopped chives

FOR THE SALMON:

3   tablespoons extra-virgin olive oil, divided

1   2 - to 3-pound (1.2- to 1.4-kg) side of wild salmon, with skin

     Kosher salt and freshly ground black pepper

Make the relish: Preheat the broiler. Cut the tomatoes in half crosswise. Squeeze the tomato halves to release the seeds and discard the seeds. Cut the tomatoes into 1-inch dice.

In a bowl, combine the tomatoes, jalapeños, scallions and garlic and season generously with salt, pepper and the sumac. Add the oil and toss to coat the tomatoes. Spread the mixture out in single layer on a rimmed baking sheet. Broil the tomatoes until they're caramelized and the jalapeños and scallions are charred, about 8 minutes. Transfer the contents of the baking sheet to a bowl and add the vinegar and chives. Toss well and season to taste with salt and pepper.

Cook the salmon: Preheat the oven to 350°F (175°C). Brush a large baking sheet with 1 tablespoon of oil. Season both sides of the salmon generously with salt and pepper and place it, skin-side down, on the baking sheet. Generously brush the salmon with the remaining oil. Bake the salmon until the edges are golden brown and the flesh just turns opaque, about 10 to 12 minutes.

Transfer the fish to a serving tray, spoon the roasted-tomato relish over the top and serve whole. (You can also divide the cooked fish into portions and distribute them among plates before topping with the relish and serving.)

Room-Service Tomato Sandwich

MAKES 1 SERVING

1   very ripe slicing tomato, such as beefsteak

     Salt and freshly ground black pepper

2   slices white bread (any bread with a little bit of sweetness will work—Pullman, brioche, potato bread, etc.)

¼   cup (60 ml) mayonnaise, homemade (see page 204) or store-bought, divided

½   cup (50 g) finely grated Parmesan cheese

¼   cup (12 g) alfalfa sprouts

There's an entire genre of recipes dedicated to curing hangovers, which is bogus, really, because who wants to cook while hungover? Nobody, that's who.

This recipe won't cure a hangover, but it was born from one. On the room service menu of the Ace Hotel in New York, there's a breakfast sandwich that contains an army of greasy, headache-fighting ingredients: eggs, cheese, bacon—the works. But the most defining article of this morning-after meal (besides the fact that someone will bring it to your bedside) is the broiled cheese that lines the outside walls of the sandwich, *croque-monsieur*-style.

The version we make at home isn't quite so salacious; the tomato and sprouts could even fool someone into thinking it was healthy. But make no mistake: This sandwich has a night of heavy drinking in its bones, and it's all the better for it.

Preheat the broiler.

Cut the tomato crosswise into ½-inch-thick slices and lay them flat on a plate. Sprinkle each slice with salt and pepper and let sit for 10 to 15 minutes.

Arrange the bread on a baking sheet. Spread about 2 teaspoons of mayonnaise on each slice. Sprinkle the Parmesan on top of the mayonnaise and toast the bread under the broiler until the cheese is melted and golden brown, about 3 minutes (watch it carefully, as some broilers are hotter than others).

Let the toast cool slightly. When it's cool enough to handle, turn the bread over and spread the remaining mayonnaise on the untoasted sides of each slice. On one slice, arrange the seasoned tomato slices; on the other slice, arrange the sprouts. Place the slices together, with the cheesy sides facing out. Cut the sandwich in half and serve.

Tomato Sangrita

MAKES 4 SERVINGS

Sangrita is the ultimate chaser. Customarily sipped alongside a glass of blanco tequila, this citrusy, spicy drink hails from tequila's birthplace, in Jalisco, Mexico. Legend has it that the original formula came from the dregs of a popular fruit salad from the same region that contained Sevilla oranges and chile powder. Somehow, tomato juice ended up in the recipe that was later popularized in America, and we're not ashamed of this break from tradition. Our version combines fresh tomato juice—basically an impatient tomato water—with magical pomegranate molasses in place of the usual grenadine. We frequently make this refresher by the pitcherful and serve it instead of Bloody Marys or alongside a bottle of top-shelf agave-based spirits.

If you don't already have a bottle of pomegranate molasses in your kitchen, get one: This tart, musky syrup has limitless potential in cocktails and adds a mysterious punch to sauces and dressings.

2	pounds (910 g) ripe tomatoes
½	cup (120 ml) fresh orange juice
¼	cup (60 ml) fresh lime juice
1	tablespoon pomegranate molasses (available at Middle Eastern markets or online)
½	teaspoon Worcestershire sauce
½	teaspoon Tabasco, or another hot sauce

Cut the tomatoes into quarters and place in a food processor. Puree until smooth. Pass the tomato puree through a fine-mesh strainer into a measuring glass, pressing on the solids to extract as much juice as possible.

Measure out 1¼ cups (300 ml) of juice and pour it into a pint-size (480-ml) jar. Add the remaining ingredients, seal the jar and shake well. Refrigerate until ready to serve.

Tomato & Peach Salad with Tomato Vinaigrette

MAKES 6 SERVINGS

There's a quote attributed to the British humorist Miles Kington that goes "Knowledge is knowing that tomato is a fruit. Wisdom is not putting it in a fruit salad." To this we counter, "Ignorance is never giving it a try."

It's true that tomatoes are usually paired with other vegetables in salads, but we've become fond of matching them with watermelon, strawberries and other summer fruits, most especially peaches. To keep any of these fruit-fruit combinations from tasting like dessert, you need an extra-savory dressing and plenty of herbs. While you should only make this salad during peak season, the tomato vinaigrette can be made year-round with supermarket tomatoes and makes a great no-cook sauce for fish, leafy greens and vegetable side dishes.

1½ pounds (680 g) mixed heirloom tomatoes, sliced crosswise ½ inch thick

2 ripe peaches, pitted and sliced into ¼-inch-thick wedges

½ cup (120 ml) Tomato Vinaigrette (recipe at right)

8 medium basil leaves, torn

1 tablespoon chopped parsley

Coarse sea salt and freshly ground black pepper

On a platter, arrange the tomatoes and peaches in a single, interspersed layer. Drizzle the tomato vinaigrette over the fruit. Scatter the herbs on top, season with salt and pepper and serve.

Tomato Vinaigrette

MAKES 1 CUP (236 ML)

½ cup (90 g) diced ripe tomatoes

1 teaspoon chopped garlic

3 tablespoons fresh lemon juice

3 tablespoons sherry vinegar

Pinch red pepper flakes

¼ cup plus 3 tablespoons (105 ml) extra-virgin olive oil

Salt and freshly ground black pepper

In a bowl, combine all the ingredients and let them sit for 1 hour. Transfer the mixture to a blender or food processor and process until smooth. Refrigerate the vinaigrette until ready to use. The vinaigrette can be made up to 1 day ahead.

Fresh Tomato Bloody Mary

MAKES 1 DRINK

8 ounces (225 g) ripe tomatoes (about 2 medium or 4 small), cut into 1-inch pieces

¼ teaspoon fine sea salt

Coarse salt, for rimming the glass

1½ ounces vodka

2 dashes hot sauce, or more to taste

This is an austere Bloody Mary, meant to highlight the flavor of fresh tomatoes. It's probably more refreshing than you're used to; most Bloody Marys are like street fights in a glass, with aggressive flavors such as horseradish, pepper, pickle brine and other ingredients bullying the poor tomato juice (which itself is often a highly preserved and augmented ingredient). This Bloody Mary is not. The most—the only—important thing is to choose the right tomato. This is a cocktail that you should make only when you can get the most flavorful fruit (and stick with canned or bottled juice the rest of the year).

Place the tomatoes in a large measuring cup. Using a muddler or wooden spoon, muddle the tomatoes thoroughly, until all of the pieces have been broken up and a coarse puree remains. Pass the tomato mixture through a fine-mesh sieve into another measuring cup, pressing and stirring the puree until very little liquid remains in the strainer. You should have about ½ cup (120 ml) of fresh juice (if you're short, muddle another tomato or two). Add the fine sea salt and stir until it's dissolved.

Wet the rim of a highball glass with water and lightly coat it with kosher salt. Fill the glass with ice cubes. Add the vodka, tomato juice, and hot sauce. Stir with a mixing spoon until combined and chilled, then serve.

WILD SHRIMP

There isn't anything particularly new about our collective love of shrimp. Since the 1990s, it's been the most popular seafood in the United States, surpassing even canned tuna by a fair margin. That popularity has led to ubiquity, which isn't necessarily a good thing when you're talking about seafood. Shrimp is cheap and available everywhere a truck or plane can travel. It's not out of place on a buffet, or synthesized as flavoring for a bag of potato chips.

In its rise to prominence, though, shrimp—at least in this country—has had a bit of an identity crisis. Too often, it's stripped of any real seafood flavor, leaving a rubbery, shrimp-shaped lobe of protein behind.

So we've included wild shrimp here not as a directive to eat more of it—actually, quite the contrary. Shrimp shouldn't be a staple: Our oceans can't keep up with that demand. And that's OK with us, because it determines the kind of shrimp we buy and how we prepare it. Wild shrimp from the Atlantic and off the Gulf Coast is usually a safe bet, as are prawns from either coast; avoid shrimp from China and Mexico, which consistently rank very low on sustainability ratings due to the bottom-trawling methods that are used to catch them.

When shrimp is fresh, it's buttery and sweet with a definitive note of salinity. Its shells hold endless flavor that can be harnessed to enrich sauces or stews. It's an ingredient that should elicit a craving, demand an occasion or incite an opportunity to take a break from the other constants of our days and pay attention.

Rock Shrimp Dumplings

MAKES 30 DUMPLINGS

The most famous shrimp dumpling is known to dim sum lovers as *har gow*, and it comes with a mood ring–worthy special effect. When it's steamed, the tapioca flour–based dough turns translucent, allowing the flamingo pink hues of the cooked shrimp to shine through.

This take on shrimp dumplings cribs the simplicity of *har gow*'s filling (shrimp and pork fat) but sidesteps the elaborate process of making dough; we'll take pre-rolled dumpling wrappers, thanks. The trade-off for the time saved? None of *har gow*'s blush-like coloring. But we usually eat these too quickly to even notice.

½   pound (225 g) small shrimp (31 to 40 count) or rock shrimp, peeled

½   teaspoon baking soda

     Fine sea salt

     Ice

1   3-by-3-inch square pork fatback (usually available in the deli section of the grocery store; you can substitute unsmoked bacon here too)

2   scallions, finely chopped

1   garlic clove, finely chopped

1   teaspoon finely chopped fresh ginger

¼   teaspoon ground white pepper

1   teaspoon toasted sesame oil

2   teaspoons rice wine vinegar

1   teaspoon dark soy sauce

30   round or square dumpling wrappers

¼   cup (60 ml) canola oil, optional

Cut each shrimp into 3 pieces and place them in a medium bowl. In a measuring cup, mix ½ cup (120 ml) of water with the baking soda and ½ teaspoon of salt. Stir until the salt has dissolved, then add an additional ½ cup (120 ml) of water and 1 cup (140 g) of ice. Add the shrimp and set aside. This ice brine will help protect the integrity of the shrimp's texture (meaning no rubbery shrimp) and season it to the core.

While the shrimp is brining, bring a small saucepan of water to a boil. Add the fatback and boil for 2 minutes to soften. Drain the fatback, then remove the tough layer from the top and discard. Finely dice the remaining fatback and add it to a medium bowl. Add the scallions, garlic, ginger, white pepper, oil, vinegar and soy sauce. Drain the shrimp, add them to the scallion mixture and toss to combine. Place half of the mixture in a food processor and pulse until it forms a paste. Return it to the bowl and fold the paste into the rest of the shrimp.

On a clean work surface, lay a dumpling wrapper flat. With wet fingers dampen half of the perimeter of the wrapper. Place 1 teaspoon of the filling in the center of the wrapper, then fold it in half; press the sides together firmly and crimp to seal. Repeat with the remaining wrappers and dumpling filling.

Decide if you want to boil, fry or steam the dumplings. To boil them, bring a skillet full of water to a simmer. Working in batches, add the dumplings and cook for 4 minutes. Using a slotted spoon or fine-mesh skimmer, remove the dumplings from the water and serve.

To fry: Heat the canola oil in a skillet over medium heat. Working in batches, add the dumplings to the oil and fry for 2 minutes per side. Transfer to a paper towel–lined plate to drain, then serve.

To steam: Set a bamboo steamer basket lined with parchment paper over a saucepan filled with 1 inch of simmering water. Add the dumplings in an even layer, close the lid and steam for 7 minutes. Serve immediately.

Coconut-Poached Shrimp with Chorizo

MAKES 4 SERVINGS

In our imagination, this recipe reunites high school sweethearts—coconut and shrimp—as accomplished and elegant adults. Their prom photo was full of braces and bad hair in a sweet and adorable way (yes, this is how we think about coconut-fried shrimp), but now they're mature and worldly and destined to rekindle a new kind of partnership.

It may seem like strange calculus to think about cooking shrimp as you would cook risotto. But shrimp appreciate patience and attention; overcooking or flashing them with high heat is the leading cause of rubbery texture. The slow-and-steady process of making risotto, which coaxes a tender creaminess out of rice, seemed like an experiment worth trying with these delicate crustaceans. Using coconut milk instead of broth brings flavor, yes, but also a high fat content that mimics butter and creates a butter-poached effect. Here's to the happy couple.

Canola oil

½   pound (225 g) fresh chorizo, casings removed

1   pound (455 g) medium shrimp (26 to 30 count), peeled, tails removed and deveined

Sea salt

½   red onion, thinly sliced crosswise (across the equator)

2   garlic cloves, smashed

1   15-ounce (430-g) can coconut milk, not shaken, divided

½   cup (20 g) chopped cilantro

Juice of 2 limes

Steamed white rice, for serving

Heat 1 tablespoon of oil in a large skillet over medium-high heat. Add the chorizo and cook, crumbling the sausage into pieces with the back of a wooden spoon, until browned. Transfer the chorizo to a plate and reserve.

Rinse the shrimp and pat them dry. Season generously with salt and place in a medium saucepan with the onion, garlic and 6 tablespoons (90 ml) of the coconut milk. (Use the thick solids that collect at the top of the can first.) Place the pan over medium-low heat and cook, stirring slowly and gently, until the shrimp have turned pink and opaque, about 12 minutes. Add the cilantro, lime juice, reserved chorizo and remaining coconut milk and cook for another minute, stirring to coat everything. Serve with rice.

Lemon- & Pepper-Pickled Shrimp Lettuce Wraps

MAKES 4 SERVINGS

We're quite fond of the country club dish on which this recipe is built. You know the one: frilly lettuce leaves on a quilted glass plate mounted by a mayonnaise-jacketed pyramid of shrimp. It first gained popularity when canned shrimp became widely available after the Civil War. The rich mayonnaise-based sauce was a worthy attempt, we're sure, to hide the tinny flavor of the canned seafood.

With all due respect to the ladies who lunched, we've reconfigured shrimp salad to highlight (and then underline three times) the flavor of shrimp, rather than mask it. First, we swapped in shrimp stock for poaching and shocking the shrimp, reuniting the meat with the intense flavor of its own shells. Then we took cues from America's most shrimp-loving regional cuisine, the Lowcountry of South Carolina, which festoons every potluck table and church picnic with lightly pickled shrimp. Bright and clean lemon juice, not mayonnaise, binds the shrimp here. The lettuce remains, a vestige of the original, but we encourage you to do something that would surely horrify the white-gloved diners of yesteryear: Use it as a wrap to eat with your hands.

2	pounds (910 g) medium shrimp (26 to 30 count)
1	medium carrot, chopped
1	celery stalk, chopped
1	lemon, halved
½	large onion, preferably Vidalia, plus 2 onions, thinly sliced
6	bay leaves, preferably fresh, divided
	Kosher salt and freshly ground black pepper
½	red bell pepper—cored, seeded and diced
2	garlic cloves, very finely chopped
½	cup (120 ml) fresh lemon juice
	Finely grated zest of 2 lemons
¼	teaspoon celery seeds
¼	teaspoon Aleppo pepper or red pepper flakes
1	tablespoon chopped dill fronds
1	head butter leaf lettuce, for serving

Peel the shrimp and place the shells in a large pot. Add 12 cups (2.8 L) of water, the carrot, celery, 1 lemon half, the onion half, 2 bay leaves and 1 tablespoon of salt. Bring the mixture to a boil over high heat, then lower the heat and simmer gently for about 10 minutes to make a flavorful broth. (Alternatively, if you have shrimp stock from page 27 on hand, you could use that.)

Devein the shrimp and set them aside. Fill a large heavy-duty resealable plastic bag with ice cubes. Transfer several cups of the broth to a large heat-proof bowl. Place the ice pack in the bowl of broth and move it around until the broth is well chilled (drain and add more ice to the bag as needed).

Return the heat to high and bring the remaining broth to a rolling boil. Add the shrimp and boil until the meat is white and opaque, 1 to 2 minutes. Do not overcook. Drain the shrimp in a colander and transfer to the chilled liquid to stop the cooking process. Reserve the shrimp stock for another use.

In another large bowl, combine the cooked shrimp, sliced onions, bell pepper, remaining bay leaves, garlic and ½ teaspoon of black pepper. Set aside.

In a large liquid measuring cup, combine the lemon juice, lemon zest, celery seeds, Aleppo pepper and dill. Pour the marinade over the shrimp mixture and stir to coat. Cover and refrigerate for at least 30 minutes and up to 1 hour. Taste and season with salt and pepper.

Divide the shrimp and vegetable mixture into the butter lettuce leaves. Serve immediately.

Prawns with Red Charmoula & Stale Bread

MAKES 4 SERVINGS

1 teaspoon red pepper flakes

1 teaspoon cumin seeds

½ teaspoon coriander seeds

1½ pounds (680 g) head-on prawns (jumbo shrimp work great here, too), shell-on deveined (see Box)

Kosher salt and freshly ground black pepper

¼ cup plus 2 tablespoons (90 ml) olive oil, divided

4 garlic cloves, thinly sliced

½ teaspoon smoked paprika (hot or sweet)

1 tablespoon fresh lemon juice

¼ cup (10 g) chopped parsley or cilantro

Sliced stale bread, preferably something hearty like a country loaf

Lemon slices, for serving

There are a few things that distinguish prawns from shrimp. Prawns are larger than most shrimp; they're harvested in freshwater rather than seawater; and they have more claws than shrimp. Finally, prawns are generally a great purchase with regard to sustainability, and they're regularly listed as a green choice on sustainable seafood watch lists.

Despite what the opposite photo shows (oops!), we prefer to serve prawns whole, heads and all, to get the full effect of their size and sweet flavor (a result of that freshwater environment). This recipe offers a heavily seasoned skillet sauce that, when mixed with the juices of the prawns, is concentrated and absolutely delicious. A note about the heads: We highly recommend slurping the liquid directly from the point of decapitation, but if that isn't for you, consider adding the head juice to the skillet as part of the sauce for soaking your bread.

Using a spice grinder (or mortar and pestle), coarsely grind the pepper flakes, cumin and coriander; set aside.

Season the prawns with salt and pepper. Heat ¼ cup (60 ml) of oil in a large skillet over medium-high heat. Sear the prawns on both sides until they're browned but not quite cooked through, about 2 minutes. Turn the heat down to medium and add the garlic, paprika, reserved spice mixture and the remaining 2 tablespoons of oil. Swirl the skillet to toast the spices and coat the prawns and finish cooking them, about 2 minutes. Remove the pan from the heat and add the lemon juice and parsley. Serve in bowls over bread, or eat right out of the skillet, with lemon slices for additional juice.

Deveining Shrimp

To devein shrimp while keeping the shell on, use a pair of scissors to cut along the back of the shrimp through the shell. Carefully make an incision along the flesh of the shrimp where the vein runs, and use a toothpick to expose it and pull it out.

Stuffed Shells with Shrimp Bolognese

MAKES 4 SERVINGS

This is one of those recipes with a title that threatens disaster but ends up rocking your world. Pristine shrimp takes the place of meat in a classic tomato ragu, adding a touch of sweet, briny flavor, while a quick stock made of the shrimp shells enriches the tomatoey base. The dish was born out of a Feast of the Seven Fishes menu (a Catholic Italian Christmas tradition that eschews meat), but it's delicious enough to eat any time of year.

1	12-ounce (340-g) box dried jumbo pasta shells
2	15-ounce (430-g) containers whole-milk ricotta, drained in a strainer
4	ounces (115 g) smoked mozzarella, grated
½	cup (20 g) basil, roughly chopped
2	eggs
	Kosher salt and freshly ground black pepper
3	tablespoons olive oil, divided, plus more for the pan
2	tablespoons unsalted butter
1	small carrot, diced (about ¼ cup/35 g)
1	medium white onion, diced (about 1¼ cups/140 g)
½	fennel bulb, diced (about ½ cup/43 g)
1	teaspoon fennel seeds
¼	teaspoon thyme leaves
¼	teaspoon chopped rosemary
¼	teaspoon chopped oregano
1	28-ounce (785-g) can crushed San Marzano tomatoes with their juices
1	pound (455 g) medium (26 to 30 count) shell-on shrimp
½	cup (50 g) freshly grated Parmesan cheese, plus more for serving

Preheat the oven to 375°F (190°C). Bring a large pot of salted water to a boil. Add the pasta and cook until al dente. Drain the pasta and spread it out on a tray to cool (discard any broken shells).

In a large mixing bowl, combine the ricotta, mozzarella, basil, eggs, 1½ teaspoons of salt and a few grinds of black pepper. When the shells have cooled enough to handle, spoon a generous tablespoon of the cheese mixture into each shell. Coat the bottom of a 9-by-13-inch pan with 1 tablespoon of oil and arrange the shells in an even layer. Cover and refrigerate while you make the Bolognese.

In a medium saucepan, melt the butter and add the carrot, onion, fennel, fennel seeds, thyme, rosemary, oregano and 1½ teaspoons of salt. Cook over low heat until the vegetables are softened and translucent but not caramelized, about 15 minutes. Stir in the canned tomatoes and simmer over low heat for 30 minutes.

Meanwhile, peel and devein the shrimp, reserving the shells. Chop the shrimp into ½-inch chunks and set aside.

Layer the shrimp shells between paper towels and squeeze to get the water out. In a medium saucepan, heat 1 tablespoon of oil until just smoking. Add the shrimp shells and cook over high heat for 5 to 7 minutes, or until browned and very fragrant. Add 2 cups (480 ml) of water and boil for 10 minutes, or until the liquid is reduced by half. Strain the shrimp stock through a fine-mesh sieve into the tomato sauce, cover and cook the sauce for 30 minutes.

Spoon about half of the sauce over the stuffed shells and top with ½ cup (50 g) of Parmesan. Transfer the pan to the oven and bake, uncovered, for 30 minutes, or until the sauce is bubbling.

While the pasta is baking, heat the remaining tablespoon of oil in the same nonstick pan you used for the shrimp shells. When it's almost smoking, add the chopped shrimp, sprinkle with 1 teaspoon of salt and cook, stirring occasionally, until the shrimp are lightly browned and cooked through, about 4 minutes. Add to the remaining sauce and toss thoroughly to warm through.

Divide the shells among four plates and top with a big scoop of the shrimp sauce. Add more Parmesan on top, if desired.

The Shrimp Stock You Should Be Making but Probably Aren't

MAKES 6 CUPS (1.4 L)

We're in a cooking era that values freshness over all else, so it's easy to overlook one of the most powerful and useful tools in your kitchen: the freezer. Let this recipe remind you that your icebox should be your ride-or-die chick.

Thanks to the freezer, we can compile this recipe piecemeal as a way to avoid wasting something full of flavor. Whenever we cook a dish that requires peeling shrimp, we freeze the shells in a resealable plastic bag. Once we've gathered enough to make this recipe, we go to work. Then we turn to the freezer again to preserve this stock, and we return to it another day to bolster a seafood pasta (in lieu of clam juice), enrich a soup or to create a pan-sauce for fish.

2	tablespoons vegetable oil
2	pounds (910 g) shrimp shells (with heads, if possible)
1	tablespoon tomato paste
2	celery stalks, chopped
1	large onion, chopped
1	fennel bulb, chopped
1	head garlic, halved crosswise
1	tablespoon black peppercorns
2	bay leaves (preferably fresh)
	Kosher salt
1	piece (about 6 by 5 inches) kombu kelp, optional

In a large heavy-bottomed pot, heat the oil over medium-high heat. When it shimmers, add the shrimp shells and cook, stirring occasionally, until they're bright pink and starting to brown, about 5 minutes. Add the tomato paste and stir to coat. Cook, stirring occasionally, until the tomato paste turns brick red, about 4 minutes. Add the celery, onion, fennel, garlic, peppercorns and bay leaves. Season with salt and cook, stirring occasionally, until the vegetables are softened and starting to brown in spots, about 10 minutes. Add 8 cups (2 L) of water and stir to loosen any browned bits from the bottom of the pan.

Reduce the heat to medium-low and simmer gently, until the liquid has reduced by about a third, about 60 to 70 minutes. Taste the broth; it should be rich, briny and flavorful. If it seems watery, let it simmer a little longer. Remove the stock from the heat and add the kombu (it's optional, but it will add another level of depth and umami to the final result). Let the kombu steep for 30 minutes before straining the stock and pouring into containers to cool and freeze for up to 3 months.

Learning to Count

Often in recipes (including many in this chapter), shrimp will be identified by a "count" that comes in a range such as 26 to 30 or 21 to 25. It refers to the size (the bigger the numbers, the smaller the shrimp—confusing, we know), but more specifically, it's an average number of shrimp per pound (455 g). So 26 to 30 means that you'll have roughly 26 to 30 shrimp in every 1-pound (455-g) measure.

Salt-&-Pepper Shrimp with Chiles

MAKES 4 SERVINGS

1 cup (130 g) cornstarch

½ teaspoon black peppercorns

½ teaspoon Szechuan peppercorns

1 teaspoon kosher salt

¼ teaspoon Chinese five-spice powder

Canola oil, for frying

1 pound (455 g) medium shrimp (26 to 30 count), shell-on, deveined (see the box on page 266)

1 large jalapeño chile, thinly sliced crosswise

For most, shrimp shells are waste, just a wrapper that protects the tender meat of the shrimp. But this recipe, which takes cues from San Francisco chef Charles Phan's fried squid with pineapple and chiles, exaggerates the shells and shows off their merits. By cutting through the back of each shrimp, all sides of the shells are exposed to the hot fry oil, and they crisp up into edible glass that shatters with each bite. The Szechuan peppercorns in the dredge and fried jalapeño chile rings add a kick; if you want less heat, remove the seeds of the fresh chile.

Place the cornstarch in a medium bowl. Using a spice grinder (or mortar and pestle), coarsely grind the black and Szechuan peppercorns. Add the salt and five-spice powder and mix to combine. Add 1 teaspoon of the salt mixture to the cornstarch and whisk to combine. Reserve the remaining salt mixture.

Heat 3 inches of oil in a large heavy-bottomed pot. Line a bowl with paper towels and set aside. Add half of the shrimp to the bowl containing the cornstarch and dredge, turning to coat on all sides. When the oil registers 375°F (190°C) on a deep-fry thermometer, add the dredged shrimp to the oil and fry until the shrimp are bright pink and the cornstarch coating is crisp and light golden, about 3 minutes. Using a slotted spoon, transfer the shrimp to the paper towel–lined bowl. Repeat the dredging and frying process with the remaining shrimp, allowing the oil to return to temperature between each batch.

Add the second batch of fried shrimp to the bowl with the first batch and let drain briefly. Add the chile rings to the oil and fry for 10 seconds; using a slotted spoon, remove them from the oil and transfer to the bowl with the shrimp. Remove the paper towels from the bowl and discard. Add the remaining salt-and-pepper mixture to the shrimp and toss to coat. Serve right away (we can't resist eating these with our hands, but you could serve them with chopsticks, too).

Shrimp Cocktail with Sauce Verte

MAKES 4 SERVINGS (WITH 1½ CUPS/360 ML SAUCE)

Salt and freshly ground black pepper

1 pound (455 g) large to jumbo shrimp (21 to 25 count), shell-on

4 ounces (115 g) bagged or 1 large bunch watercress, tough stems removed (1½ cups/55 g)

2 cups (100 g) parsley sprigs, large stems removed

¼ cup (11 g) chopped chives

1 tablespoon chopped tarragon

1 cup (240 ml) mayonnaise

2 tablespoons sour cream

1 tablespoon Dijon mustard

1 teaspoon fresh lemon juice

¼ teaspoon hot sauce

Most of the time, room-temperature seafood sends us packing. We'll take it piping hot or nicely chilled, but nothing in between. Shrimp cocktail is the exception to that rule: The middle ground is a boon to the shrimp's sweet flavor and keeps the texture from turning fibrous. Since there's nothing but salt in the poaching liquid, the key to this recipe is using the freshest, most pristine shrimp you can buy. Poach them, let them rest while you make the bright green sauce, then enjoy immediately.

Cook the shrimp: In a medium saucepan, bring 2 quarts (2 L) of water to a boil, and set up a large bowl of ice water next to the stove. Add 4 tablespoons (67 g) of salt to the boiling water. Add the shrimp and cook, stirring occasionally, until they turn opaque, about 5 to 6 minutes. Using a slotted spoon, transfer the shrimp to the ice bath to stop the cooking. Let the shrimp sit for about 5 minutes, then drain.

Make the sauce: In a medium saucepan, bring 2 quarts (2 L) of water to a boil, and set up a large bowl of ice water next to the stove. Liberally salt the boiling water, then add the watercress and blanch it for 30 seconds. Strain the watercress and transfer it to the ice water to stop cooking. Drain the cooled watercress and squeeze out any excess water.

Transfer the watercress to a blender along with the parsley, chives, tarragon, mayonnaise, sour cream, mustard, lemon juice, hot sauce, and ¼ teaspoon each of salt and pepper. Pulse a few times, then blend until smooth. Cover and refrigerate until ready to use.

Peel the shrimp and serve at room temperature or just lightly chilled with the sauce verte.

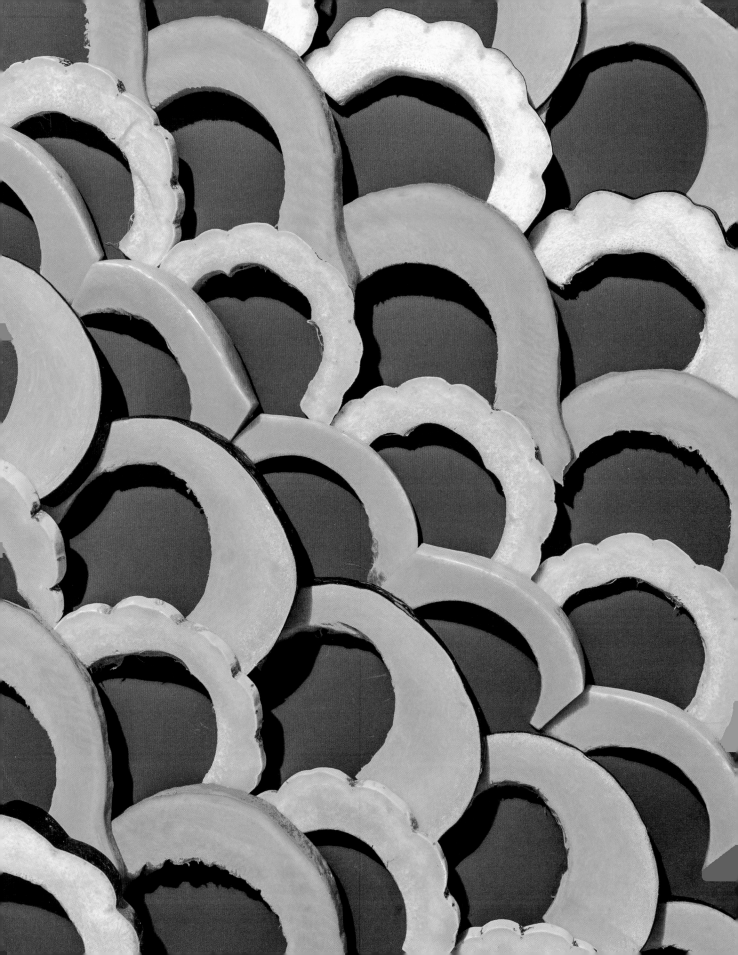

WINTER SQUASH

Of all the ingredients featured in this book, winter squash is the most deeply rooted in American food culture. It was a staple crop for Native Americans centuries before the Europeans bullied their way onto the continent, and it was one of the foodstuffs that allowed the settlers to survive those precarious first years.

Today, squash still helps us get through many a winter, especially when we're trolling the aisles of a giant supermarket in February, hunting for fresh produce that hasn't been shipped halfway across the world or picked weeks ahead of ripeness. And it seems as though every year we get new varieties to play with: delicata and kabocha have become more pervasive of late, while hubbard, ambercup and sweet dumpling are finding their place in the rotation. Although these squash have the advantage of being mostly interchangeable in recipes, each has distinct characteristics that create allegiances. Spaghetti squash, has that unmistakable shredded flesh that we take as Mother Nature's directive to make latkes (see page 280). Tender delicata, meanwhile, is the low-maintenance, jeans and T-shirt member of the bunch, with a thin flesh that doesn't require peeling and seeds that make excellent snacks.

Winter squash's seasonal designation didn't make much sense to us in the past: It's grown in the spring and summer and harvested in the fall. But we've come to rely on the misnomer as a reminder that, come December, we'll have plenty of fresh, nutrient-packed vegetables to get us through another winter.

Roasted Delicata Squash & Seeds with Za'atar

MAKES 4 SERVINGS

1 medium delicata squash (about 1 pound/455 g), sliced into ¼-inch rings (with seeds)

2 garlic cloves, smashed

1 teaspoon za'atar (or vadouvan), plus more for serving

¼ cup plus 2 tablespoons (90 ml) extra-virgin olive oil, divided

Kosher salt and freshly ground black pepper

1 cup (40 g) cilantro leaves, coarsely chopped

½ cup (25 g) mint leaves, torn

¼ cup (13 g) dill, roughly chopped

¾ cup (180 ml) full-fat Greek yogurt or labne (see page 156)

1 lemon, cut into wedges, for serving

Flaky sea salt, such as Maldon

We don't usually roast squash seeds along with the flesh. Honestly, we don't roast squash seeds much at all (too much picking through slimy flesh, too many chewy hulls). But Alison Roman (Vol. 13: Lemons) taught us that delicata squash seeds are, as the name implies, delicate and quite crunchy when roasted. The extended roasting time first softens, then firms up the thin slices of squash, resulting in a concentrated sweet flavor that can take on a bunch of other bright flavors (herbs, zesty za'atar, rich yogurt) without getting lost.

Preheat the oven to 425°F (220°C). In a medium bowl, toss the squash, garlic and za'atar with ¼ cup (60 ml) of oil and season with salt and pepper. Transfer the squash to a rimmed baking sheet and roast, turning the squash occasionally, until it's caramelized and golden brown on both sides and the seeds are crispy, 35 to 45 minutes.

Let the squash cool in the pan, then sprinkle with the cilantro, mint and dill and toss gently with a spatula, making sure you get all the crispy seeds from the pan. Spoon a bit of yogurt onto four plates or all of it on the bottom of a serving platter. Scatter the squash, seeds and herbs on top of the yogurt, then drizzle the remaining 2 tablespoons of oil over that. Squeeze a lemon wedge over the whole thing, sprinkle with more za'atar and flaky salt and serve with more lemon wedges alongside.

Maple-Roasted Squash Tartines

MAKES 4 SERVINGS

The combination of caramelized onions and cider vinegar creates a lively sweet-and-sour base for mashed squash. Adapt the serving vessel to your desire: Spread on large slices of toasted bread, this can be served as an open-faced sandwich; use thinner baguette rounds and it becomes crostini. Or skip the bread altogether for a big-flavored side dish.

1	2½- to 3-pound (1.2- to 1.4-kg) winter squash, such as butternut, kabocha or cheese pumpkin
½	cup (120 ml) extra-virgin olive oil, divided
½	teaspoon red pepper flakes
	Kosher salt and freshly ground black pepper
2	medium onions, halved and cut into ¼-inch slices
¼	cup (60 ml) maple syrup
¼	cup (60 ml) apple cider vinegar
4	large slices toasted rustic bread
	Thyme and/or mint leaves

Preheat the oven to 450°F (230°C). Peel and seed the squash, then cut into roughly 1-inch pieces. In a bowl, toss the squash with ¼ cup (60 ml) of oil, the red pepper flakes, 1 teaspoon of salt and ¼ teaspoon of pepper. Scatter on a rimmed baking sheet and roast for 20 minutes, or until tender when pierced with a knife.

While the squash cooks, heat the remaining ¼ cup (60 ml) of oil in a large heavy skillet over medium-high heat. Stir in the onions and ½ teaspoon of salt; cover and cook for 15 minutes. Uncover the skillet and continue cooking, stirring occasionally, until the onions are caramelized, about 25 to 35 minutes longer. Stir in the maple syrup and vinegar and simmer until the mixture is jammy, about 10 minutes. Remove the skillet from the heat. Using a fork, mash the squash into the onion mixture, then season to taste with salt and pepper.

Spread the squash on the toast and sprinkle with the thyme. Serve.

Pickled Butternut Squash

MAKES 2 PINTS (TK G)

We're not sure why pickled winter squash isn't more abundant, particularly when its warm-weather equivalent, summer squash, is preserved in vinegar with such zeal (here's looking at you, chowchow). But hopefully this recipe can be the beginning of a campaign in your kitchen to even the scales. We like to shave the butternut squash very thinly so that it softens up in the brine, but you could cut the squash into thicker sticks if you want to preserve a little bit of crunch. We love these pickles slotted into sandwiches; as the centerpiece of a salad with caramelized onions, pecans and feta; or served with charcuterie.

1	butternut squash (1½ to 2 pounds)
2	cups (480 ml) red wine vinegar
1	cup (200 g) sugar
2	tablespoons salt
1	tablespoon black peppercorns
4	whole allspice berries
4	whole cloves
2	cardamom pods, smashed
2	whole star anise
1	tablespoon yellow mustard seeds
1	¼-inch-thick coin fresh ginger

Peel the squash and halve lengthwise. Scoop out and discard the seeds. Very thinly slice the squash and cut each piece into 2-inch lengths. Place the squash in a nonreactive container.

In a saucepan over medium heat, stir the vinegar, 2 cups (480 ml) water, the sugar and salt together until the sugar has dissolved. Add the peppercorns, allspice, cloves, cardamom, star anise, mustard seeds and ginger and bring to a boil. Remove the brine from the heat and pour over the squash. Let the mixture cool completely, then cover and refrigerate overnight before using. The pickles will keep in an airtight container in the refrigerator for up to 1 month.

Spaghetti Squash Latkes

MAKES 6 SERVINGS

1	medium spaghetti squash (about 3 pounds/1.5 kg)
1	tablespoon olive oil
8	scallions, minced
1	jalapeño chile, stem and seeds removed, minced
1	garlic clove, minced
1	teaspoon ground coriander
1	teaspoon ground cumin
1	teaspoon red pepper flakes
2	small russet potatoes, peeled
3	large eggs, beaten
¼	cup (30 g) all-purpose flour
	Fine sea salt
2	cups (480 ml) canola oil
	Sour cream, for serving

If we're being honest, spaghetti squash isn't our favorite member of the winter squash family; its flavor and color are far more muted than other varieties. But the delightful formation of its flesh, resembling the noodles for which it's named, is a characteristic worth playing up in the kitchen. When the squash is matched with grated potato in a spice-forward version of a latke, the squash's natural strands operate like a tightly choreographed drill team, keeping the batter together with a minimum of added flour. For a gluten-free version, swap chickpea flour in for all-purpose.

Preheat the oven to 375°F (190°C). Prick the spaghetti squash all over with the tip of a knife, then place it on a baking sheet and cook for 1½ hours, until tender. Let the squash cool slightly, then cut the squash in half lengthwise and carefully spoon out the flesh. Measure 4 cups (980 g) of the squash and reserve; save any remaining squash for another use.

Heat the olive oil in a medium skillet over medium heat. Add the scallions, jalapeño and garlic and cook until softened, about 5 minutes. Add the coriander, cumin and pepper flakes and cook until the spices are fragrant, about 2 minutes. Transfer the mixture to a large bowl and let cool.

Grate the potatoes on the large holes of a box grater (you should have about 2 cups/340 g), then place in the center of a kitchen towel or a piece of cheesecloth. Bring the ends of the towel together to form a bundle and twist to drain all excess moisture from the potatoes. Add the potatoes to the spice mixture, along with the reserved squash, eggs, flour and 1 teaspoon salt.

Wipe out the skillet and add the oil so that the pan is a quarter full. Heat on medium-high heat until the oil is shimmering, then, working in batches, add ¼-cup (60-ml) scoops of batter to the oil, taking care not to crowd the pan. Cook the latkes until golden brown on both sides, 3 to 4 minutes a side. Transfer to a paper towel–lined plate and keep warm while you fry the remaining latkes.

Serve the latkes immediately with sour cream on the side.

Kabocha Squash & Dashi Soup

MAKES 4 SERVINGS

Kabocha (aka Japanese pumpkin) is the golden retriever of the squash family: fluffy, sweet and exceptionally eager to please. We like it best without a lot of adornment, a predilection we picked up from a strikingly simple dish of dashi-steamed kabocha served at Chiyono, a now-defunct Japanese restaurant in Manhattan's East Village. Remember the hullabaloo about "figs on a plate"? Well, this was literally squash on a plate. But it tasted like so much more.

Here, we simmer the squash in dashi, the seaweed-based broth that's elemental in Japanese cooking, and puree everything into a soup. Like chicken stock, dashi is so much better when it's homemade—and can be used in just as many ways as its poultry counterpart. Think of it as liquid umami, and you'll have no problem coming up with other applications.

3½ cups (840 ml) Dashi (recipe at right)

3 tablespoons mirin

1 tablespoon low-sodium soy sauce

1 teaspoon sugar

1 2-pound (910-g) kabocha squash—halved, seeded and cut into 1½-inch wedges (1¼ pounds/570 g peeled butternut or acorn squash can be used as a substitute)

Kosher salt

Finely chopped scallion greens and chile oil, for serving

In a medium saucepan, bring the dashi, mirin, soy sauce and sugar to a boil. Add the squash, cover and simmer over moderately low heat until tender, about 10 minutes. (It's OK if it's not fully submerged.) Using tongs, transfer the squash to a work surface. When the squash is cool enough to handle, scoop the flesh off of the skin and return to the saucepan and let cool until warm.

Use an immersion blender or transfer the mixture to a stand blender to puree. Season with salt. Heat to the desired serving temperature and ladle into bowls. Garnish the soup with scallion greens and a few drops of chile oil and serve.

Dashi

MAKES ABOUT 3½ CUPS (840 ML)

Many Japanese cooks make this savory stock using an instant powder (and you can as well), but the flavor is so much more complex when you use dried bonito (flakes of smoked, dried skipjack tuna) and kombu (dried sea kelp). It takes a little more time but very little effort. The only tricky part can be finding the ingredients, which are usually available at Asian markets or the Asian section of well-stocked supermarkets.

1 2-inch piece of kombu

2 cups (30 g) bonito shavings

In a medium saucepan, cover the kombu with 4 cups (960 ml) of water and let stand for 1 hour.

Bring the water to a simmer over moderate heat and remove the kombu before it boils. Add the bonito and simmer for 1 minute. Cover the saucepan, remove from the heat and let stand for 10 minutes. Strain the dashi through a fine-mesh sieve or cheesecloth. The dashi can be refrigerated for up to 1 week or frozen up to 1 month.

Cheese-Stuffed Roasted Pumpkin

MAKES 10 TO 12 SERVINGS

This recipe comes from Ian Knauer (Vol. 1: Eggs), who adapted it from Ruth Reichl, his former boss at *Gourmet* magazine. As the pumpkin roasts, it shrivels and shrinks slightly as its rich filling mingles with the softened flesh and forms a self-contained fondue that will make an arresting centerpiece at your next fall-winter holiday or dinner party.

1   baguette, cut into ½-inch slices

1   cheese pumpkin (about 7 pounds/3.2 kg)

    Salt and freshly ground black pepper

1½ cups (360 ml) heavy cream

½   teaspoon grated nutmeg

1   cup (240 ml) white wine

5   cups (550 g) coarsely grated Gruyère or Cheddar cheese

1   tablespoon olive oil

Preheat the oven to 450°F (230°C).

Arrange the bread on two baking sheets and toast until the tops are crisped (the bread might not take on any color), about 7 minutes. Transfer to a rack to cool.

Remove the top of the pumpkin by cutting a circle around the stem with a small knife (like you did as a kid when carving pumpkins); reserve the pumpkin top. Scrape out the seeds and loose fibers with a large spoon (including from the top of the pumpkin; save these seeds for roasting if desired). Season the inside of the pumpkin with a few pinches of salt. In a bowl, whisk together the cream, nutmeg, 1 teaspoon of salt and ½ teaspoon of pepper.

Add a layer of toasted bread to the bottom of the pumpkin, then sprinkle some of the wine over the bread and cover the bread with about 1 cup (110 g) of cheese. Drizzle about ½ cup (120 ml) of the cream mixture over everything. Continue layering the bread, wine, cheese and cream mixture until the pumpkin is filled almost to the top. Pour any leftover cream mixture over the filling, letting it seep in.

Cover the pumpkin with its lid and place it inside a small roasting pan or on a baking sheet. Brush the outside of the pumpkin all over with oil. Bake the pumpkin until it's tender and the filling has puffed, 75 to 90 minutes. Serve the pumpkin whole with a large spoon for scooping out the filling.

Farro Salad with Roasted Squash

MAKES 4 TO 6 SERVINGS

1	small butternut squash (about 1½ pounds/680 g)—peeled, seeded and cut into ½-inch cubes
1	large red onion, halved and cut into ½-inch slices
3	tablespoons olive oil
	Kosher salt and freshly ground black pepper
3	rosemary sprigs
4	cups (960 ml) apple cider
4	cups (960 ml) chicken or vegetable stock
2	cups (400 g) farro
⅓	cup (75 ml) cider vinegar
2	tablespoons pure maple syrup
½	cup (120 ml) extra-virgin olive oil
1	cup (50 g) coarsely chopped parsley
½	cup (55 g) chopped roasted almonds
½	cup (50 g) shaved hard cheese (Parmigiano-Reggiano, aged goat cheese, a good Cheddar, etc.)

The rice pilaf of our era, farro salad is something we cook more often than we'll ever admit. It's become something of a Sunday ritual: Cook some farro, scan our refrigerator for fading produce, combine with farro. So turning this leftover catchall into a recipe was kind of weird, but we're using it to highlight our favorite way to pack more flavor into the salad: Cook the grains in a mixture of apple cider and chicken (or vegetable) stock. Take that method and tweak the rest of the recipe as you like, though the sweet roasted squash (and any kind works in this, really) is a great backbone for making this a meal.

At the store, you might encounter three versions of this ancient grain: whole, pearled and semi-pearled. Whole farro contains more nutrients but cooks more slowly, and it often needs to be soaked before cooking. Most of what we find at the store is semi-pearled. If your package doesn't say, then you'll find out when you cook it! Whole farro takes about 60 minutes to cook; semi-pearled around 30 minutes and pearled as little as 15 minutes.

Preheat the oven to 450°F (230°C). In a large bowl, toss the squash with the onion and olive oil and season with salt and pepper. Spread the squash in an even layer on a rimmed baking sheet and top with the onion slices and rosemary sprigs. Roast, stirring a few times, until the squash is tender and caramelized in spots, about 30 minutes. Remove the squash from the oven and discard the rosemary.

Meanwhile, in a saucepan, combine the cider, stock and 1 tablespoon of salt. Bring the mixture to a boil and skim any foam that rises to the surface. Add the farro, reduce the heat to medium and simmer until the farro is cooked through but still has some bite (it should be pleasant to chew), about 15 to 60 minutes depending on the kind of farro you're using. (If you run out of liquid, add small amounts of water as needed.) While the farro cooks, whisk together the vinegar, maple syrup and extra-virgin olive oil in a small bowl and season to taste with salt. Drain the farro in a strainer and let it cool, giving it the occasional stir.

In a serving bowl, toss the farro with the vinaigrette. Add the squash, onion, parsley, almonds and cheese; toss again and serve.

Chai Hummingbird Cake

MAKES ONE 9-INCH CAKE

Hummingbird cake is a 1970s-born convergence of spice cake, banana bread and fruitcake. A combination of bananas and pineapple usually keeps the cake moist, while nuts puncture each bite with crunch. Using acorn squash in lieu of bananas and upping the spice quotient with cardamom and ginger works on two levels: It modernizes this dessert while redeeming an object of pop-culture absurdity: the pumpkin spice latte. As with any cake, make sure that the layers are completely cool before attempting to frost and assemble.

Make the cake: Preheat the oven to 400°F (205°C). Place the squash halves cut-side up in a baking pan. Drizzle 2 tablespoons of oil over the halves and rub all over to coat. Cook for 1 hour, until the squash is fork-tender. Let cool. Spoon the flesh out of the skins and mash it in a bowl. Measure 2 cups (490 g) of squash flesh and set aside (you can save any leftover flesh for another use; it'll keep for 3 to 4 days in the refrigerator).

Reduce the oven heat to 350°F (175°C). Grease three 9-inch cake pans and dust them with flour.

In a large bowl, whisk together the flour, baking soda, salt, sugars and spices. Add the remaining oil and the eggs and stir until incorporated. Add the vanilla, pineapple, almonds, coconut and reserved squash flesh. Mix until combined, then divide the batter among the three pans. Bake for 30 minutes, until a cake tester inserted in the center comes out clean. Let the cakes cool for 10 minutes, then carefully flip them out onto wire racks and let cool completely.

Make the frosting: In a stand mixer fitted with the paddle attachment, combine the confectioners' sugar, cream cheese, butter and vanilla and beat until thoroughly combined.

Assemble the cake: Set 1 cake layer on a platter. Spread with ¾ cup (180 ml) of the frosting. Stack another layer on top, and repeat with another layer of frosting. Add the final cake layer, and use the remaining frosting to cover the top of the cake (and the sides, if you like). The leftover cake can be covered and refrigerated for up to 3 days.

FOR THE CAKE:

- 2 acorn squash, halved, seeds removed
- 1⅓ cups plus 2 tablespoons (390 ml) canola oil, divided
- 3 cups (375 g) all-purpose flour, plus more for dusting
- 1 teaspoon baking soda
- 1½ teaspoons salt
- 1½ cups (300 g) granulated sugar
- ½ cup (55 g) packed dark brown sugar
- 1 teaspoon ground cardamom
- 1 teaspoon ground ginger
- ½ teaspoon ground cinnamon
- ¼ teaspoon black pepper
- ¼ teaspoon ground nutmeg
- ¼ teaspoon ground cloves
- 3 eggs
- 1 teaspoon pure vanilla extract
- 1 8-ounce (225-g) can crushed pineapple, with its juices
- 1 cup (110 g) chopped almonds
- 1 cup (85 g) unsweetened coconut flakes

FOR THE FROSTING:

- 4 cups (500 g) confectioners' sugar
- 2 8-ounce (225-g) packages cream cheese, softened
- ½ cup (1 stick/115 g) unsalted butter, softened
- 1½ teaspoons pure vanilla extract

MENUS

BRUNCH

We get why brunch gets a bad rap: sourpuss waitstaff, the same old tired offerings and endless lines make us wonder why on earth we got out of bed. The solution? Make brunch at home, and have your guests pick up coffee en route.

TRYING TO EAT HEALTHY WITHOUT BEING ANTISOCIAL

One of the most difficult parts about a specific diet is that it makes cooking for a group more challenging. These recipes are among those we turn to most frequently to satisfy the gluten-free or red-meat eschewers of the bunch.

PEACOCK IN THE KITCHEN

Cooking is one of our favorite ways to strut our stuff, whether we're trying to impress a date or a parent. This menu requires some time to execute, but it'll make you look like a rock star, and lots of the components can be made ahead.

BEYOND THE HAMBURGER

Come summer, we hit our burger stride hard. So hard, in fact, that by August we're pretty maxed out on beef patties and coleslaws. These recipes keep the spirit of everyone's favorite summer dishes while providing much-needed variation.

GAME DAY

We may squabble internally about NFL teams (Kaitlyn is a die-hard Packers fan; Nick roots for the Vikings), but at least we can agree on the snacks. Pick one or all of these recipes, add beer and breathe in the victory.

THINGS TO BRING TO A DINNER PARTY INSTEAD OF WINE

Wine is a default hostess gift for good reason, but sometimes the one-size-fits-all approach falls short. We lean on these recipes as thoughtful alternatives to the bottle.

TUESDAY NIGHT QUICKIE

This dinner doesn't require much active kitchen time, but you'd never know it by the end result, which feels (and tastes) carefully produced.

A MEAL MADE OF SNACKS

We can get annoyed by the ubiquity of the "small bite" approach that so many restaurants seem to take these days, but sometimes it's exactly how we like to eat—more grazing than dining. When you're in that "can't make up my mind" mood, here's an array that will satisfy. (All of these also make great party snacks.)

DINNER AS A BAND-AID

We mark both the good and the bad moments in life at the dinner table. These recipes do a particularly good job at ameliorating the pain of the latter. Whether it's breakups, job losses or deaths in the family, let your fork soothe.

WEEKEND RENTAL

Cooking on vacation can be relaxing, if you know how to accurately assess the (often very limited) tools at your disposal. Our rule: Keep it simple. Our worst beach- or ski-house meals were the ones where we expected too much of the electric range or dull knives.

"SURE, BRING THE KIDS."

There's that moment in life when suddenly you and/or all your friends have babies, and socializing comes with certain requisites. These recipes are kid-tested and family-approved.

MAKE IT AHEAD

We all have those friends who pull together a dinner party with what seems like an effortless flick of the wrist. What we've discovered, though, is that these people all share a reliance on recipes that can be made almost entirely ahead of time. Want to join their ranks? Start here.

APPLES

SOURCING

Selecting apples for cooking is largely a matter of preference. Most types work well in both raw and cooked preparations, but where they lie on the sweet-tart spectrum varies and depends on individual taste. There are, however, a few varieties—namely Fuji and Honeycrisp—that are best eaten raw because of their crisp texture and the fact that their subtle aromas don't hold up as well as other varieties during cooking. Conversely, there are a few varieties—including McIntosh, Rome and Empire—that have less appealing textures when raw and really benefit from cooking.

When buying apples, give them a sniff; they should have an appley aroma. Then give them a squeeze: If you're not going to cook the apples, avoid any with bruises or soft spots (bruised apples are fine for cooking). If the entire apple feels soft, it's overripe or old.

STORING

Apples will keep for months in the crisper drawer of your refrigerator. To keep them fresh for extended periods of time, store them in a sealed plastic bag to keep the humidity level high. Because apples release ethylene gas, keep them away from other produce that's sensitive to ethylene, such as broccoli, carrots, cucumbers, leafy greens, parsley, squash and strawberries.

YIELDS & CONVERSIONS

1 pound (455 g) apples = 2 large or 3 medium apples

1 large apple = 2 cups coarsely chopped = 1½ cups finely chopped

1 medium apple = 1⅓ cups coarsely chopped = 1½ cups finely chopped

FLAVOR BUDDIES

Bay leaf	Chives	Parsley
Butter	Cinnamon	Pork
Cabbage	Cumin	Poultry
Caramel	Ginger	Raisins
Cardamom	Hazelnuts	Rhubarb
Celery	Maple syrup	Rosemary
Cheese (Gruyère, Cheddar)	Nuts	
	Olive oil	

BACON

SOURCING	STORING
There are many styles of bacon but, as with other types of meat, the best will be made from organic pork raised without antibiotics (the package will say so). In order to be considered bacon, pork belly must cured—even so-called uncured bacon has been cured, albeit without the use of sodium nitrate or sodium nitrite (for more on this, see page 47). Most commercial bacon is wet cured in a brine or injected with brine (called "pumped" bacon). Dry-cured bacon has been rubbed with salt, sodium nitrite, sugar and spices. Not all bacon is smoked, but unsmoked bacon won't taste as bacony. Hickory-smoked bacon is usually the most smoky tasting, while other woods yield a more mild flavor.	Bacon can be wrapped tightly in plastic and refrigerated for up to 10 days. If the bacon smells off or is slimy, discard it. You can also freeze individual slices of bacon: layer them in wax or parchment paper and store them inside a resealable plastic bag for up to 2 months. Rendered bacon fat can be refrigerated for up to 1 week or frozen for several months.

YIELDS & CONVERSIONS

Bacon comes in various thicknesses. We like to buy slab bacon.
1 pound (455 g) bacon = 30 to 35 thin (about $\frac{1}{32}$ inch) strips = 16 to 20 regular (about $\frac{1}{16}$ inch) strips = 12 to 16 thick-cut (about $\frac{1}{8}$ inch) strips

1 pound (455 g) bacon = about 1 cup (240 g) of rendered fat

FLAVOR BUDDIES

Apples	Maple syrup	Salmon
Avocados	Mayonnaise	Scallops
Brussels sprouts	Mushrooms	Shallots
Butter	Onions	Spinach
Greens	Parsnips	Tomatoes
Lentils	Potatoes	

BRUSSELS SPROUTS

SOURCING	STORING
The freshest brussels sprouts will be those that come still attached to the stalk. Heads should be bright green with tightly packed leaves; avoid any with yellowing leaves. If you can't find a stalk, look for sprouts that have been freshly cut (the stem end shouldn't be brown and dried up). While sprouts range in size from ½ inch to 2 inches, we usually go for ones about 1 inch in diameter.	Fresh brussels sprouts should be stored in a plastic bag and refrigerated for up to 5 days. Don't wash sprouts until just before using. Blanched sprouts can be frozen for up to 1 year.

YIELDS & CONVERSIONS

1 pound (455 g) brussels sprouts = 4 cups

FLAVOR BUDDIES

Apples
Apple cider
Bacon
Bread crumbs
Butter
Cheese (especially blue, goat and Parmesan)
Chives
Cream
Dijon mustard

Garlic
Lemon
Nutmeg
Nuts
Parsley
Potatoes
Shallots
Thyme
Vinegar

BUTTER

SOURCING	STORING
By law, all butter in America contains at least 80 percent butterfat. European-style butter often contains more fat, up to 87 percent. We typically save the fancier European butter for spreading and cook with the standard stuff; if you use a high-fat butter when baking, keep in mind that it will have a slightly lower moisture content. Uncultured or "sweet cream" butter is the supermarket standard; cultured butter is made from fermented cream and contains "good" bacteria that also gives it a tangier flavor. We usually buy unsalted butter, which gives us more room to season food to our liking, and it contains less moisture than salted butter.	Butter loves to absorb other flavors, so keep it tightly wrapped or covered. It can be refrigerated for up to 1 month (it'll keep longer if you don't store it in the dedicated butter compartment on the refrigerator door, where the temperature fluctuates more). Frozen, it will keep for up to 9 months. If you are going to use butter within a few days, you can store it (tightly covered) at room temperature, as long as your kitchen is below 70°F (21°C).

YIELDS & CONVERSIONS

1 stick butter = 4 ounces = 1/2 cup (115 g) = 8 tablespoons

1 pound (455 g) butter = 4 sticks = 2 cups

FLAVOR BUDDIES

Pretty much everything!

CHEDDAR

SOURCING

Cheddar comes in a variety of colors and ages. Color-wise, there isn't much difference; historically, the color was a mark of origin (white Cheddar was produced exclusively in New England, while all other Cheddar was dyed orange with annatto), but now both colors are produced to cater to shoppers' preference.

Where Cheddar does differ significantly is age. Cheddar often comes with labels like mild, sharp or extra sharp: These designations relate directly to how long the cheese has been aged. Mild Cheddars are the youngest, at only 2 to 3 months; sharp Cheddar clocks in at 6 to 9 months, while extra-sharp Cheddars span from 1½ to 2 years old. As the artisan domestic cheese industry has grown, even more mature Cheddars have entered the market, aged 3 years and beyond. The older the Cheddar, the more briny its flavor. Aged Cheddars also have less moisture, which gives them a crumbly texture.

STORING

Store your cheddar wrapped in wax paper or plastic wrap, and keep it in the crisper or cheese drawer of the refrigerator. Mild cheddar will keep for 3 to 4 weeks in the refrigerator; more mature cheddars will last 2 to 3 weeks longer. You can freeze cheddar, but as it affects the texture and moisture content, we avoid doing it.

YIELDS & CONVERSIONS

8 ounces (225 g) cheddar = 3 cups large grate = 4 cups small grate

FLAVOR BUDDIES

Apples	Mushrooms	Turkey
Beef	Mustard	
Broccoli	Peppers	
Celery	Pickles	
Eggs	Potatoes	
Garlic	Rye	
Grapes	Sour cream	
Ham	Sourdough	
Horseradish	Tomatoes	
Mayonnaise	Tuna	

CHICKEN

SOURCING	STORING
These days, chicken comes with as many labels as a Kardashian closet. It can be tough to sort out the difference between free-range and farm raised, since the definitions are constantly shifting. If you only remember one though, let it be "certified organic." Birds under this set of stipulations are free of chemical pesticides, additives and animal byproducts and also meet certain humane guidelines. And since it's one of the most popular proteins on the planet, chicken is usually sold in multiple cuts, from boneless, skinless breasts to thighs and wings. We prefer purchasing the whole bird and breaking it down ourselves—it tends to be cheaper, and it leaves you with the carcass for making stock.	Like most raw proteins, chicken has a very short shelf life. Raw chicken should always be kept cold, and it will keep in the refrigerator for no more than 2 days. However, you can freeze chicken for up to 6 months. For best results, freeze it in a resealable plastic bag, taking as much air out of the bag as possible before sealing. Leftover cooked chicken will keep in the refrigerator for 3 to 4 days. Trust your nose to tell if chicken has gone off; the odor is the first thing that will change.

YIELDS & CONVERSIONS

1 pound (455 g) chicken = 12 wings = 3 boneless thighs = 2 small breasts

1 whole (3½- to 4-pound / 1.6 to 1.8 kg) chicken yields about 3 cups cooked meat

FLAVOR BUDDIES

Apples	Ginger	Tomato
Bacon	Leeks	Turmeric
Black pepper	Lemon	
Butter	Mustard	
Celery	Onions	
Cranberries	Rosemary	
Fennel	Sage	
Fish sauce	Soy sauce	
Garlic	Thyme	

CHILE PEPPERS

SOURCING

The majority of recipes call for chile peppers that are either fresh or dry. Certain varieties, such as jalapeño, are available fresh all year round. Other, more specific chile peppers, such as shishitos, are easiest to find at farmers' markets in mid to late summer, when peppers are in season.

Chile peppers take very well to various methods of preservation, most notably drying. Most grocery stores carry a selection of the most common varieties, including guajillo, ancho and chipotle. Head to a Latin or Asian market for an expanded selection, including chiles de àrbol, morita, pasilla, japones, Tien Tsin and *gochugaru*.

STORING

Fresh peppers will keep in the refrigerator for 1 to 2 weeks. Store them in a resealable plastic bag in the crisper drawer to extend their shelf life. Treat your dried peppers like spices; store them in a dry, cool place in a sealed container, and replace every 6 to 12 months.

SUBSTITUTIONS

We grouped together chiles with similar-enough flavor profiles to be easily substituted for one another:
- Chipotle, guajillo, morita
- Ancho, mulato, pasilla
- Japones, Tien Tsin
- Àrbol, Calabrian, pequin

YIELDS & CONVERSIONS

1 pound (455 g) fresh jalapeños = about 20 medium jalapeños

FLAVOR BUDDIES

Avocado	Corn	Sweet potatoes
Beans	Cucumber	Tomatoes
Beef	Cumin seed	Zucchini
Butter	Eggs	
Butternut squash	Chocolate	
Carrots	Garlic	
Cheese (goat cheese, feta, cream cheese)	Lime	
Chicken	Pork	
Chickpeas	Shellfish (shrimp, crab, oysters)	

EGGS

SOURCING	STORING
Like chicken, eggs have an entire glossary of labels that are supposed to give us insight into how the bird was treated. Whenever possible, skip the grocery store altogether and get fresh eggs from a farmers' market. The difference between fresh local eggs and store-bought ones is unmistakable—even the color of the yolk is strikingly different (a deep orange as opposed to pale yellow). But since most of us buy our eggs from the supermarket, "certified organic" is the label that covers the most ground. Free-range "certified humane" eggs rank high too, as the birds must have access to the outdoors for 6 hours a day.	Whole eggs will keep in the refrigerator for about 4 weeks. To tell if your eggs are fresh, place them in a bowl of water; a fresh egg will sink to the bottom, but an old one will float. Cooked eggs, refrigerated, will last 2 to 4 days.
	To save leftover egg whites, add one to each cell of an ice cube tray and freeze them. Once frozen, pop the egg whites out of the tray and store in a resealable plastic bag for up to 4 months. Let thaw completely before using.

YIELDS & CONVERSIONS

1 cup = 5 large whole eggs = 7 large whites = 14 large yolks

Large	Jumbo	X-Large	Medium	Small
1	1	1	1	1
2	2	2	2	3
3	2	3	3	4
4	3	4	5	5
5	4	4	6	7
6	5	5	7	8

FLAVOR BUDDIES

Pretty much everything!

GREEK YOGURT

SOURCING

Read the label: The only ingredients in Greek yogurt should be milk and live cultures. If you see any thickeners or additives, choose another brand. Or make your own: Line a strainer with a couple layers of cheesecloth and place it over a bowl, then add a quart or so of unflavored yogurt to the strainer. Place everything in the refrigerator and let the yogurt drain (squeeze the cheesecloth occasionally to speed up the process); when it's reached the consistency of sour cream, transfer the strained yogurt to a container and refrigerate.

STORING

Greek yogurt usually stays fresh in the refrigerator for about a week after its "sell by" date. If the yogurt starts to get clumpy, smell sour or, obviously, if mold forms, discard it. You can also freeze yogurt for up to 2 months.

SUBSTITUTIONS

You can swap Greek yogurt in for many other ingredients, including mayonnaise, milk or heavy cream, sour cream and, in baked goods, butter or oil. When cooking with yogurt, keep in mind that it can curdle when exposed to high temperatures.

FLAVOR BUDDIES

Apricots
Bananas
Blueberries
Chickpeas
Cilantro
Coconut
Cucumber
Dill
Eggplant
Garlic
Grapes
Honey
Lemon
Maple syrup
Mint
Nuts
Parsley
Peaches
Pineapple
Rhubarb
Strawberries
Vanilla
Zucchini

HONEY

SOURCING

The most important thing to do when purchasing honey is read the label for the list of ingredients. (There should just be one: honey.) The easiest way to ensure this is by purchasing honey from a local, reliable source. Avoid the bear-shaped mass-produced bottles in the supermarkets, which are frequently filled with honey that has been filtered so much that it no longer contains pollen, or worse, that isn't honey at all.

STORING

Honey is about 80 percent sugar and 20 percent water. Store honey in a cool, dark place. It keeps indefinitely—millennia-old samples found in King Tut's tomb were still edible, despite more than 2,000 years beneath the desert sand—although it may crystallize over time. If it does, heat it briefly by placing the jar in a pan of warm water, or by blasting it for 10-second intervals in the microwave.

YIELDS & CONVERSIONS

Swapping honey for sugar: As a general rule, honey is sweeter than granulated sugar. Mild honey varietals such as acacia and wildflower will mimic the flavor of sugar best, while darker, more flavorful honeys will lend their notes to the finished product.

Use equal amounts of honey for sugar up to 1 cup (240 ml / 200 g). For measurements over 1 cup, replace with $\frac{2}{3}$ to $\frac{3}{4}$ cup (165 to 180 ml / 200 g) honey for every cup (200 g) of sugar, depending on desired sweetness. When swapping honey in baking recipes, reduce your oven temperature by 25°F (about 15°C) and take a few minutes off your bake time, since honey caramelizes more quickly than granulated sugar.

FLAVOR BUDDIES

Apples	Chiles	Rhubarb
Bacon	Corn	Rosemary
Bananas	Eggplant	Salmon
Basil	Lavender	Seaweed
Butter	Peaches	Soft cheese
Carrots	Peanut butter	Tea
Chicken	Plums	Tomatoes

KALE

SOURCING	STORING
Kale grows well from summer through December, though it tastes better if its leaves have been exposed to the first frost. Thus, for most climates, late-autumn kale is the sweet spot. A member of the cabbage family, kale comes in a number of different varieties. The most popular is Lacinato kale (aka cavelo nero, Tuscan kale or dinosaur kale), which has dark green quilted leaves. Curly kale is also widely available, with green leaves that curl around the edges. Keep an eye out for other varieties, such as Russian red and frilly purple kale.	For the longest shelf life, don't wash your kale until you're ready to use it, and store in a resealable plastic bag in the crisper drawer, where it will keep for 1 to 2 weeks. Toss it if the leaves have blackened in spots or become slimy.

YIELDS & CONVERSIONS

1 pound (455 g) kale = 6 cups trimmed and chopped leaves = 1 cup cooked leaves

How much in a bunch? One bunch of kale varies a bit, but in general you can estimate that most bunches weigh between 12 and 16 ounces (340 and 455 g).

FLAVOR BUDDIES

Almonds	Mushrooms
Avocado	Olive oil
Beans	Parmesan
Chiles	Sausage
Chorizo	Sesame
Eggs	Soy sauce
Garlic	Tahini
Lemons	Tomatoes

LEMONS

SOURCING

Look for lemons that are heavy for their size and have firm, smooth skin. Give them a squeeze; they should give a little bit, but they shouldn't be spongy.

If you're planning on zesting your lemons, buy organic (the skin is where pesticides and other crap like to hang out). If you're only juicing lemons, conventional ones are OK.

STORING

Store lemons at room temperature for up to 1 week, or seal in a plastic bag and refrigerate for up to 3 weeks. You can also freeze whole lemons in a plastic bag: While they can be zested straight out of the freezer, the texture of the flesh will get mushy once thawed, so they'll be best for juicing. To thaw frozen lemons quickly, microwave them for a few seconds at a time or submerge in cold water for 15 to 20 minutes.

YIELDS & CONVERSIONS

1 pound (455 g) = 4 to 5 medium lemons

1 medium lemon yields 2 to 3 tablespoons of juice and 1 tablespoon of zest

FLAVOR BUDDIES

Artichokes	Ginger	Plums
Basil	Grapes	Rhubarb
Black pepper	Honey	Rice
Blueberries	Leafy greens	Ricotta
Butter	Maple syrup	Rosemary
Buttermilk	Mint	Thyme
Capers	Nuts	Yogurt
Chocolate	Parsley	
Coconut	Pears	

MAYONNAISE

SOURCING	STORING
As far as store-bought mayonnaise goes, most of the major brands (Hellmann's, Kraft, Duke's, Best Foods) are pretty interchangeable. It's really more a matter of personal preference than any quality guidelines. That's not the case with Kewpie, a Japanese mayonnaise that has more sugar than typical American mayonnaise, and Miracle Whip, which is, well, something else; both of these have distinct flavors that will affect your final recipe if you try to substitute. Homemade mayonnaise depends on the quality of your eggs (see our sourcing guidelines on page 299); since they aren't cooked, it's even more critical to use the best you can find.	Store-bought mayonnaise contains stabilizers that make it safe to keep in the refrigerator for 2 to 3 months after opening (sealed, it'll keep indefinitely at room temperature). Homemade mayonnaise will keep for 3 to 4 days in the refrigerator.

YIELDS & CONVERSIONS

Mayonnaise can be substituted for eggs in basic baking recipes: Just omit the eggs and oil, and add the same amount of mayonnaise as oil is called for in the recipe. (So if your brownie recipe calls for 3 eggs and ⅓ cup (75 ml) of oil, swap with just ⅓ cup (75 ml) of mayonnaise.)

FLAVOR BUDDIES

Artichokes	Corn	Porcini mushrooms
Bacon	Eggs	Potatoes
Bonito	Garlic	Salmon
Cabbage	Herbs (parsley, basil, dill,	Sprouts
Caraway	cilantro, chives)	Tomatoes
Cheddar	Lemon	Tuna
Chicken	Peppers	Vinegar

RICE

SOURCING

Rice is one of the most readily available ingredients we can think of. It's a mass-produced crop and ubiquitous in cuisines across the world. You can find rice in any grocery store, but the varieties vary widely. There are also an increasing number of purveyors who focus on heirloom varietals.

Most rice can be broken down into three categories:

SHORT GRAIN: Squat and plump, short-grain rice is most known for dishes that require the grains to stick together, such as sushi, sticky rice or rice pudding. These grains typically produce more starch, making them chewy when cooked.

MEDIUM GRAIN: Arborio, the standard rice used to make risotto, falls into this category, as does bomba rice, the standard-bearer for paella. Two to three times longer than it is wide, medium-grain rice is just a touch chewier than long grain, without being sticky like short-grain sushi rice.

LONG GRAIN: Skinny, long varieties such as jasmine and basmati fall into this category. When cooked, these grains have a dry, feathery bite and don't clump together, which makes them ideal for dishes like pilaf. Most brown and wild rice also falls into this category.

STORING

Most uncooked rice will keep indefinitely when stored in an airtight container. The exception to this is brown rice, which has a higher oil content—it'll only keep for about 6 months in an airtight container at room temperature. Cooked rice will keep for about 1 week in the refrigerator or 6 months in the freezer.

YIELDS & CONVERSIONS

1 cup (180 g) long-grain or medium-grain rice yields 3 cups (528 g) cooked rice
1 cup short-grain rice yields 2⅔ cups cooked rice
1 cup brown rice yields 3½ to 4 cups cooked rice

One 2-pound (910 g) bag white rice = 4 cups (910 g) uncooked = 12 cups (2.1 kg) cooked

FLAVOR BUDDIES

Beans	Cream	Peppers
Bok choy	Eggs	Scallions
Broccoli	Garlic	Soy
Butter	Herbs	Tomatoes
Cinnamon	Onions	

SOURDOUGH BREAD

SOURCING	STORING
Sample a bunch of sourdough breads until you find a bakery or brand you like. A good loaf will have a dark, hardened crust that thumps when tapped. Inside, the crumb should be moist and chewy with some spring and relatively large air pockets.	The best way to keep bread fresh is to use fresh bread! But most sourdough loaves will keep at room temperature (wrapped in plastic or a paper bag, or placed inside a sealed container) for 4 days or so. Refrigerators are bread's worst enemy; they dry the bread out quickly. We usually freeze any leftover bread—wrapped in plastic, then aluminum foil—after a couple of days. If we know the bread is destined for sandwiches, we'll slice it before freezing, then thaw individual slices in a toaster. Discard frozen bread after 3 months.

YIELDS & CONVERSIONS

1 pound (455 g) loaf = 15 regular slices = 12 cups small croutons

One 1-inch (2.5 g) slice bread = ½ to 1 cup croutons
= ⅓ to ½ cup (35 to 50 g) fine crumbs

FLAVOR BUDDIES

Avocados	Dijon mustard	Parsley
Bacon	Eggs	Shellfish
Butter	Garlic	Tomatoes
Capers	Honey	
Cinnamon	Leafy greens	
Cream	Mayonnaise	
Cheese (all kinds)	Olive oil	
Cured meats	Onions	

TOMATOES

SOURCING

If you aren't able to taste a tomato before buying it, your nose is the best tool for finding great ones; fresh tomatoes should give off a sweet, earthy, tomato-y aroma. Reach for tomatoes that are deeply colored and firm, but not hard. They should also feel heavy for their size. Avoid any small tomatoes (grape, cherry, etc.) that are wrinkled.

STORING

Store tomatoes at room temperature for up to 5 days. To speed up the ripening process, place them in a pierced paper bag along with an apple, which will release ethylene gas. Most folks will tell you to never refrigerate tomatoes; this is true for crappy commercial or under-ripe tomatoes, but we've found that ripe heirloom tomatoes will hold up well in the refrigerator for a couple of days, especially if your kitchen is hot during tomato season.

YIELDS & CONVERSIONS

1 medium tomato = 4 to 6 ounces (115 to 170 g) = 1 cup chopped

1 pound (455 g) tomatoes = 2 large tomatoes = 3 medium tomatoes = 8 plum tomatoes = 2 to 2½ cups chopped

1 pint small tomatoes = 45 to 50 grape tomatoes = 25 to 30 cherry tomatoes

FLAVOR BUDDIES

Anchovies	Cilantro	Leafy greens
Arugula	Corn	Mayonnaise
Avocados	Crab	Olive oil
Bell peppers	Cucumbers	Parsley
Capers	Eggplant	Rosemary
Cauliflower	Eggs	Tarragon
Cheese (blue, cheddar, feta, goat, mozzarella, Parmesan, ricotta)	Fennel	Thyme
	Garlic	Vinegar
Chile peppers	Honey	Watermelon
	Lamb	

WILD SHRIMP

SOURCING

Shrimp can rank among the least sustainable types of seafood, so it pays to read up on current ratings of sites like SeafoodWatch.org.

Shrimp also have a very short shelf life, so pay extra care to freshness at the time of purchase. Look for shrimp that has the label "IQF," which stands for "individually quick frozen." This means that the shrimp were flash frozen immediately after they were caught, so they're more likely to be fresh. Avoid any shrimp with an ammonia scent, which is a sign of spoilage, and pick shrimp with fully intact, taut bodies.

When purchasing shrimp, you can choose from a spectrum of sizes (called counts) and varieties. Size-wise, the bigger the count number, the smaller the shrimp (learn more about shrimp counts on page 269).

STORING

Fresh shrimp should be cooked or frozen within a day or two of purchase; head-on shrimp decay faster than headless shrimp, so use them as close to the time of purchase as possible. Frozen shrimp will keep for up to 1 year. To thaw, set the shrimp in a bowl covered with plastic wrap and refrigerate overnight.

YIELDS & CONVERSIONS

There are between 18 and 36 shrimp in a pound (455 g), depending on the size. The shrimp "count" will give an average range for the quantity of individual shrimp per pound.

1 pound (455 g) shell-on shrimp = ½ pound (225 g) shells

FLAVOR BUDDIES

Bay leaf	Grits	Sherry
Celery	Lemon	Soy
Coconut	Mayonnaise	Tomatoes
Cream	Mushrooms	White pepper
Curry	Peppers	
Garlic	Pineapple	
Ginger	Scallions	

WINTER SQUASH

SOURCING	STORING
Generally speaking, a winter squash should be deeply colored compared to others of its same variety. It should also feel heavy for its size, with a dry, intact stem. If possible, avoid squash with cracks or soft spots. Its skin should be dull; shiny skin indicates it was harvested prematurely.	Whole squash will keep well in a cool, dark place for 1 to 2 months. Refrigeration isn't recommended until the squash is cut up (even then its texture and flavor will deteriorate quickly). You can freeze cooked squash for up to 10 months.

YIELDS & CONVERSIONS

NOTE: Squash vary widely in size and weight by variety, and even among the same variety, so we're offering approximate yields by the pound.

1 pound (455 g) squash = 2 cups 1-inch cubes
= 1 cup (240 ml) cooked puree

FLAVOR BUDDIES

Avocados	Cured meats	Olive oil
Bacon	Dijon mustard	Onions
Butter	Eggs	Parsley
Capers	Garlic	Shellfish
Cinnamon	Honey	Tomatoes
Cream	Leafy greens	
Cheese (all kinds)	Mayonnaise	

AUTHORS

NICK FAUCHALD is the publisher of Short Stack Editions. He's worked as an editor at *Food & Wine*, *Wine Spectator* and *Every Day with Rachael Ray* magazines, and was the editor in chief of TastingTable.com from its launch in 2008 until 2011. His writing has been featured in numerous publications, and he's authored several books about cooking and cocktails. In 2016, he teamed up with W&P Design to start Dovetail, a Brooklyn-based publishing and product design company.

ROTEM RAFFE is the creative director of Short Stack Editions. She has worked as an art director on advertising campaigns for Baskin Robbins and Johnson & Johnson brands, among others. In 2012 she became a creative consultant, contributing art direction, illustration and design work to clients that range from small bars and restaurants to large global brands.

KAITLYN GOALEN is the editor of Short Stack Editions. Based in Raleigh, North Carolina, she has contributed to a number of national publications, including *Southern Living*, *Food & Wine* and *Garden & Gun*, and was formerly an editor at TastingTable.com. Recently she co-wrote *The Craft Cocktail Party* with Clover Club's Julie Reiner.

CONTRIBUTORS **SUSIE HELLER** is the author/producer of more than 12 award-winning cookbooks, including five with Thomas Keller, and the producer of PBS programming, including cooking series with Julia Child, Jacques Pépin and José Andres. She is presently Chief of Global Content of Feast, a cooking app that features recipes and techniques from the world's greatest food minds. She is the author of Short Stack Editions Vol. 18: Chocolate.

JULIA SHERMAN is the vegetable-obsessed artist, photographer, writer and editor behind the website SaladforPresident.com, an evolving project that draws a meaningful connection between food, art and everyday obsessions. She is the creator of the first-ever MoMA PS1 rooftop Salad Garden, a project that traveled to Los Angeles's Getty Center in fall 2015. **MICHAEL HARLAN TURKELL** is an award-winning photographer who captured the inner workings of kitchens for his James Beard–nominated Back of the House project. Since 2010, Michael has been recording his weekly food podcast, The Food Scene, at HeritageRadioNetwork.org. He's photographed more than a dozen cookbooks and is now writing his first, *Acid Trip: A Fermented Look Into Vinegar's Soured Past and Bright Future*, due out from Abrams in spring 2017. **SCOTT HOCKER** is a writer, editor, recipe developer and content and editorial consultant. He is currently the editor in chief of Liquor.com and is based in New Orleans. Someday, he wants to live in Mexico. He is the author of Short Stack Editions Vol. 6: Sweet Potatoes. **KRISTIN DONNELLY** is the author of *The Modern Potluck* and co-owner of Stewart & Claire, a line of small-batch lip balms. A former editor at *Food & Wine* magazine, she works as a writer, editor and recipe developer and lives in Pennsylvania.

REBEKAH PEPPLER is a writer and food stylist based in Brooklyn and Paris. Her clients include various cookbooks as well as online, print and television outlets such as the *New York Times*, *Real Simple*, *Every Day with Rachael Ray*, Epicurious and Food Network. She is the author of Short Stack Editions Vol. 8: Honey. **JULIA TURSHEN** has been cooking since before she can remember and writes about food. She has co-authored a number of bestselling cookbooks, has been a radio host, and moderates food-centered panels and conversations around the country. Her own cookbook, *Small Victories*, was published by Chronicle Books in 2016. **SOA DAVIES** is the executive chef of Maple, a new kind of food company that reimagines what a restaurant can be. She is also the founder of Salt Hospitality, an advisement firm that works with brands on hospitality concepts, operations and menu development. She produced and styled the Emmy-award winning television show *Avec Eric*, wrote the companion cookbook and was responsible for the menus and food styling on the HBO series *Treme*. She is the author of Short Stack Editions Vol. 2: Tomatoes. **RAQUEL PELZEL** is an award-winning food writer and cookbook collaborator and has co-authored more than a dozen cookbooks in addition to writing her first solo cookbook, *Toast: The Cookbook*, published by Phaidon in 2015. She was an editor and recipe developer at *Cook's Illustrated* and the senior food editor for Tasting Table. She lives in Brooklyn and is the author of Short Stack Editions Vol. 22: Eggplant.

VICTORIA GRANOF, whose creative vision is both unique and fiercely passionate, is one of the most respected and sought-after food stylists working today. She has joined forces with many of the photo world's best-known photographers and directors, and she launched her career with a decade-long collaboration with the great Irving Penn. She lives in Brooklyn with her son, Theo, where she indulges her passion for pickling, preserving and fermenting. She is the author of Short Stack Editions Vol. 17: Chickpeas. **ANGIE MOSIER** is a food stylist and photographer who started her career as a baker making pastries and wedding cakes in Atlanta. Over the past 25 years, Angie has styled and photographed food for editorial, commercial and film projects, including cookbooks for chefs Sean Brock, Vivian Howard and Eric Ripert. She is the author of Short Stack Editions Vol. 4: Buttermilk. **MEGAN SCOTT** is a freelance recipe developer and tester and food photographer who lives in Portland, Oregon. She is currently working, with her husband John Becker, on the next major revision of *Joy of Cooking*. **VIRGINIA WILLIS**—a Southern chef, cookbook author, award-winning food writer and blogger—is one of the most popular and respected voices on Southern food and cooking. Georgia-born and French-trained, Virginia is known for reimagining Southern favorites and giving classic French dishes a down-home comfort feel. She is the author of Short Stack Editions Vol. 5: Grits. **IAN KNAUER** was a food editor at *Gourmet* magazine for nearly a decade. His first cookbook, *The Farm: Rustic Recipes for a Year of Incredible Food*, was published in 2012 and nominated for an IACP cookbook award; it prompted a companion PBS television series of the same name. Most recently, he has opened a cooking school in Pennsylvania, where he teaches hands-on night cooking classes and hosts seasonally inspired dinners. He is the author of Short Stack Editions Vol. 1: Eggs. **SUSAN SPUNGEN** is a cookbook author, culinary consultant and food stylist for both print and film. She was the founding food editor at *Martha Stewart Living* and is a frequent contributor to publications such as *Bon Appétit*, *Food & Wine* and *More*. Susan has published two cookbooks, *Recipes: A Collection for the Modern Cook* and *What's a Hostess to Do?* She is the author of Short Stack Editions Vol. 3: Strawberries. **MARTHA HOLMBERG** is a Portland, Oregon–based writer, editor, cook and undisciplined-but-avid home gardener. After training in France, she served as editor-in-chief of *Fine Cooking* magazine for 10 years, followed by five years as food editor of *The Oregonian* newspaper. Martha has written several cookbooks, including the James Beard– and IACP-nominated *Modern Sauces*. She is the author of Short Stack Editions Vol. 9: Plums. **SARA JENKINS** is the highly accomplished chef and owner of Porsena restaurant in New York's East Village. Billed as a "pasta restaurant," Porsena has been met with excellent reviews and much enthusiasm. Sara has been featured in *Bon Appétit* and on NPR and contributes regularly to *The Atlantic*'s food blog. She is the author of Short Stack Editions Vol. 14: Prosciutto di Parma. **SHERI CASTLE** is an award-winning food writer and cooking teacher. She hails from the Blue Ridge Mountains of North Carolina but now lives near Chapel Hill. She is fueled by mountains, farmers' markets, bourbon and storytelling. Sheri is the author of Short Stack Edition Vol. 20: Rhubarb.

JESSICA BATTILANA is a writer, cook and recipe developer. She has collaborated on cookbooks with chef Charles Phan, baker Chad Robertson, butcher Ryan Farr and entrepreneur Anya Fernald. Jessica's writing and recipes have appeared in myriad publications. She lives in San Francisco with her wife and two sons, with whom she shares a deep love of ice cream. She is the author of Short Stack Editions Vol. 10: Corn. **TYLER KORD** is chef-owner of the No. 7 restaurant group in New York. He earned a master's degree in English from Oberlin College before attending the French Culinary Institute, where he stayed on to be sous chef to Alain Sailhac for four years. He then worked as sous chef at Jean-Georges Vongerichten's restaurant Perry St. before opening No. 7. He is the author of Short Stack Editions Vol. 7: Broccoli.

ANDREA ALBIN is a chef, recipe developer, tester and food stylist with more than 10 years of culinary experience. She has worked in some of New York's top kitchens, as well as the test kitchens of *Gourmet* magazine and the *Food Network Magazine*. Andrea recently relocated to her hometown of Houston, where she continues to write and test recipes. She is the author of Short Stack Editions Vol. 11: Apples. **LIBBIE SUMMERS** earned her culinary chops below deck as a chef on private yachts. Today she is an award-winning producer and artistic director of her own lifestyle brand, A Food-Inspired Life. Libbie is the author of two cookbooks, and her blog, *Salted and Styled*, has won two IACP awards. Libbie lives in Savannah, Georgia, with one husband, one son and one opinionated dog. She is the author of Short Stack Editions Vol. 12: Brown Sugar. **ALISON ROMAN** is a food editor, writer, maker and eater. Before joining the editorial world, she worked as a pastry chef at such places as Quince in San Francisco and Momofuku Milk Bar in New York. Originally from Los Angeles, she lives in Brooklyn, where she tries to eat pizza for every meal, sometimes successfully. She is the author of Short Stack Editions Vol. 13: Lemons. **KEMP MINIFIE** is a freelance recipe developer/tester and food writer. She worked in the food department at *Gourmet* magazine for almost 32 years, testing and developing recipes and styling them for photography. She ended her run at the magazine as the executive editor and went on to become the senior editor of Epicurious.com.

SARAH BAIRD is a food writer and culinary anthropologist living in New Orleans. Her writing regularly appears online and in print for publications that include PUNCH, First We Feast, Eater, *AFAR*, *The Atlantic* and more. She is the former restaurant critic for New Orleans's alt-weekly *The Gambit* and author of the cookbook *Kentucky Sweets: Bourbon Balls, Spoonbread and Mile High Pie*. She is the author of Short Stack Editions Vol. 15: Summer Squash. **PAUL GRIMES** is a food stylist working in advertising and editorial. He was formerly senior stylist at *Gourmet* as well as one of the magazine's food editors. A graduate of La Varenne in France, with a degree in Fine Arts from Kenyon College, Paul won a Watson Fellowship, which landed him on the steps of Simone "Simca" Beck, helping her run her cooking school in the south of France.

BETH LIPTON is the food director for *Health* magazine, where she writes, edits and develops recipes. Her writing has appeared in print and online for publications such as *People, Travel + Leisure and Time*, and her first cookbook, *You Made That Dessert?*, was released in 2009. She also works as a health coach and is the author of Short Stack Editions Vol. 16: Peaches.

ACKNOWLEDGMENTS
—

This book wouldn't exist if it weren't for the success of Short Stack Editions, and for that we have so many people to thank. But the first bouquet goes to our authors—past, present and future. We created Short Stack to showcase your talents, and you've rewarded us and our readers with your best work and recipes. We're honored to work with each of you.

Equally vital to Short Stack's existence is our brilliant creative director, Rotem Raffe. You gave this series—and this cookbook—its identity and personality, and you've been the most patient and dedicated business partner anyone could ever ask for. To the rest of our Short Stack staff, thank you for keeping us in business. And to our many bookbinders, for keeping us in stitches (ha!).

Short Stack Editions are lucky enough to share shelf space with an ever-growing array of independent food publications. We've enjoyed collaborating and sharing war stories with you all, and we hope more folks will join us to keep growing the paper-publishing business.

Infinite thanks to our agent and offensive coordinator, David Black, for your counsel, negotiation skills, generosity (and use of your lake house to write this thing). And to the folks at Abrams—especially our editor, Camaren Subhiyah —thanks for overseeing a book that we can all be proud of. And we can't forget our indefatigable copy editor, Abby Tannenbaum, who has scrubbed clean this manuscript as well as every Short Stack Edition to date. Also instrumental in the making of this book were recipe tester Rachel Sozynski, researcher Parker Brown, and Ashley Christensen, who provided instrumental feedback, general moral support . . . and pimento cheese.

The funky photography you see here was made possible by a trio of talent: photographer Noah Fecks (that's his real name! Sort of!), food stylist–artista Victoria Granof, prop stylist Alex Brannian and their assistants. This was the most intense, crazy fun we've had on a photo shoot. Thanks for being such a generous and tenacious bunch.

Finally, to anyone who cooks from this book, Short Stack Editions, or any other cookbook, magazine or newspaper food section. You're keeping the printed recipe relevant. If you keep reading and cooking, we'll keep producing.

—Nick and Kaitlyn

Editor: Camaren Subhiyah
Designers: Heesang Lee and Deb Wood
Production Manager: Denise LaCongo
Food Stylist: Victoria Granof
Prop Stylist: Alex Brannian

Library of Congress Control Number: 2015955677

ISBN: 978-1-4197-2241-7

Printed and bound in the United States
10 9 8 7 6 5 4 3 2 1

Abrams books are available at special discounts when purchased
in quantity for premiums and promotions as well as fundraising or
educational use. Special editions can also be created to specification.
For details, contact specialsales@abramsbooks.com or the address below.

ABRAMS The Art of Books
115 West 18th Street, New York, NY 10011
abramsbooks.com